The Macroeconomics of
Imperfect Competition and
Nonclearing Markets

The Macroeconomics of Imperfect Competition and Nonclearing Markets

A Dynamic General Equilibrium Approach

Jean-Pascal Bénassy

The MIT Press

Cambridge, Massachusetts

London, England

This book was set in Times Roman by Interactive Composition Corporation.

Printed and bound in the United States of America.

Library of Congress Cataloging-in-Publication Data

Bénassy, Jean-Pascal.
    The macroeconomics of imperfect competition and nonclearing markets : a dynamic gerneral equilibrium approach / Jean-Pascal Bénassy.
    p. cm.
    Includes bibliographical references and index.
    ISBN 0-262-02528-0 (hc. : alk. paper)
    1. Macroeconomics—Mathematical models. 2. Rational expectations (Economic theory)—Mathematical models. 3. Equilibrium (Economics) 4. Keynesian economics—Mathematical models. 5. Competition, Imperfect—Mathematical models. I. Title

HB172.5 .B454   2003
339 ′.01 ′ 5195—dc21   2002021922

Contents

Preface

The purpose of this book is to build a consistent family of dynamic macroeconomic models whose structure is firmly grounded in rigorous microeconomic principles. The models we will present all come from a synthesis of four central paradigms in economic theory:

- General equilibrium theory, in the line of Walras (1874) and Arrow and Debreu (1954).
- Keynesian theory, as exemplified by Hicks's famous IS-LM model (1937), and later revisited by Patinkin (1956), Clower (1965), and Leijonhufvud (1968).
- Imperfect competition, especially of the monopolistic competition variety due to Chamberlin (1933), and its general equilibrium formalization by Negishi (1961).
- And finally rational expectations, as developed by Muth (1961) and their integration into dynamic general equilibrium macroeconomic models by Lucas (1972) or Kydland and Prescott (1982).

At first sight this list may seem like a contradiction in terms. Everybody in the profession recalls indeed the long battles between classicals and Keynesians, and then between new-classicals and Keynesians, and finally between new-classicals and new-Keynesians. Although such controversies did provide excitement in the field, it seems that the profession has grown beyond these, and that the time is ripe for a more synthetic paradigm within which ideas can be rigorously debated on a common scientific ground. This is why a synthesis of paradigms such as the one outlined above should be particularly welcome.

This strategy of synthesis is not entirely new, however. It began indeed in the early 1970s, a time when opposition between schools was particularly acute. There were then, and there still are, several ways one could envision a unified theory. Our strategy consisted in starting with what was at the time the most rigorous and well-specified theory, that is, the Walrasian one, and enriching it to encompass nonclearing markets and imperfect competition. At the time when the research leading to this book was started, the Walrasian paradigm was essentially the Arrow-Debreu model of general equilibrium. This was soon enriched on the macroeconomic side by Lucas's (1972) reconsideration of the Phillips curve in a rational expectations framework and later by the dynamic stochastic general equilibrium models in the "real business cycles" tradition (Kydland and Prescott 1982; Long and Plosser 1983). All these models have the rigor and microfoundations that were long missing in macroeconomics, and therefore they are a most useful starting point. Still they have nothing to say about what might happen outside Walrasian equilibrium, an obviously too severe restriction.

So the strategy that was followed then, and that which I will continue to follow in this book, consisted in starting from rigorous market-clearing models and generalizing them to various non-Walrasian situations. This way we will obtain a whole new class of models that combine the rigor of traditional Walrasian models with the generality and relevance of models with nonclearing markets and imperfect competition. In this book we will notably construct many dynamic models whose Walrasian versions are similar in spirit to those of real business cycles, but which we will study under much more general, non-Walrasian, conditions.

Plan of the Book

The book is divided into six autonomous parts.

Part I aims at presenting in a simple and pedagogical way some basic concepts and macroeconomic applications. Chapter 1 starts with a simple market-clearing paradigm as a benchmark, and shows how rationing and quantity signals occur when markets do not clear, how the theory of demand and supply must be modified to take into account these quantity signals, and finally how a rational theory of price setting in nonclearing markets can be developed. Chapter 2 immediately applies these concepts to a very simple macroeconomic framework, and develops in a two-market economy a Walrasian version, a fixprice-fixwage version, and a model where prices and wages are set by imperfect competitors. Equilibrium allocations and the effects of public policies are studied.

Part II consists of the longer chapter 3, which develops the same concepts as chapter 1, but in a full general equilibrium framework. The starting point this time is the multimarket Walrasian equilibrium model, and we integrate into this framework the concepts of rationing, quantity signals, effective demand, and price setting. We further define a few non-Walrasian equilibrium concepts, notably fixprice equilibria and imperfectly competitive equilibria where agents determine prices on the basis of objective demand curves. The efficiency (or rather, inefficiency) properties of these equilibria are thoroughly investigated.

Part III presents macroeconomic models that bring together the various elements described at the beginning of this preface. At this point, and in order to gradually introduce difficulties, I restrict these models to deterministic ones. Chapter 4 constructs an intertemporal model of imperfect competition based on objective demand curves, and asks a question that has puzzled researchers in the field for a while: are imperfect competition models Keynesian or classical? Chapter 5 builds a traditional model of decentralized trade unions and investigates how bargaining powers affect welfare, both at the sectoral and aggregate levels. A notable result is that too much bargaining power on the side of trade unions creates not only underemployment but inefficiencies detrimental to the workers themselves.

Part IV introduces stochastic elements in the preceding models, in the same way as in real business cycles models, but generalizing them to imperfectly competitive environments. Chapter 6 constructs a benchmark model of a dynamic economy with money and imperfect competition and submits it to real and monetary shocks. Although it endogenously generates underemployment, the dynamic behavior of this model is found to be somewhat similar to that of traditional RBC models. Things change drastically in chapter 7, which shows that one can actually generate highly persistent unemployment in such a model, even when the underlying shocks are themselves not persistent, by an adequate combination of imperfect competition and capital-labor complementarities. Chapter 8 introduces endogenous growth, and shows that in such a circumstance imperfect competition modifies the rate of growth as well.

The rigidities considered in part IV are "real." Part V introduces nominal rigidities into the picture. Chapter 9 considers one-period wage contracts and shows that this can create employment imbalances, with the resulting output-employment dynamics having characteristics intermediate between those of Keynesian and traditional RBC models. At this stage unemployment is not persistent at all, and chapter 10 introduces a new type of staggered wage contract. This type of contract can generate a highly persistent response of employment and output to money shocks, and even the "hump" response that traditional models fail to reproduce. The wage contracts of chapters 9 and 10 make the traditional assumption that labor suppliers always adapt their supply to demand. Chapter 11 describes a dynamic model where wages are rationally determined by trade unions maximizing the welfare of their constituents, and under the assumption of voluntary exchange. As a result the model naturally displays nonlinearities, and the variability of shocks has a direct effect on the average rate of unemployment.

Finally, part VI deals with policy issues, and notably with a problem that stirred enormous controversy at the inception of rational expectations: should government lead activist policies and, if so, which ones? Chapter 12 starts with the simple case where wages are preset and only fiscal policy is available to the government. A central result is that even if the government has no more information than the private sector (this was a central point in the debate), it is nevertheless possible to design activist policies that do much better than nonactivist ones. Chapter 13 extends the argument to the case where wages are set by maximizing trade unions and shows that the results extend readily to that case. Chapter 14 generalizes the argument to the determination of the optimal combination of monetary and fiscal policy. This optimal policy mix turns out to have an activist fiscal policy. Finally chapter 15 investigates the topical issue of optimal monetary policy rules and shows that the widespread neglect of the accompanying fiscal policies is likely to lead to highly distorted recommendations.

Modeling

All the chapters of this book share a common methodology based on a rigorous general equilibrium approach to nonclearing markets and imperfect competition. This methodology is applied to a wide range of macroeconomic issues.

The dynamic models that are used, however, differ according to the chapter topics. Some use the infinitely lived consumer paradigm, some the two-period overlapping generations model, and chapter 7 an hybrid between the two. Of course, it would have been tempting to use throughout the book a single model, such as the infinitely lived consumer model which is popular with dynamic macroeconomists working in the real business cycles line of thought. It turned out that such a strategy was not feasible for at least two reasons: (1) computations in some cases would have been infeasible, or so clumsy, as to preclude an explicit solution or a reasonable exposition, and (2) the infinitely lived consumer model has the property of Ricardian equivalence, which makes it unfit to study the effects of fiscal policy. Since this is a central theme of the last four chapters on optimal policy, clearly a different model had to be used.

Since treating all problems with a single model was not a feasible option, in each chapter I decided on a model with the purpose to treat the issue at stake in a way that would yield the results in the simplest manner and lead to an elegant and effective exposition. Of course, whatever the issue the underlying methodology remains fully unified throughout the book.

A Reading Guide

A central interest of this book is clearly in the construction of rigorously microfounded models. However, I wanted also this book to be accessible to the less technical macroeconomist. For that purpose the book provides a number of shortcuts that can be taken in a first reading without impairing the understanding of concepts and results.

First, a number of important results of the various models are described as "propositions," followed by a proof where these results are rigorously demonstrated. Although this may look at first sight like a mathematization of the exposition, this is actually quite the contrary. The reader can entirely skip the proofs in a first reading without loss of continuity.

Second, chapter 3, which is the most technical and set in the format of Walrasian general equilibrium, can also be skipped in a first reading. Many of the essential concepts were already described in a less technical manner in chapter 1.

In order not to break the continuity of reading the text, references in the text have been kept to a strict minimum. Relevant references are gathered at the end of each chapter. The bibliography includes additional references that are not directly related to a particular chapter's material but present models or results in a spirit similar to those in this book.

Acknowledgments

In writing this book I have incurred an enormous debt to Fabrice Collard and Franck Portier. They read the entire manuscript, and their insightful comments brought many improvements. I also benefited from the comments of Pierre Cahuc and Rafael Munoz. Finally Josselyne Bitan cheerfully and efficiently helped me with the practical details of preparing the manuscript.

Part I

From Microeconomics to Macroeconomics

1

Basic Concepts

1.1 Introduction

In this chapter we will develop in the simplest manner possible the central concepts of the theories we will be using in this book. It is actually convenient to start the exposition with the polar case of a Walrasian market-clearing model. This will allow us to identify a number of important elements that are obviously missing if one wants to extend the analysis to more general environments. We will then see how the concepts can be generalized to nonclearing markets and imperfect competition. We will look at how transactions are organized when demands and supplies do not match (section 1.3), how quantity signals are formed in the process (section 1.4), how demands and supplies themselves react to market imbalances (section 1.5), and finally how prices are determined in such an imperfectly competitive environment (section 1.6). So before venturing any further, let us scrutinize the Walrasian model in order to precisely identify the missing elements.

1.2 Walrasian Theory: The Missing Parts

We will first briefly describe the characteristics of the Walrasian model, and then outline how it has to be generalized to deal with nonclearing markets and imperfect competition.

1.2.1 The Walrasian Paradigm

Consider an economy where goods indexed by $h = 1, \ldots, \ell$ are exchanged among agents indexed by $i = 1, \ldots, n$. Call p_h the price of good h, and p the price vector:

$$p = (p_1, \ldots, p_h, \ldots, p_\ell) \tag{1}$$

All private agents receive the same price signal, the vector of prices p, and assume that they will be able to exchange whatever they want at this price system (a belief which will actually be validated ex post). Denote by d_{ih} and s_{ih} the demand and supply of good h by agent i. Each agent i sends to the market his Walrasian demands and supplies, obtained through maximization of his own objective function. Of course, demand and supply depend on the price system. So we denote them as

$$d_{ih} = d_{ih}(p), \quad s_{ih} = s_{ih}(p) \tag{2}$$

In this economy there is an "auctioneer" who changes the price system by some unspecified mechanism (the famous "tâtonnement" process) until a Walrasian equilibrium price vector p^* is reached. This equilibrium price p^* is characterized by the equality of aggregate demand and aggregate supply in all markets:

$$\sum_{i=1}^{n} d_{ih}(p^*) = \sum_{i=1}^{n} s_{ih}(p^*) \qquad \text{for all } h = 1, \ldots, \ell \tag{3}$$

Transactions are equal to the demands and supplies at this price system. No quantity constraint is experienced by any agent, since demands and supplies match on all markets.

1.2.2 The Missing Elements

The Walrasian story is a good description of reality for the few real world markets, such as the stock market which inspired Walras, where the equality between demand and supply is ensured institutionally by an actual auctioneer. For all other markets with no auctioneer in attendance, the Walrasian story is clearly incomplete, something pointed out by Arrow (1959) himself. Two important characteristics of the Walrasian model deserve to be stressed here:

• All agents receive price signals (actually the *same* price vector) but no agent actually sends any price signal, as price setting is left to the implicit Walrasian auctioneer.
• Though all agents send quantity signals (their Walrasian demands and supplies), no agent makes any use of the quantity signals available on the market.

Our purpose will be to fill these gaps, and to build a consistent theory of the functioning of decentralized market economies when no auctioneer is present, market clearing is not axiomatically assumed, and quantity signals have to be considered in addition to price signals.

1.2.3 The Generalization

The consequences of abandoning the assumption that all markets clear at all times turn out to be quite far-reaching:

• Transactions cannot be all equal to demands and supplies expressed on markets. As a consequence some agents experience rationing, and quantity signals are formed in addition to price signals.
• Demands and supplies must be substantially modified on account of these quantity signals. Walrasian demand, which takes only prices into account, must be replaced by a more general *effective demand,* which takes into account *both* price and quantity signals.
• Price theory must also be amended in a way that integrates the possibility of nonclearing markets, the presence of quantity signals, and makes agents themselves responsible for rational price-making decisions. As we will see, the resulting framework is reminiscent of the traditional theories of imperfect competition.

Full general equilibrium concepts embedding these features will be developed in chapter 3. Later in this chapter we will study in a simpler setting the essential microeconomic elements of the theory. Notably we will be concerned with quantity signals, demand-supply theory, and price setting. Before that we must clarify which institutional structure we are dealing with.

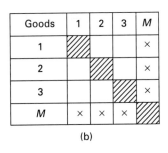

(a)   (b)

Figure 1.1   Barter and money

1.2.4   The Organization of Markets: Monetary Exchange

A relatively neglected issue in Walrasian general equilibrium models is the problem of the actual institutions of exchange. In his initial model Walras (1874) referred to a barter economy, with a market for each pair of goods. Other authors have assumed that all exchanges are monetary.

The difference between these two systems appears quite clearly in figure 1.1, adapted from Clower (1967), which shows which markets for various pairs of goods may be open or closed in each system. In the figure the existence of a market for the exchange between two goods is indicated by a cross in the corresponding box.[1] In a barter economy (panel a) a market exists for every pair of goods. So, for ℓ goods, there are $\ell(\ell - 1)/2$ markets. In a monetary economy, on the contrary (panel b), all exchanges must go through a medium of exchange, money, which we assume to be an additional good denoted M, so that there are ℓ markets.

Clearly, for a large number of goods, the cost of operating a barter structure would be prohibitive, and this explains why barter is almost never observed nowadays. Thus, for evident reasons of realism, we will work within the framework of a monetary economy.[2] Money is the medium of exchange. It is also the numéraire and a reserve of value. There are ℓ nonmonetary goods indexed by $h = 1, \ldots, \ell$ in addition to money. The money price of good h is p_h. An agent i may make a purchase d_{ih}, for which he pays $p_h d_{ih}$ units of money, or a sale s_{ih}, for which he receives $p_h s_{ih}$ units of money.

---

1 Since there is no such thing as the market for a good against itself, the boxes along the diagonal have been eliminated.

2 The theories presented here have been developed in nonmonetary exchange structures as well, but the formalization is both less realistic and more complex. See, in particular, Bénassy (1975b, 1982).

1.3 Transactions in Nonclearing Markets

A most important element of the theory is obviously to show how transactions can occur in a nonclearing market and how quantity signals are generated in the decentralized trading process.

1.3.1 Demands and Transactions

In nonmarket-clearing models we must make an important distinction that by nature is not made in market-clearing models: that between demands and supplies, on the one hand, and the resulting transactions, on the other. We distinguish them by different notations. Demands and supplies, denoted $\tilde{d}_{ih}$ and $\tilde{s}_{ih}$, are signals sent by each agent to the market (i.e., to the other agents) before an exchange takes place. They represent, as a first approximation, the exchanges agents wish to carry, and so do not necessarily match on the market. Transactions, namely purchases and sales of goods, are denoted d_{ih}^* and s_{ih}^*. They are the actual exchanges carried on markets, and as such they are subject to all traditional accounting identities. In particular, in each market h, aggregate purchases must be equal to aggregate sales. With n agents in the economy, this is written

$$D_h^* = \sum_{i=1}^{n} d_{ih}^* = \sum_{i=1}^{n} s_{ih}^* = S_h^* \tag{4}$$

As we indicated earlier, no such equality holds a priori for demands and supplies. We will study in this section the functioning of a market for a particular good h, where a price p_h has already been quoted. Since everything pertains to the same market, we can suppress the index h for the rest of this chapter.

1.3.2 Rationing Schemes

Since the price is not necessarily a market-clearing one, we may have

$$\tilde{D} = \sum_{i=1}^{n} \tilde{d}_i \neq \sum_{i=1}^{n} \tilde{s}_i = \tilde{S} \tag{5}$$

From any such set of possibly inconsistent demands and supplies, the exchange process must generate consistent transactions satisfying equation (4). Evidently, as soon as $\tilde{D} \neq \tilde{S}$, some demands and supplies cannot be satisfied in the exchange process and some agents must be rationed. In real life this is done through a variety of procedures, such as uniform rationing, queueing, proportional rationing, and priority systems, depending on the particular organization of each market. We will call rationing scheme the mathematical representation of the exchange process in the market being considered. This rationing scheme gives the transactions of each agent as a function of the demands and supplies of all agents present in that market (a general formalization appears in chapter 3). Before describing the various properties that rationing schemes may have, we give a simple example.

1.3.3   Example: A Queue

In a queueing system the demanders (or the suppliers) are ranked in a predetermined order and served according to that order. Let there be $n - 1$ demanders ranked in the order $i = 1, \ldots, n - 1$, each having a demand $\tilde{d}_i$, and a supplier, indexed by n, who supplies $\tilde{s}_n$. When the turn of demander i comes, the maximum quantity he can obtain is what demanders before him (i.e., agents $j < i$) have not taken, namely

$$\tilde{s}_n - \sum_{j<i} d_j^* = \max\left(0, \tilde{s}_n - \sum_{j<i} \tilde{d}_j\right) \tag{6}$$

The level of his purchase is simply the minimum of this quantity and his demand:

$$d_i^* = \min\left[\tilde{d}_i, \max\left(0, \tilde{s}_n - \sum_{j<i} \tilde{d}_j\right)\right] \tag{7}$$

As for the supplier, he sells the minimum of his supply and of total demand:

$$s_n^* = \min\left(\tilde{s}_n, \sum_{i=1}^{n-1} \tilde{d}_i\right) \tag{8}$$

It is easy to verify that whatever the demands and supplies, aggregate purchases and sales always match.

We now turn to study successively a number of properties of rationing schemes.

1.3.4   Voluntary Exchange and Market Efficiency

The first property we consider is a very natural one in a free market economy, namely that of *voluntary exchange,* according to which no agent can be forced to purchase more than he demands, or to sell more than he supplies. This will be expressed by

$$d_i^* \leq \tilde{d}_i \tag{9}$$

$$s_i^* \leq \tilde{s}_i \tag{10}$$

Such a condition is quite natural and actually verified in most markets, except maybe for some labor markets regulated by more complex contractual arrangements. It is clearly satisfied by the queueing example above.

Under voluntary exchange agents fall into two categories: rationed agents, for which $d_i^* < \tilde{d}_i$ or $s_i^* < \tilde{s}_i$, and nonrationed ones, for which $d_i^* = \tilde{d}_i$ or $s_i^* = \tilde{s}_i$. We say that a rationing scheme on a market is *efficient* or *frictionless* if there are not both rationed demanders and rationed suppliers in that market. The intuitive idea behind this is that in an efficiently organized market, a rationed buyer and a rationed seller should be able to meet and exchange until one of the two is not rationed anymore. Together with the voluntary exchange assumption, the efficiency assumption implies the "short-side" rule, according to which agents on the short side of the market can realize their desired transactions

$$\tilde{D} \geq \tilde{S} \Rightarrow s_i^* = \tilde{s}_i \qquad \text{for all } i \tag{11}$$

$$\tilde{S} \geq \tilde{D} \Rightarrow d_i^* = \tilde{d}_i \qquad \text{for all } i \tag{12}$$

This also yields the "rule of the minimum," which says that the aggregate level of transactions is equal to the minimum of aggregate demand and supply:

$$D^* = S^* = \min(\tilde{D}, \tilde{S}) \tag{13}$$

The market efficiency assumption is quite acceptable when one considers a small decentralized market where each demander meets each supplier (as in the queue of section 1.3.3). Market efficiency becomes a less fitting assumption when we consider a wide and decentralized market where some buyers and sellers might not meet pairwise. One may note in particular that the efficiency property is usually lost through the aggregation of submarkets. As a result the global level of transactions may be smaller than both total demand and supply. Figure 1.2 shows indeed how the aggregation of two frictionless submarkets yields an inefficient aggregate market, at least in some price range.

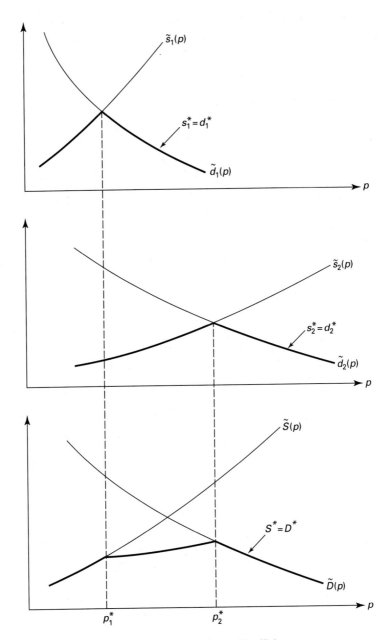

Figure 1.2   Aggregation and inefficiency

In the macroeconomic examples of the subsequent chapters we will assume frictionless markets, but we should note that the concepts that follow do not actually depend on this assumption.

1.4 Quantity Signals

Now it is quite clear that, since they cannot trade what they want, at least the rationed agents must perceive some quantity signals in addition to the price signals. Let us look at an example of how this occurs.

1.4.1 An Example

In order to see how quantity signals are formed in the transaction process, we begin with the simplest possible example, where only two agents are present in the market considered. Agent 1 demands $\tilde{d}_1$, and agent 2 supplies $\tilde{s}_2$. In such a simple market the "rule of the minimum" applies:

$$d_1^* = s_2^* = \min(\tilde{d}_1, \tilde{s}_2) \tag{14}$$

Now, as transactions take place, quantity signals are sent across the market: faced with a supply $\tilde{s}_2$, and under voluntary exchange, demander 1 knows that he will not be able to purchase more than $\tilde{s}_2$. Symmetrically supplier 2 knows that he cannot sell more than $\tilde{d}_1$. Each agent thus receives from the other a "quantity signal," respectively denoted $\bar{d}_1$ and $\bar{s}_2$, that tells him the maximum quantity he can respectively buy and sell. In this example, we have

$$\bar{d}_1 = \tilde{s}_2, \quad \bar{s}_2 = \tilde{d}_1 \tag{15}$$

so the rationing scheme (14) can be alternatively be expressed as

$$d_1^* = \min(\tilde{d}_1, \bar{d}_1) \tag{16}$$

$$s_2^* = \min(\tilde{s}_2, \bar{s}_2) \tag{17}$$

1.4.2 Quantity Signals

It turns out that many rationing schemes, and actually those we shall study in that follows, share the simple representation given by equations (16) and (17). Every agent i receives in the market a quantity signal, respectively $\bar{d}_i$ or $\bar{s}_i$ on

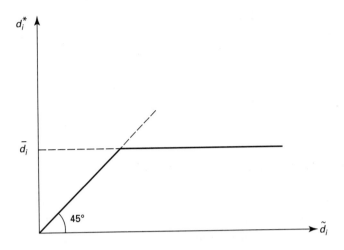

Figure 1.3   Nonmanipulable rationing scheme

the demand or supply side, which tells him the maximum quantity he can buy or sell. So the rationing scheme is simply written

$$d_i^* = \min(\tilde{d}_i, \bar{d}_i) \tag{18}$$

$$s_i^* = \min(\tilde{s}_i, \bar{s}_i) \tag{19}$$

where the quantity signals are functions of the demands and supplies of the *other* agents in the market. The relation between the demand $\tilde{d}_i$ and purchase d_i^* would appear as in figure 1.3.

As an example, for the queueing scheme of section 1.3.3 (equations 7 and 8), the quantity signals are given by

$$\bar{d}_i = \max\left(0, \bar{s}_n - \sum_{j<i} \tilde{d}_j\right), \qquad i = 1, \dots, n-1 \tag{20}$$

$$\bar{s}_n = \sum_{j=1}^{n-1} \tilde{d}_j \tag{21}$$

We may note that under the representation given by (18) and (19), the rationing scheme displays obviously voluntary exchange, but also another important property, that of nonmanipulability. A scheme is called *nonmanipulable* if, once rationed, an agent cannot increase his transaction by increasing the size of his demand. This property is quite evidently present in figure 1.3: once the transaction level $\bar{d}_i$ is attained, no increase of demand can yield a greater transaction. This assumption of nonmanipulability will be maintained in what follows.[3]

It is further clear that the quantity signals perceived by the agents should have an effect on demand, supply, and price formation. This is the relationship we explore next.

1.5 Effective Demand and Supply

As indicated above, demands and supplies are "signals" that agents send to the market in order to obtain the best transactions according to their own criteria. The traditional Walrasian demands and supplies are constructed on the assumption (which is verified ex post in Walrasian equilibrium) that every agent can buy and sell as much as he wants in the marketplace. Demands and supplies are thus functions of price signals only. We must now look more closely at how demands and supplies are formed when markets do not clear, and for that purpose we develop a theory of *effective demands and supplies,* which are functions of both price and quantity signals.

1.5.1 A Definition

When formulating his effective demands and supplies, agent i knows that his transactions will be related to them by equalities like (18) and (19) above, that is,

$$d_i^* = \min(\tilde{d}_i, \bar{d}_i) \tag{22}$$

$$s_i^* = \min(\tilde{s}_i, \bar{s}_i) \tag{23}$$

Maximizing the expected utility of these resulting transactions may lead to complex calculations (especially if constraints are stochastic). In the case of deterministic constraints, which is what we will consider here, there exists a simple

---

3 Of course, there exist some rationing schemes, like the proportional rationing scheme, that are *manipulable* in the sense that an agent can, even when rationed, continue to increase the level of his transaction by overstating his demand. Such schemes are studied in the appendix to this chapter where it is shown that they typically lead, in a nonclearing market, to divergent demands or supplies and possibly no equilibrium.

and workable definition that generalizes Clower's (1965) seminal insight: effective demand (or supply) of a particular good is the trade that maximizes the agent's criterion subject to the usual constraints *and* to the quantity constraints on the *other* markets. A more formal definition is given in chapter 3, but before we get to it, we will study a well-known example.

1.5.2   The Employment Function

A good illustrative example of our definition of effective demand and supply is the employment function due to Patinkin (1956) and Barro and Grossman (1971). We take a firm with a diminishing returns to scale production function $Y = F(N)$ faced with a price P and wage W. The Walrasian labor demand is equal to $F'^{-1}(W/P)$. Assume now that the firm faces a constraint $\bar{Y}$ on its sales of output (in a complete model, such as will be developed in chapter 2, $\bar{Y}$ is equal to total demand from the other agents). By the definition of section 1.5.1, the effective demand for labor $\tilde{N}^d$ is the solution in N of the program

$$\max PY - WN \quad \text{s.t.}$$

$$Y = F(N)$$

$$Y \leq \bar{Y}$$

This yields

$$\tilde{N}^d = \min \left\{ F'^{-1}\left(\frac{W}{P}\right), F^{-1}(\bar{Y}) \right\} \tag{24}$$

We see that the effective demand for labor may actually have two forms: the Walrasian one $F'^{-1}(W/P)$ if the sales constraint is not binding, or, if this constraint is binding, a more "Keynesian" form equal to the quantity of labor just necessary to produce the output demand $F^{-1}(\bar{Y})$. We immediately see in this example that effective demand may take various functional forms, which intuitively explains why non-Walrasian models often have multiple regimes, as we will discover in the next chapter.

We also see that the definition of effective demand above naturally includes the well-known *spillover effects:* we say indeed that there is a spillover effect when an agent who is constrained to exchange less than he wants in a market because of rationing modifies his demands or supplies in the other markets. Here insufficient sales in the goods market "spill" into the labor market, resulting in a reduction of labor demand. We shall see in the next chapter how the combination of such spillover effects can lead to the famous "multiplier" effects.

1.6 The Formation of Prices

We are now ready to address the problem of price setting by agents internal to the system, and we will see that as in demand and supply theory, quantity signals play a fundamental role. The general idea relating the concepts of this section to those of the preceding ones is that price setters change their prices so as to "manipulate" the quantity constraints they face, that is, so as to increase or decrease their possible sales or purchases.

As a result of this introduction of quantity signals into the price-setting process, the theory bears, at least formally, some strong resemblance to the traditional theories of imperfect competition. This will be so even if the market is highly competitive. As was pointed out by Arrow (1959), the absence of quantity signals is characteristic only of an auctioneer-engineered market, and not of the more or less competitive market structure.

1.6.1 The Institutional Framework

Various price-setting scenarios integrating the above ideas can actually be envisioned. We will focus here on a particular (and realistic for many markets) pricing process where agents on one side of the market (usually the sellers) quote prices and agents on the other side are price takers.[4]

Consider thus, to fix ideas, the case where sellers set the price (the exposition would be symmetrical if demanders were setting the price). In order to have a single price per market, as was the case in all we said before, we will characterize a good not only by its physical and temporal attributes, but also by the agent who sets its price (this way two goods sold by different sellers are considered as different goods, which is a fairly usual assumption in microeconomic theory since these goods differ at least by location, quality, etc.). With markets so defined, each price setter is alone on his side of the market, and thus appears formally as a monopolist. Note, however, that this does not imply anything about to his actual monopoly power because there may be competitors' markets where other agents sell goods that are very close substitutes.

---

4 An alternative is for prices to be bargained between the two sides of the market. A model with such bargaining is developed in chapter 5.

1.6.2   Perceived Demand and Supply Curves

Consider thus a seller i who sets the price P in a certain market.[5] As we saw above, once he has posted his price, demands are expressed, transactions occur, and this seller faces a constraint $\bar{s}_i$ which is equal to the sum of all other agents' demands:

$$\bar{s}_i = \sum_{j \neq i} \tilde{d}_j = \tilde{D} \tag{25}$$

Now, if we consider the market *before* seller i set price P, we see that he does not, contrarily to a price taker, consider his quantity constraint $\bar{s}_i$ as parametric. Rather, and this is how the price-setting theory developed here relates to what we saw previously, he will use the price P to "manipulate" the quantity constraint $\bar{s}_i$ he faces, that is, so as to increase or decrease the demand addressed to him. The relation between the maximum quantity seller i expects to sell and the price he sets is called the perceived demand curve. If expectations are deterministic (which we assume here) the perceived demand curve will be denoted[6]

$$\bar{S}_i(P) \tag{26}$$

In view of equation (25), this perceived demand is what the price setter expects the aggregate demand of the other agents to be, conditional on the price P that he sets. Now, depending on what the price setter knows about the economy, two main forms of perceived demand curves can be considered, objective or subjective:

• In the "objective demand curve" approach, which we will be using in most of this book, it is assumed that the price setter knows the *exact* form of the other agents' demand functions, so that

$$\bar{S}_i(P) = \tilde{D}(P) \tag{27}$$

where $\tilde{D}(P)$ is the exact aggregate effective demand of agents facing the price

5 Although the price P is set by agent i, we do not index it by i because it is the (unique) market price.

6 Although it may seem odd that the perceived *demand* curve is denoted $\bar{S}_i(P)$, this is fully logical since it is a constraint on the *supply* of the price setter. The connection with the actual demand is expressed in formula (27) below.

setter. Although the construction of such an objective demand curve in a partial equilibrium framework is a trivial matter, things become much more complicated in a multimarket situation, as this requires a sophisticated general equilibrium argument. We will see in chapter 3 how to use the concepts developed here to rigorously construct an objective demand curve in a full general equilibrium system. Simple macroeconomic applications will be developed explicitly in chapters 4 and 5.

· In the "subjective demand curve" approach, it is assumed that the price setter does not have full information about the form of the demand curve facing him, so his perceived demand curve $\bar{S}_i(P)$ is partly "subjective." Most often isoelastic subjective demand curves are used, with the following form:

$$\bar{S}_i(P) = \xi_i P^{-\eta} \tag{28}$$

It should be noted that although the elasticity η is somewhat arbitrary, the position parameter ξ_i is not, since each realization $(P, \bar{s}_i)$ is a point on the "true" demand curve, and the subjective demand curve must pass through this point (Bushaw and Clower 1957). For example, with the isoelastic curves (28), if the price setter faces a quantity constraint $\bar{s}_i$ after setting a price $\bar{P}$, the parameter ξ_i must be such that

$$\bar{s}_i = \xi_i \bar{P}^{-\eta} \tag{29}$$

The functional form and the elasticity may be wrong, but at least the position must be right, as shown in figure 1.4. An example of equilibria using the subjective demand curve approach is found in chapter 2.

The subjective and objective demand curves approaches are not actually antagonistic, at least not in our theory. Knowing the exact objective demand curve requires very high amounts of information and computational ability, and the subjective demand curve should be thought of as what the price setter expects the "true" curve to be in an ongoing learning process. Whether this learning will lead to a good approximation of the "true" objective demand curve is still an unresolved problem.

1.6.3 Price Setting

Once the parameters of the perceived demand curve are known, price setting proceeds along lines that are traditional in imperfect competition theories: the price setter maximizes his objective function subject to the constraint that his

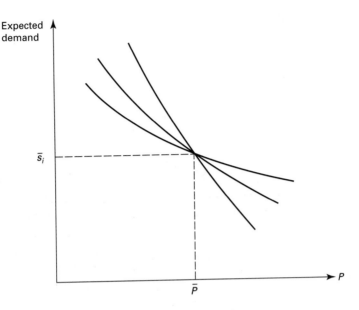

Figure 1.4 Subjective demand curves

sales can be no greater than the amount given by the perceived demand curve on the markets he controls (in addition to the usual constraints).

For example, take a firm with a cost function $\Gamma(Y)$, and assume that it faces an *objective* demand curve $\tilde{D}(P)$. The program giving the optimal price of the firm is thus written:

$$\max PY - \Gamma(Y) \quad \text{s.t.}$$

$$Y \leq \tilde{D}(P)$$

To solve this, we first note that the price setter will always choose a combination of P and Y such that he is "on" the demand curve, meaning such that $Y = \tilde{D}(P)$. If he were not, he could increase price P without modifying Y, thus increasing his profits. The solution is thus first characterized by

$$Y = \tilde{D}(P) \tag{30}$$

Now inserting (30) into the expression of profits and maximizing, we obtain the first-order condition

$$\Gamma'(Y) = \frac{\eta(P) - 1}{\eta(P)} P \tag{31}$$

where

$$\eta(P) = -\frac{\partial \log \tilde{D}(P)}{\partial \log P} > 0 \tag{32}$$

Equation (31) is the well-known "marginal cost equals marginal revenue" condition, in which we see that the firm will choose a price high enough so that it will not only want to serve the actual demand, but would even be willing to serve more demand at the price it has chosen. In fact the firm would be content to meet demand up to $\Gamma'^{-1}(P) > Y$. There is thus in our sense an "excess supply" of the good, although this excess supply is fully voluntary on the part of the price setter.

The imperfectly competitive price and production are determined by equations (30) and (31). They are drawn together in figure 1.5, where

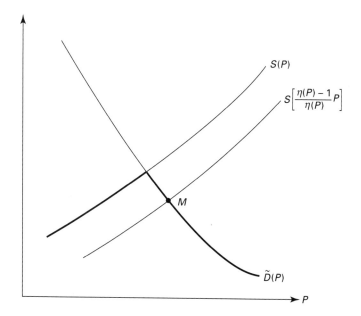

Figure 1.5 Imperfect competition equilibrium

$S(P) = \Gamma'^{-1}(P)$ is the "competitive" supply of the firm. The resulting equilibrium corresponds to point M.

Figure 1.5 also shows the "fixprice allocations" given by the minimum of supply and demand, that is,

$$Y = \min[\tilde{D}(P), S(P)] \tag{33}$$

In the figure we see that the imperfectly competitive solution corresponds to one of the "fixprice" points, and one that is clearly in the excess supply zone.

1.7   Conclusions

We reviewed in this chapter the most basic elements for a rigorous theory of nonclearing markets. We saw how quantity signals are naturally formed in such markets, and how demands and supplies are responsive to these quantity signals. We also considered the issue of rational price setting, and we saw clearly that there is a natural relation between the functioning of nonclearing markets and the theory of price setting in circumstances of imperfect competition. This relation between nonclearing markets and imperfect competition will appear throughout the book.

For the simplicity of exposition we described all the above in a somewhat partial equilibrium framework. Obviously the next step is to move to a general equilibrium framework. Chapter 2 will start with the simplest macroeconomic model embedding the features of chapter 1, and show the rich variety of results that can be obtained. Chapter 3 will integrate the same concepts in a full-fledged multimarket general equilibrium setting. Finally the subsequent chapters will introduce successively time and uncertainty, moving to dynamic general equilibrium macromodels.

1.8   References

This chapter is based on Bénassy (1976c, 1982, 1993).

The starting point of many works on nonclearing markets is found in the article by Clower (1965), where he showed how to reinterpret the Keynesian consumption function through some type of effective demand, and in the book by Leijonhufvud (1968). Early elements of theory in the same direction are found in Hansen (1951), who introduced the ideas of active demand, close in spirit to that of effective demand, in Patinkin (1956), who studied the employment function of firms unable to sell their Walrasian output, and Hahn and

Negishi (1962), who studied nontâtonnement processes where trade takes place outside Walrasian equilibrium.

The representation of rationing schemes and quantity signals in this chapter are taken from Bénassy (1975a, 1977b, 1982). The voluntary exchange and market efficiency properties had been discussed under various forms in Clower (1960, 1965), Hahn and Negishi (1962), Barro and Grossman (1971), Grossman (1971), and Howitt (1974). The problem of manipulability was studied in Bénassy (1977b). The theory of effective demand originates in Clower (1965), and the more general definition is found in Bénassy (1975a, 1977b).

As we noted, the model of price setting is quite reminiscent of the imperfect competition line of thought (Chamberlin 1933; Robinson 1933; Triffin 1940; Bushaw and Clower 1957; Arrow 1959) and more particularly of the theories of general equilibrium with monopolistic competition, as developed notably by Negishi (1961, 1972). Their relation to the above non-Walrasian theories was developed in Bénassy (1976a, 1977a).

Appendix 1.1: Manipulable Rationing Schemes

Throughout this chapter we implicitly studied nonmanipulable rationing schemes. These are rationing schemes where an agent, once rationed, cannot increase his transaction by overstating his demand. In this appendix we will look at the opposite case of *manipulable* rationing schemes where a rationed agent can increase his transaction by overstating his demand, hence the name "manipulable." This is represented in figure 1.6, which represents the relation between the demand $\tilde{d}_i$ of a demander i and the transaction $d_i^* = \phi_i(\tilde{d}_i)$ he will obtain from the market.

An Example

We begin with a well-known example of a manipulable rationing scheme, that of proportional rationing. In a proportional rationing scheme, total transactions are equal to the minimum of aggregate demand and aggregate supply. These trades are allocated among the various agents proportionately to their demand or supply. This is expressed mathematically as

$$d_i^* = \tilde{d}_i \times \min\left(1, \frac{\tilde{S}}{\bar{D}}\right) \tag{34}$$

$$s_i^* = \tilde{s}_i \times \min\left(1, \frac{\tilde{D}}{\bar{S}}\right) \tag{35}$$

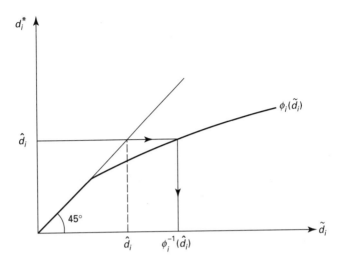

Figure 1.6   Manipulable rationing scheme

It is easy to verify that whatever the demands and supplies, the trades realized always match at the aggregate level.

Manipulation and Overbidding

We will now see that manipulable rationing schemes lead to a perverse phenomenon of overbidding, which may totally jeopardize the existence of an equilibrium in demands and supplies. The mechanism is easy to understand: consider an agent i who would like to obtain a transaction $\hat{d}_i$, but who would be rationed if he announces that level. As shown in figure 1.6, he will be naturally led to overstate his demand to the level $\phi_i^{-1}(\hat{d}_i)$ in order to reach $\hat{d}_i$. The problem is that all rationed demanders will do exactly the same thing, and as a result the perceived rationing schemes will move in time in such a way that the same demand yields an ever lower transaction. It is easy to see that because of this overbidding phenomenon, demands may grow without bound, so that no equilibrium with finite demands and supplies exists, as we will now observe in a simple example.

An Example

Let us consider the case of a supplier facing two demanders, indexed by 1 and 2. In each period t we have, respectively, a supply $\tilde{s}(t)$ and demands $\tilde{d}_1(t)$ and

$\tilde{d}_2(t)$. The rationing scheme is thus written as

$$d_i^*(t) = \tilde{d}_i(t) \times \min\left[1, \frac{\tilde{s}(t)}{\tilde{d}_1(t) + \tilde{d}_2(t)}\right], \qquad i = 1, 2 \qquad (36)$$

$$s^*(t) = \min[\tilde{s}(t), \tilde{d}_1(t) + \tilde{d}_2(t)] \qquad (37)$$

Let us assume that each trader knows the rationing rule and the demands and supplies of the others after they have been expressed. Moreover he expects these to remain the same from period $t - 1$ to period t. The perceived rationing scheme is thus for demander 1,

$$\phi_{1t}(\tilde{d}_1) = \tilde{d}_1 \times \min\left[1, \frac{\tilde{s}(t-1)}{\tilde{d}_1 + \tilde{d}_2(t-1)}\right] \qquad (38)$$

and similarly for demander 2. Now let us assume that the agents have "target transactions" $\hat{d}_1, \hat{d}_2$, and $\hat{s}$ such that the supplier could serve each demander individually, but not both, that is,

$$\hat{d}_1 < \hat{s}, \quad \hat{d}_2 < \hat{s}, \quad \hat{s} < \hat{d}_1 + \hat{d}_2 \qquad (39)$$

Under these conditions the supplier will never be rationed and will express his target transaction as effective supply:

$$\tilde{s}(t) = \hat{s} \qquad (40)$$

The demanders, in the contrary, will be rationed, and they will in each period overstate their demands in a way such that they (wrongly) believe to reach their target transaction.[7] Their effective demands will thus be given by

$$\phi_{1t}[\tilde{d}_1(t)] = \hat{d}_1 \qquad (41)$$

$$\phi_{2t}[\tilde{d}_2(t)] = \hat{d}_2 \qquad (42)$$

7 This belief is false simply because each demander computes his demand assuming that the other demander will not change his demand from the previous period, whereas, as we will soon see, these demands will generally increase over time.

In view of (38), and the corresponding formula for demander 2, these two equations yield

$$\tilde{d}_1(t) = \tilde{d}_2(t-1) \times \frac{\hat{d}_1}{\hat{s} - \hat{d}_1} \tag{43}$$

$$\tilde{d}_2(t) = \tilde{d}_1(t-1) \times \frac{\hat{d}_2}{\hat{s} - \hat{d}_2} \tag{44}$$

Combining (43) and (44), we obtain

$$\tilde{d}_1(t) = \tilde{d}_1(t-2) \times \frac{\hat{d}_1}{\hat{s} - \hat{d}_1} \times \frac{\hat{d}_2}{\hat{s} - \hat{d}_2} \tag{45}$$

which is an indefinitely divergent sequence since $\hat{s} < \hat{d}_1 + \hat{d}_2$.

2

A Simple Macroeconomic Example

2.1 Introduction

We show in this chapter how the concepts described in chapter 1 can be used to construct a wide variety of macroeconomic models. We thus consider a simple economy and study successively macroeconomic equilibria under the following assumptions on price and wage formation: (1) Walrasian equilibrium, (2) rigid prices and wages, and (3) imperfect competition in the goods and labor markets.

We will learn that employment and output determination, as well as the effects of economic policies, can be very different, depending not only on the pricing scheme but, for a given pricing scheme, even on the endogenously determined regime of the economy. All these models will be studied in the framework of the *same* economy, which we now describe.

2.2 The Economy

Let us consider a very simple monetary economy with three goods-money, output, and labor-and three agents-an aggregate firm, an aggregate household, and the government. There are two markets where output and labor are exchanged against money at the price P and wage W, respectively. We assume that these markets are frictionless so that transactions in each one are equal to the minimum of supply and demand. We denote by Y and N, respectively, the output and labor transactions.

The aggregate firm has a strictly concave production function $F(N)$. The firm maximizes profits $\Pi = PY - WN$. These profits are fully redistributed to the household.

The household has an initial endowment of money $\bar{M}$. It consumes a quantity C of output, works an amount N, saves an amount of money M, and its budget constraint is

$$PC + M = WN + \Pi + \bar{M} - PT \tag{1}$$

where T is the real value of taxes levied by the government. The household has the simple utility function:

$$\alpha \log C + (1 - \alpha) \log \left(\frac{M}{P^e} \right) - V(N) \tag{2}$$

where α will be naturally interpreted as the propensity to consume and P^e is an expected price. $V(N)$ is the disutility of labor, with

$$V'(N) > 0, \quad V''(N) > 0 \tag{3}$$

The utility function (2) can be justified as follows:[1] imagine that the household lives two periods. The second period is indexed by e, as expected. The household's utility function is

$$\alpha \log C + (1 - \alpha) \log C^e - V(N) \tag{4}$$

where C^e is the second period's consumption. Assuming that the household earns nothing in the second period, then the only way it can consume is to save under the form of money, so the second-period consumption is

$$C^e = \frac{M}{P^e} \tag{5}$$

Inserting (5) into (4), we obtain the utility function (2).

Last the government has a demand for output G and, as already seen, taxes an amount T in real terms from the household. As a consequence its budget

---

1 A fully self-contained model along this line is actually developed in chapter 4.

constraint is

$$M - \bar{M} = P(G - T) \tag{6}$$

So we can describe government policy by any two of the three variables G, T, and M, the third being deduced through the government budget constraint (6). In what follows we will take G and T as our exogenous variables, the value of M proceeding from (6).

2.3 Walrasian Equilibrium

We will derive as a benchmark the Walrasian equilibrium of this economy. We begin by computing the Walrasian demands and supplies in the output and labor markets. Maximization of the firm's profits under the production function $F(N)$ yields

$$N^d = F'^{-1}\left(\frac{W}{P}\right) \tag{7}$$

$$Y^s = F\left[F'^{-1}\left(\frac{W}{P}\right)\right] \tag{8}$$

Maximization of the household's utility function (2), subject to the budget constraint (1), yields the first-order conditions

$$\frac{\alpha}{PC} = \frac{1 - \alpha}{M} = \frac{V'(N)}{W} \tag{9}$$

We also have the equilibrium condition on the goods market:

$$Y = C + G \tag{10}$$

Combining equations (7) to (10), we find that the values of N, Y, P, and W in Walrasian equilibrium (whenever it exists) are given by

$$\alpha F'(N) = [F(N) - G]V'(N) \tag{11}$$

$$Y = F(N) \tag{12}$$

$$\frac{W}{P} = F'(N) \tag{13}$$

$$P = \frac{\alpha \bar{M}}{(1 - \alpha)Y + \alpha T - G} \tag{14}$$

From (14) we see that a necessary condition for the existence of a Walrasian equilibrium is

$$G < (1 - \alpha)Y(G) + \alpha T \tag{15}$$

where $Y(G)$ denotes the solution in Y to equations (11) and (12). This condition says that the real spending of the government must not be too high. From these equations we learn a few things. First, money is "neutral" (i.e., the price and wage are proportional to $\bar{M}$, whereas Y and N do not depend on it). Furthermore from (10), (11), and (12) we deduce

$$-1 < \frac{\partial C}{\partial G} < 0 \tag{16}$$

So there is crowding out of private consumption by government expenditures, though at less than 100 percent.

2.4   Fixprice-Fixwage Equilibria

We can study the model above under an assumption that is polar to that of the Walrasian model, namely that the price P and wage W are completely rigid in the period considered. We will obtain the "fixprice" model originally developed by Barro and Grossman (1971, 1976). A remarkable feature of such models is that they endogenously produce multiple regimes. As is well-known now, this particular model has three possible regimes.[2]

2 Note that the terminology of the three regimes is not fully satisfactory, as it tends to associate the idea of classical unemployment with an excess demand for goods, which is not necessarily the case (Bénassy 1982). We nevertheless retain this terminology as many people are accustomed to using it.

- Keynesian unemployment, with excess supply of both output and labor
- Classical unemployment, with excess supply of labor and excess demand for goods
- Suppressed inflation, with excess demand for both labor and output

We will now consider these three regimes in turn.

2.4.1 Keynesian Unemployment

The Keynesian regime exhibits excess supply in both markets. In particular the household faces a binding constraint $\bar{N}^s$ in the labor market, so that its effective consumption demand $\tilde{C}$ is the solution in C of the following program:

$$\max \alpha \log C + (1 - \alpha) \log \left(\frac{M}{P^e} \right) - V(N) \quad \text{s.t.}$$

$$PC + M = \bar{M} + WN + \Pi - PT$$

$$N \leq \bar{N}^s$$

This yields, since the second constraint is binding,

$$\tilde{C} = \alpha \left(\frac{\bar{M} + W\bar{N}^s + \Pi - PT}{P} \right) \tag{17}$$

Equation (17) can be rewritten, using the definition of Π and the fact that $\bar{N}^s$ is equal to the actual sale of labor,

$$\tilde{C} = \alpha \left(\frac{\bar{M}}{P} + Y - T \right) \tag{18}$$

This is a standard Keynesian consumption function, with a propensity to consume equal to α. Because of excess supply on the goods market, transactions Y are equal to total output demand:

$$Y = \tilde{C} + G = \alpha \left(\frac{\bar{M}}{P} + Y - T \right) + G \tag{19}$$

This equation yields the level of equilibrium transactions on the goods market:

$$Y^* = \frac{1}{1-\alpha}\left(\frac{\alpha \bar{M}}{P} + G - \alpha T\right) = Y_k \qquad (20)$$

We recognize in (20) a traditional Keynesian multiplier formula where $1/(1-\alpha)$ is the multiplier and the term in parentheses is the so-called autonomous demand. This multiplier results from the interaction of two spillover effects. First, in view of the employment function (this we derived in chapter 1, formula 24), less demand for goods creates a reduced demand for labor. Second, and in view of the consumption function (17), less demand for labor results in less demand for goods. The compounding of these two mutually reinforcing effects will "multiply" autonomous demand variations.

Labor transactions are equal to the firm's demand. Since the firm is constrained in its output sales to Y_k, this labor demand (and therefore the transaction) is equal, as we saw in chapter 1, to the quantity of labor just necessary to produce Y_k:

$$N^* = \tilde{N}^d = F^{-1}(Y_k) = N_k \qquad (21)$$

We can also compute private consumption $C^* = Y^* - G$:

$$C^* = \frac{\alpha}{1-\alpha}\left(\frac{\bar{M}}{P} + G - T\right) \qquad (22)$$

Let us now make a few observations. The first is that money is not neutral any more: an increase in $\bar{M}$ increases production, employment, and private consumption. Second, these will also be increased by decreases in taxes or increases in government spending. The traditional results of Keynesian "multiplier" analysis are thus fully valid in this regime.

Perhaps the most striking fact is that an increase in government spending will increase private consumption (formula 22). There is thus no crowding-out, quite on the contrary: although the government collects real output from the private sector, more of it is available for private consumption. This is a remarkable by-product of the inefficiency of the Keynesian multiplier state.

2.4.2 Classical Unemployment

In this case there is an excess supply of labor and an excess demand for goods. The firm is thus on the "short" side in both markets, so it is able to carry out its

Walrasian plan, so that

$$N^* = F'^{-1}\left(\frac{W}{P}\right) = N_c \tag{23}$$

$$Y^* = F\left[F'^{-1}\left(\frac{W}{P}\right)\right] = Y_c \tag{24}$$

We immediately see that Keynesian policies have no impact on employment and production. In fact it is easy to check that the main effect of a Keynesian policy would be to aggravate excess demand on the goods market, as we can easily check. If we further assume that government has priority in the goods market, then the actual consumption is equal to

$$C^* = Y^* - G = Y_c - G \tag{25}$$

There is a 100 percent crowding-out effect of government expenditures. However, this time the crowding-out does not occur through prices (as in the Walrasian equilibrium above) but by direct quantity rationing.

The only thing that affects employment and production is the level of real wages, thus this validates the classical view that there is unemployment because real wages are too high.

2.4.3 Suppressed Inflation

In this regime there is excess demand in both markets. In particular, the consumer is faced to a binding constraint $\bar{C}$ in the goods market. His effective supply of labor $\tilde{N}^s$ is thus given by the solution in N to the program

$$\max \alpha \log C + (1 - \alpha) \log\left(\frac{M}{P^e}\right) - V(N) \quad \text{s.t.}$$

$$PC + M = \bar{M} + WN + \Pi - PT$$

$$C \leq \bar{C}$$

where the last constraint is binding. The first-order condition for this program gives the effective supply of labor $\tilde{N}^s$:

$$V'(\tilde{N}^s) = \frac{(1-\alpha)\,W}{\bar{M} + WN + \Pi - PT - P\bar{C}} \tag{26}$$

Formula (26) shows a new spillover effect: if $\bar{C}$ diminishes, so does $\tilde{N}^s$. In other words, a household that does not succeed in consuming what it wants will be led to reduce its supply of labor.

Now suppose again that government has priority in the goods market and that production is high enough to satisfy G (the reader can easily work out the case where it is not). Then $\bar{C}$ is equal to the household's purchases on the goods market, namely

$$\bar{C} = C^* = Y^* - G \tag{27}$$

Since there is excess demand for labor, the transaction N^* is equal to the effective labor supply $\tilde{N}^s$. Combining this with equations (26), (27), and the definition of profits, we obtain the equilibrium amount of labor in this regime, denoted as N_i:

$$V'(N_i) = \frac{(1-\alpha)W}{\bar{M} + PG - PT} \tag{28}$$

Because there is excess demand for goods, transactions in the goods market are equal to the supply of output. This supply of output is itself equal (since the firm is constrained in its labor purchases) to the maximum quantity producible with available labor supply, namely

$$Y^* = F(N_i) = Y_i \tag{29}$$

We may note that in this regime the economic policy variables have effects completely opposite to those in the Keynesian regime. In particular, increases in the quantity of money or in government spending *diminish* employment and production, whereas higher taxes increase production! furthermore, under the above assumptions private consumption is equal to

$$C^* = Y^* - G = Y_i - G \tag{30}$$

Since an increase in G reduces Y_i, there is a more than 100 percent crowding-out effect. An increase in G reduces C^* by an even greater amount! The mechanism at work in this regime is a type of "supply multiplier" (Barro-Grossman 1974) by which a reduction in the quantity of goods available for consumption reduces the supply of labor, which itself reduces further the amount of goods produced, and so on.

2.4.4 The Complete Picture

As we have seen above, the three regimes of our model display strikingly different properties concerning the determination of employment and production, and the economy's response to policy variables. It is therefore important to know for which values of the "exogenous" parameters $\bar{M}$, P, W, G, and T each of the three regimes obtains. We can easily check that both the employment level and the nature of the regime are determined by finding the lowest of the three possible employment levels computed above (equations 20, 21, 23, 24, 28, and 29), that is,

$$N^* = \min(N_k, N_c, N_i) \tag{31}$$

$$Y^* = \min(Y_k, Y_c, Y_i) \tag{32}$$

We now depict the three regimes in the $(\bar{M}/P, W/P)$ space, G and T being parametric. Figure 2.1 shows the case where G and T are both equal to zero, a case where we are sure that the Walrasian equilibrium always exists. The triangles are iso-employment or iso-output lines. The highest level of employment and production occurs at W, the Walrasian equilibrium point. Region K corresponds to Keynesian unemployment, region C to classical unemployment, and region I to suppressed inflation.

In the figure we see particularly well that the spillover effects from the goods market to the labor market matter a lot: even if the real wage is "right" (i.e., equal to its Walrasian equilibrium level, which corresponds to the horizontal line going through W), we may have inefficiently low values of employment due to insufficient or excessive demand in the output market.

2.4.5 Inefficiency Properties

We now want to highlight in this particular macroeconomic example some inefficiencies that we will study in more generality in the next chapter. A property we will find is that in cases of generalized excess demand or supply, which lead to the existence of multiplier effects, there are most likely potential Pareto

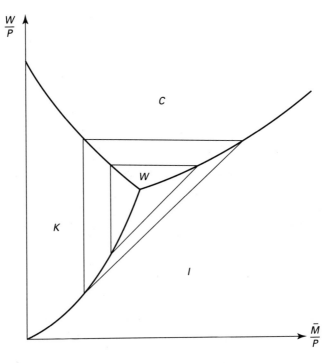

Figure 2.1   The three regimes

improving trades at the given price system. We want to verify this fact in the two regimes concerned, those of Keynesian unemployment and suppressed inflation.

Let us begin with the interior of the Keynesian regime. Since $N_k < N_c$, we have

$$F'(N) < \frac{W}{P} \tag{33}$$

so the firm could increase its real profit by trading directly labor for output. Consider now the household. Since it is unconstrained in the goods market and constrained on the labor market, we have

$$\frac{1}{P}\frac{\partial U}{\partial C} = \frac{\partial U}{\partial M} > -\frac{1}{W}\frac{\partial U}{\partial N} \tag{34}$$

so that the household would also gain in selling directly labor for output. So both the firm and household would strictly gain in exchanging directly output for labor. Nevertheless, this simple Pareto-improving trade remains unattained in equilibrium.

Symmetrically in the interior of the suppressed inflation regime, we have

$$F'(N) < \frac{W}{P} \tag{35}$$

$$\frac{1}{P}\frac{\partial U}{\partial C} > \frac{\partial U}{\partial M} = -\frac{1}{W}\frac{\partial U}{\partial N} \tag{36}$$

Clearly, again both the firm and household could profitably exchange directly output for labor.

This result means that multiplier equilibria do not only fail to be Pareto optimal. One could actually, starting from these equilibria, improve consumers' utilities *and* firms' profits, and all that while carrying exchanges at the *given* prices. This very striking inefficiency explains the surprising effects of Keynesian policies that we saw above.

2.5 An Imperfectly Competitive Model

We will here endogenize prices and wages in a framework of imperfect competition similar to that described in chapter 1, section 1.6. We will assume that firms set prices, and that households set wages. In order to make exposition more compact, we will use the subjective demand curve approach. It turns out that highly similar results can be obtained with objective demand curves and rational expectations (see chapter 4).

2.5.1 The Equilibrium

To characterize the equilibrium, we will successively consider the optimal actions of the firm and household. Consider first the firm, and assume that it perceives demand curves of the form $\xi P^{-\eta}$, where $\eta > 1$ is given and ξ is a variable "position" parameter. The optimal actions of the firm are given by the program

$$\max PY - WN \quad \text{s.t.}$$

$$Y = F(N)$$

$$Y \leq \xi P^{-\eta}$$

The first-order conditions for this program yield, after elimination of ξ,

$$F'(N) = \frac{\eta}{\eta - 1} \frac{W}{P} \qquad (37)$$

Suppose now that the household similarly perceives demand curves of the form $\xi W^{-\epsilon}$, where $\epsilon > 1$ is given and ξ is again a position parameter. The program yielding the household's optimal actions is

$$\max \alpha \log C + (1 - \alpha) \log \left(\frac{M}{P^e} \right) - V(N) \quad \text{s.t.}$$

$$PC + M = \bar{M} + WN + \Pi - PT$$

$$N \leq \xi W^{-\epsilon}$$

The first-order conditions yield

$$\frac{\alpha}{PC} = \frac{1 - \alpha}{M} = \frac{\epsilon - 1}{\epsilon} \frac{V'(N)}{W} \qquad (38)$$

We may note that except for the factor $(\epsilon - 1)/\epsilon$, these equations resemble the competitive ones (equation 9).

To complete the model, we add to the first-order conditions (37) and (38) three equations that hold in all versions of the model. These are the production function:

$$Y = F(N) \qquad (39)$$

the budget constraint of the household:

$$PC + M = \bar{M} + WN + \Pi - PT \qquad (40)$$

and the equality between production and total demand:

$$Y = C + G \qquad (41)$$

Solving the system of equations (37) to (41), we find that the values of Y, N, P, and W in equilibrium (when it exists) are given by

$$\alpha F'(N) = \frac{\epsilon}{\epsilon - 1}\frac{\eta}{\eta - 1}[F(N) - G]V'(N) \tag{42}$$

$$Y = F(N) \tag{43}$$

$$\frac{W}{P} = \frac{\eta - 1}{\eta}F'(N) \tag{44}$$

$$P = \frac{\alpha \bar{M}}{(1 - \alpha)Y + \alpha T - G} \tag{45}$$

We may note that the Walrasian equilibrium is a particular limit case of this equilibrium when both η and ϵ go to infinity (compare equations 11 to 14 and equations 42 to 45), that is when the perceived demand curves become infinitely elastic, as one would naturally expect.

2.5.2 Properties of the Equilibrium

We can first remark that the allocation in our imperfectly competitive equilibrium has, at first sight, properties similar to those of a "Keynesian" allocation, as described in section 2.4, and notably that we are somehow in a "general excess supply" regime. Indeed equation (37) shows that the firm would be willing, at the equilibrium price and wage, to produce and sell more goods if the demand was forthcoming. Similarly equation (38) shows that the household would like to sell more labor at the going price and wage if there was more demand for it. In figure 2.1 the equilibrium values of W and P would yield a point *within* region K. We want to learn next whether this similarity extends to the effects of government policy.

2.5.3 Government Policy

We now want to ask whether the Keynesian-style government policies that are successful in the regime of Keynesian unemployment are still as successful in this imperfectly competitive framework.

Let us consider first the effects of money. We see that money is now fully neutral: An increase in $\bar{M}$ brings about an equiproportionate rise in P and

W, whereas Y and N do not move. Next we see that a tax decrease does not have any impact on Y and N but does increase prices and wages (equations 44 and 45). If we finally consider an increase in government spending G, we see that it increases employment and production but actually crowds out private consumption.

All in all, we see that this model yields an allocation that has "Keynesian" inefficiency properties but reacts to government policy in a somewhat similar way to that of a Walrasian model. All this will be studied in more depth in chapter 4, where we will consider a model of similar inspiration but with rational expectations and objective demand curves.

2.6   Conclusions

Although highly simplified, the model of this chapter has shown us the potential richness of the approach outlined in chapter 1, since we can obtain within the *same* model results belonging to the Walrasian, Keynesian, and imperfect competition paradigms, and still a few others (see notably section 2.4).

Although this is quite encouraging, the model of this chapter is clearly only a first step. So we will see in the next chapter that the theory extends far beyond this simple example, and that all important concepts can be developed in a full-fledged general equilibrium setting.

2.7   References

The model in this chapter is based on Barro and Grossman (1971, 1976) and Bénassy (1977a, 1993).

The first fully worked out fixprice-fixwage macroeconomic model is due to Barro and Grossman (1971, 1976). They succeeded putting together Patinkin's (1956) contribution on the employment function and Clower's (1965) one on the consumption function. Early attempts in that direction are found in Glustoff (1968) and Solow and Stiglitz (1969).

The particular adaptation of the fixprice model in this chapter comes from Bénassy (1976b, 1977a). Subsequent adaptations and extensions are found in Malinvaud (1977), Hildenbrand and Hildenbrand (1978), Muellbauer and Portes (1978), Honkapohja (1979), Neary and Stiglitz (1983), Persson and Svensson (1983), and Bénassy (1986).

Macroeconomic models with imperfect competition of the type presented here were initially developed in Bénassy (1977a) and Negishi (1977).

Subsequent contributions include Bénassy (1978, 1982, 1987), Negishi (1979), Hart (1982), Weitzman (1982, 1985), Snower (1983), Svensson (1986), Blanchard and Kiyotaki (1987), Dixon (1987), Sneessens (1987), and many more since. The particular version in this chapter comes from Bénassy (1977a, 1993). Surveys of the field are found in Silvestre (1993, 1995) and Dixon and Rankin (1994).

In this chapter we concentrated on the standard three goods model and the problems of employment and policy. Several other issues have been treated with this methodology, including foreign trade (Dixit 1978; Neary 1980; Cuddington, Johansson, and Lofgren 1984), growth (Ito 1980; Picard 1983; D'Autume 1985), business cycles (Bénassy, 1984), and the specific problems of planned socialist economies (Portes 1981). A large number of applied econometric models have been developed as well (Quandt 1982, 1988; Sneessens 1981).

Part II

General Equilibrium

3

General Equilibrium Concepts

3.1 Introduction

We developed in the previous chapter an example of a macroeconomic model which showed the variety and richness of the non-Walrasian approach. However, in times when the emphasis is on the microeconomic foundations of macroeconomics, one may legitimately inquire whether the concepts outlined in the two preceding chapters can be developed in a full general equilibrium framework such as the one students of Walrasian economics are accustomed to. We shall give a positive answer to this question by constructing a number of general equilibrium concepts with price rigidities and imperfect competition. These concepts are developed in the traditional multimarket and multiagent Walrasian framework which we will first briefly outline.

3.2 Walrasian Equilibrium

3.2.1 The Institutional Framework

As already indicated in chapter 1, we will describe the various concepts of non-Walrasian economics in the framework of a monetary economy, where one good, called money, serves as the numéraire, the medium of exchange and a reserve of value. There are ℓ active markets in the period considered. In each of these markets one of the ℓ nonmonetary goods, indexed by $h = 1, \ldots, \ell$, is exchanged against money at the price p_h. We call p the ℓ-dimensional vector of these prices.

To simplify the exposition, and although all our later macroeconomic applications include explicitly production, we consider here a pure exchange economy. The agents in this economy are indexed by $i = 1, \ldots, n$. At the beginning of the period considered, agent i has a quantity of money $\bar{m}_i \geq 0$ and holdings of nonmonetary goods represented by a vector ω_i, with components $\omega_{ih} \geq 0$ for each good.

An agent i in market h may make a purchase $d_{ih} \geq 0$, or a sale $s_{ih} \geq 0$. We define his net purchase of good h as $z_{ih} = d_{ih} - s_{ih}$, and the ℓ-dimensional vector of these net purchases as z_i. Agent i's final holdings of nonmonetary goods and money, x_i and m_i, are, respectively,

$$x_i = \omega_i + z_i \tag{1}$$

$$m_i = \bar{m}_i - p z_i \tag{2}$$

Note that equation (2), which describes the evolution of money holdings, is simply the conventional budget constraint for a monetary economy.

3.2.2   Equilibrium

Having described the basic institutional structure of the economy, we now describe its Walrasian equilibrium, in order to contrast it with the non-Walrasian equilibrium concepts that will follow. We still have to describe the preferences of the agents. Agent i has a utility function $U_i(x_i, m_i) = U_i(\omega_i + z_i, m_i)$, which we will assume throughout strictly concave in its arguments.[1]

As indicated above, each agent is assumed to be able to exchange as much as he wants in each market. He thus transmits demands and supplies that maximize his utility subject to the budget constraint. The Walrasian net demand function $z_i(p)$ is the solution in z_i of the following program:

$$\max U_i(\omega_i + z_i, m_i) \quad \text{s.t.}$$

$$p z_i + m_i = \bar{m}_i$$

---

1 Money enters the utility function because it is valuable both as a store of value and as a medium of exchange. These functions will appear in more detail in subsequent dynamic macroeconomic models. We should also note that some form of "real money," and not nominal money as here, should enter the utility function. This would entail adding some further price arguments in the utility function. Since these arguments do not play a role in what follows, they are omitted for the sake of simplicity.

We have as a result a vector of Walrasian net demands $z_i(p)$. We may note that there is no "demand for money," since there is no such thing as a market for money but only markets of various goods against money. A Walrasian equilibrium price vector p^* is defined by the condition that all markets clear, namely

$$\sum_{i=1}^{n} z_i(p^*) = 0 \tag{3}$$

The vector of transactions realized by agent i is equal to $z_i(p^*)$. Walrasian equilibrium allocations possess a number of good properties. By construction, they are consistent both at the individual and market levels. They are also Pareto optimal, so it is impossible to find an allocation that would be as good for all agents, and strictly better for at least one. We will later contrast this property with the suboptimality properties of non-Walrasian equilibria.

3.3   Rationing Schemes and Quantity Signals

We know from chapter 1 that when markets do not clear, we have to distinguish carefully between transactions and effective demands. Take a particular market h. Transactions carried out by agent i are denoted as $d_{ih}^* \geq 0$ (for a purchase) or $s_{ih}^* \geq 0$ (for a sale). Aggregate purchases and sales are identically equal:

$$D_h^* = \sum_{i=1}^{n} d_{ih}^* = \sum_{i=1}^{n} s_{ih}^* = S_h^* \qquad \forall h \tag{4}$$

However, in this market effective demands and supplies, denoted $\tilde{d}_{ih}$ and $\tilde{s}_{ih}$, do not necessarily balance in the aggregate, so that we will often have

$$\tilde{D}_h = \sum_{i=1}^{n} \tilde{d}_{ih} \neq \sum_{i=1}^{n} \tilde{s}_{ih} = \tilde{S}_h \tag{5}$$

In order to keep the notations more compact, we will work with net demands $\tilde{z}_{ih}$ and net transactions z_{ih}^* defined by

$$\tilde{z}_{ih} = \tilde{d}_{ih} - \tilde{s}_{ih}, \quad z_{ih}^* = d_{ih}^* - s_{ih}^* \tag{6}$$

Now from any set of possibly inconsistent demands and supplies the exchange process generates consistent transactions. Some rationing necessarily occurs, which may take various forms, depending on the particular organization of market h. We call *rationing scheme* the mathematical representation of each specific organization. More formally:

Definition 1 *The rationing scheme in market h is described by a set of n functions:*

$$z_{ih}^* = F_{ih}(\tilde{z}_{1h}, \ldots, \tilde{z}_{nh}), \qquad i = 1, \ldots, n \qquad (7)$$

such that

$$\sum_{i=1}^{n} F_{ih}(\tilde{z}_{1h}, \ldots, \tilde{z}_{nh}) = 0 \qquad \text{for all } \tilde{z}_{1h}, \ldots, \tilde{z}_{nh} \qquad (8)$$

We will generally assume that F_{ih} is continuous, nondecreasing in $\tilde{z}_{ih}$ and nonincreasing in the other arguments. We already saw the example of a queue in chapter 1.

3.3.1 Properties of Rationing Schemes

We now review again briefly, in this more general framework, three important properties that a rationing scheme may potentially satisfy: voluntary exchange, market efficiency and nonmanipulability.

There is *voluntary exchange* in market h if no agent can be forced to purchase more than he demands, or to sell more than he supplies. This is expressed as

$$d_{ih}^* \leq \tilde{d}_{ih}, \quad s_{ih}^* \leq \tilde{s}_{ih}, \qquad \text{for all } i \qquad (9)$$

or equivalently in algebraic terms as

$$|z_{ih}^*| \leq |\tilde{z}_{ih}|, \quad z_{ih}^* \cdot \tilde{z}_{ih} \geq 0, \qquad \text{for all } i \qquad (10)$$

In reality most markets meet this condition, and we will assume in this chapter that voluntary exchange always holds. Under this assumption agents are classified in two categories: unrationed agents, for which $z_{ih}^* = \tilde{z}_{ih}$, and rationed agents, who trade less than they want.

The second possible property is that of *market efficiency*, or *absence of frictions*. A rationing scheme is efficient, or frictionless, if one cannot find simultaneously a rationed demander and a rationed supplier in the corresponding market. Together with the voluntary exchange assumption, this implies the "short-side" rule, which is expressed in terms of net demands, as

$$\left(\sum_{j=1}^{n} \tilde{z}_{jh} \right) \cdot \tilde{z}_{ih} \leq 0 \Rightarrow z_{ih}^{*} = \tilde{z}_{ih} \tag{11}$$

As we indicated in chapter 1, market efficiency does not always hold, especially for an aggregated market. However, fortunately, this hypothesis is not necessary for most of the microeconomic concepts presented in the next sections.

We now consider a third important property of rationing schemes, that of *nonmanipulability*. A rationing scheme is nonmanipulable if an agent, once rationed, cannot increase the level of his transactions by increasing his demand or supply, as shown in figure 3.1. To characterize the nonmanipulability property more formally, it is convenient to separate $\tilde{z}_{ih}$ from the other net demands in the same market, and thus to write a rationing scheme in the form

$$z_{ih}^{*} = F_{ih}(\tilde{z}_{ih}, \tilde{z}_{-ih}), \qquad i = 1, \ldots, n \tag{12}$$

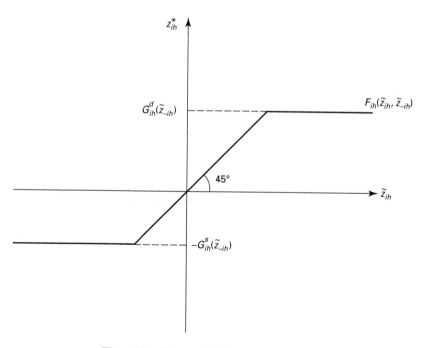

Figure 3.1 Nonmanipulable rationing scheme

with

$$\tilde{z}_{-ih} = \{\tilde{z}_{jh} \mid j \neq i\} \tag{13}$$

where $\tilde{z}_{-ih}$ is the set of all net demands on market h, except for agent i's demand. Let us now define:

Definition 2 *The rationing scheme in market h is nonmanipulable if it can be written under the following form for all agents i:*

$$F_{ih}(\tilde{z}_{ih}, \tilde{z}_{-ih}) = \begin{cases} \min \left[\tilde{z}_{ih}, G_{ih}^d(\tilde{z}_{-ih}) \right] & \text{if } \tilde{z}_{ih} \geq 0 \\ \max \left[\tilde{z}_{ih}, -G_{ih}^s(\tilde{z}_{-ih}) \right] & \text{if } \tilde{z}_{ih} \leq 0 \end{cases} \tag{14}$$

where

$$G_{ih}^d(\tilde{z}_{-ih}) = \max\{\tilde{z}_{ih}, F_{ih}(\tilde{z}_{ih}, \tilde{z}_{-ih}) = \tilde{z}_{ih}\} \geq 0 \tag{15}$$

$$G_{ih}^s(\tilde{z}_{-ih}) = -\min\{\tilde{z}_{ih}, F_{ih}(\tilde{z}_{ih}, \tilde{z}_{-ih}) = \tilde{z}_{ih}\} \geq 0 \tag{16}$$

In words, $G_{ih}^d(\tilde{z}_{-ih})$ and $G_{ih}^s(\tilde{z}_{-ih})$ are simply the largest demand and supply of agent i that can be satisfied given other agents' demands and supplies. This appears particularly clearly in figure 3.1, which shows the relations among $F_{ih}(\tilde{z}_{ih}, \tilde{z}_{-ih})$, $G_{ih}^d(\tilde{z}_{-ih})$ and $G_{ih}^s(\tilde{z}_{-ih})$ for a nonmanipulable rationing scheme. It is easy to see that the queueing system described in chapter 1 is nonmanipulable.

3.3.2 Quantity Signals

We just saw how transactions occur in a nonclearing market. In such a market each agent receives, in addition to the traditional price signal, some quantity signals. In what follows we will concentrate on markets that satisfy the properties of voluntary exchange and nonmanipulability.[2] These may be represented as

$$z_{ih}^* = \begin{cases} \min(\tilde{z}_{ih}, \bar{d}_{ih}), & \tilde{z}_{ih} \geq 0 \\ \min(\tilde{z}_{ih}, -\bar{s}_{ih}), & \tilde{z}_{ih} \leq 0 \end{cases} \tag{17}$$

2 We exclude manipulability because, as we noted in the appendix to chapter 1, manipulable schemes lead to a perverse phenomenon of "overbidding" which prevents the establishment of an equilibrium (see Bénassy 1977b, 1982).

or more compactly by

$$z_{ih}^* = \min\{\bar{d}_{ih}, \max(\tilde{z}_{ih}, -\bar{s}_{ih})\} \tag{18}$$

with

$$\bar{d}_{ih} = G_{ih}^d(\tilde{z}_{-ih}), \quad \bar{s}_{ih} = G_{ih}^s(\tilde{z}_{-ih}) \tag{19}$$

The quantities $\bar{d}_{ih}$ and $\bar{s}_{ih}$, which we will henceforth call the *perceived constraints*, are the quantity signals that agent i receives in market h in addition to the price p_h. We will see in the following sections how the introduction of these quantity signals plays a fundamental role in both demand and price theory, and that their consideration enables us to considerably enlarge the set of possible equilibria.

3.4 Fixprice Equilibria

We are ready to look at a first concept of non-Walrasian equilibrium, that of fixprice equilibrium. This concept is of interest for several reasons. First, it gives us a very general structure of non-Walrasian equilibria since, under some very mild conditions, fixprice equilibria exist for every positive price system and every set of rationing schemes. Second, as we will see in section 3.5, fixprice equilibria are an essential building block in constructing other non-Walrasian equilibrium concepts with flexible prices. Third, the study of their optimality (or rather suboptimality) properties will be applicable to the other concepts as well.

We thus assume that the price system p is given. As we indicated above, we consider nonmanipulable rationing schemes in all markets. Accordingly, transactions and quantity signals are generated on all markets according to the formulas seen above (equations 12 and 19).

We can make notation even more compact by representing the rationing functions and perceived constraints concerning an agent i (equations 12 and 19) as vector functions:

$$z_i^* = F_i(\tilde{z}_i, \tilde{z}_{-i}) \tag{20}$$

$$\bar{d}_i = G_i^d(\tilde{z}_{-i}), \quad \bar{s}_i = G_i^s(\tilde{z}_{-i}) \tag{21}$$

where $\tilde{z}_i$ is the vector of demands expressed by agent i, and $\tilde{z}_{-i}$ the set of all such vectors for all agents, except agent i.

We immediately see that all that remains to be done, in order to obtain a fixprice equilibrium concept, is to determine how effective demands themselves are formed, a task to which we now turn.

3.4.1 Effective Demand and Supply

Let us consider an agent i faced with a price vector p and vectors of perceived constraints $\bar{d}_i$ and $\bar{s}_i$. We will see how he can choose a vector of effective demands $\tilde{z}_i$ that leads him to the best possible transaction. We recall from chapter 1 the definition of effective demand in a market h, as the trade that maximizes utility after taking into account the constraints on the *other* markets. We can make this more precise through the following definition:

Definition 3   *The effective demand of agent i in market h, which we will denote as $\tilde{\zeta}_{ih}(p, \bar{d}_i, \bar{s}_i)$, is the solution in z_{ih} of the following program A_h:*

$$\max U_i(\omega_i + z_i, m_i) \quad \text{s.t.}$$

$$pz_i + m_i = \bar{m}_i \tag{A_h}$$

$$-\bar{s}_{ik} \le z_{ik} \le \bar{d}_{ik}, \qquad k \ne h$$

Because of the strict concavity of U_i, we obtain a function. In repeating this program for all markets $h = 1, \ldots, \ell$, we obtain a vector function of effective demands, $\tilde{\zeta}_i(p, \bar{d}_i, \bar{s}_i)$.

Clearly, so far this is only a definition. To qualify as a legitimate demand vector, $\tilde{\zeta}_i(p, \bar{d}_i, \bar{s}_i)$ must be shown to lead to the best transactions vector. To find this best transaction, we note that agent i's transactions in market h are limited to the interval given by the perceived constraints $-\bar{s}_{ih} \le z_{ih} \le \bar{d}_{ih}$. So his best transaction is the solution in z_i of the following program A_0:

$$\max U_i(\omega_i + z_i, m_i) \quad \text{s.t.}$$

$$pz_i + m_i = \bar{m}_i \tag{A_0}$$

$$-\bar{s}_{ih} \le z_{ih} \le \bar{d}_{ih}, \qquad h = 1, \ldots, \ell$$

Since the function U_i is strictly concave, the solution is unique and we denote it as $\zeta_i^*(p, \bar{d}_i, \bar{s}_i)$. Now there remains for us to prove that $\tilde{\zeta}_i$ leads to the best transaction ζ_i^*, that is, in mathematical terms, that the following proposition holds:

Proposition 1 *The vector of effective demands* $\tilde{\zeta}_{ih}(p, \bar{d}_i, \bar{s}_i)$ *leads to the best transaction, namely*

$$\min\{\bar{d}_{ih}, \max[\tilde{\zeta}_i(p, \bar{d}_i, \bar{s}_i), -\bar{s}_{ih}]\} = \zeta^*_{ih}(p, \bar{d}_i, \bar{s}_i) \qquad (22)$$

Although trivial, the proof is a bit clumsy, and so has been relegated to an appendix. Besides leading to the best transaction, our effective demand function has a second property: whenever a constraint is binding on a market h, the corresponding demand (or supply) is greater than the constraint or the transaction, which thus "signals" to the market that the agent trades less than he would want. It turns out that this property is important to avoid trivial equilibria (Bénassy 1982).

We see immediately from definition 3 that depending on which quantity constraints are binding, effective demand can take various functional forms. This intuitively explains why non-Walrasian models generally have multiple regimes, as we saw in the three-goods, three-regimes model of chapter 2.

3.4.2 Fixprice Equilibrium

With the preceding definition of effective demand, we can give the definition of a fixprice equilibrium (Bénassy 1975a, 1982), which we will call a K-equilibrium for short.

Definition 4 *A K-equilibrium associated with a price system p and rationing schemes represented by functions F_i, $i = 1, \ldots, n$, is a set of effective demands $\tilde{z}_i$, transactions z^*_i, and perceived constraints $\bar{d}_i$ and $\bar{s}_i$ such that*

(a) $\tilde{z}_i = \tilde{\zeta}_i(p, \bar{d}_i, \bar{s}_i)$ $\quad \forall i$
(b) $z^*_i = F_i(\tilde{z}_i, \tilde{z}_{-i})$ $\quad \forall i$
(c) $\bar{d}_i = G^d_i(\tilde{z}_{-i})$, $\bar{s}_i = G^s_i(\tilde{z}_{-i})$ $\quad \forall i$

We see that in a fixprice K-equilibrium the quantity constraints $\bar{d}_i$ and $\bar{s}_i$ from which the agents construct their effective demands (condition a) are the ones that will be generated by the exchange process (condition c). In equilibrium the agents thus have a correct perception of these quantity constraints.

Equilibria defined by the conditions above exist for all positive prices and rationing schemes satisfying voluntary exchange and non-manipulability (Bénassy 1975a, 1982). The "exogenous" data consist of the price system and the rationing schemes in all markets F_i, $i = 1, \ldots, n$. One may wonder whether for such given exogenous data the equilibrium is likely to be unique. A positive answer is provided by Schulz (1983) who showed that the equilibrium is unique if the spillover effects from one market to the other are less than 100 percent in value terms. For example, in the simplest traditional Keynesian model, this would amount to assuming a propensity to consume smaller than 1, which is quite an intuitive condition.

We will assume that the conditions for uniqueness are satisfied, and we will denote by $\tilde{Z}_i(p)$, $Z_i^*(p)$, $\bar{D}_i(p)$, and $\bar{S}_i(p)$ the values of $\tilde{z}_i$, z_i^*, $\bar{d}_i$, and $\bar{s}_i$ at a fixprice equilibrium.

We now take a simple example of a fixprice equilibrium, the traditional Edgeworth box (figure 3.2). It represents a single market where agents A and B exchange a good (measured horizontally) against money (measured vertically). Point O corresponds to initial endowments, DC is the budget line of the two agents at price p, and points A and B are the tangency points of the indifference curves with this budget line.

Measuring the level of exchanges along the line OC, we see that agent A demands a quantity OA, agent B supplies a quantity OB. They exchange the minimum of these two quantities, namely OA, and agent B is rationed. The perceived constraints are, respectively, OA for agent B and OB for agent A. Agent B is constrained on his supply, while A is not constrained.

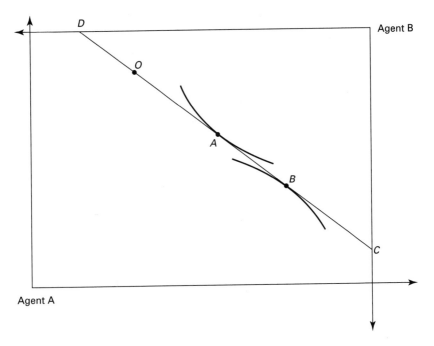

Figure 3.2 Fixprice equilibrium

We may say a few words about the properties of the allocations in a fixprice K-equilibrium. First, in a particular market h, the transactions of the various agents are, by construction, mutually consistent, since they result from the rationing schemes

$$\sum_{i=1}^{n} z_{ih}^* = 0 \qquad \forall h \tag{23}$$

Demands and supplies need not balance, however, and in a particular market one may have three different categories of agents:

1. Unrationed agents such that $z_{ih}^* = \tilde{z}_{ih}$
2. Rationed demanders such that $\tilde{z}_{ih} > z_{ih}^* = \bar{d}_{ih}$
3. Rationed suppliers such that $\tilde{z}_{ih} < z_{ih}^* = -\bar{s}_{ih}$

Note that since our concept permits inefficient rationing schemes, there can be both rationed demanders and rationed suppliers in the same market. If, however, the rationing scheme in the market considered is frictionless, at most one side of the market is rationed.

If we now consider a particular agent i, we see that his transactions vector z_i^* is the best, taking account of the perceived constraints in all markets. This is because effective demand is constructed so as to yield precisely this optimal trade (see appendix 3.1 at the end of the chapter). Mathematically z_i^* is the solution in z_i of program A_0 already seen above:

$$\max U_i(\omega_i + z_i, m_i) \quad \text{s.t.}$$

$$pz_i + m_i = \bar{m}_i \tag{A_0}$$

$$-\bar{s}_{ih} \le z_{ih} \le \bar{d}_{ih}, \qquad h = 1, \dots, \ell$$

3.4.3 An Alternative Concept

We present here an alternative concept of a fixprice equilibrium, due to Drèze (1975),[3] which we will recast using our notations. That concept deals directly with the vectors of transactions z_i^* and quantity constraints $\bar{d}_i$ and $\bar{s}_i$. The original concept by Drèze actually considered uniform rationing whereby the vectors $\bar{d}_i$ and $\bar{s}_i$ were the same for all agents.

---

3 Drèze (1975) actually proves existence of such an equilibrium in the more general case of prices variable between given limits.

Definition 5   *A fixprice D-equilibrium for a given set of prices p is defined as a set of vectors of transactions z_i^*, and quantity constraints $\bar{d}_i$ and $\bar{s}_i$, such that*

(a) $\displaystyle\sum_{i=1}^{n} z_{ih}^* = 0 \quad \forall h$

(b) *The vector z_i^* is a solution in z_i of*

$$\max U_i(\omega_i + z_i, m_i) \quad \text{s.t.}$$

$$p z_i + m_i = \bar{m}_i$$

$$-\bar{s}_{ih} \le z_{ih} \le \bar{d}_{ih}, \qquad h = 1, \dots, \ell$$

(c) $\forall h$,

$$z_{ih}^* = \bar{d}_{ih} \quad \text{for some } i \text{ implies} \quad z_{jh}^* > -\bar{s}_{jh} \qquad \forall j$$

$$z_{ih}^* = -\bar{s}_{ih} \quad \text{for some } i \text{ implies} \quad z_{jh}^* < \bar{d}_{jh} \qquad \forall j$$

Let us interpret these conditions. Condition (a) is the natural requirement that transactions should balance in each market. Condition (b) says that transactions must be individually rational, that is they must maximize utility subject to the budget constraint and the quantity constraints on all markets. In the notations of the preceding subsections, $z_i^* = \zeta_i^*(p, \bar{d}_i, \bar{s}_i)$. We should note at this stage that using quantity contraints under the form of maximum upper bounds and lower bounds on trades implicitly assumes rationing schemes that exhibit both voluntary exchange and nonmanipulability, as we saw in section 3.3.

Condition (c) basically says that rationing may affect either supply or demand but not both simultaneously. We recognize here, with a different formalization, the condition of market efficiency that is thus built into this definition of equilibrium (whereas it was not in the previous definition).

Drèze (1975) proved that an equilibrium according to definition 3 exists for all positive price systems and for uniform rationing schemes, under the traditional concavity assumptions for the utility functions. The concept is easily extended to some nonuniform bounds (Grandmont and Laroque 1976; Greenberg and Müller 1979), but in this last case it is not specified in the concept how shortages are allocated among rationed demanders or rationed suppliers. Because of this, usually there will be an infinity of fixprice equilibria corresponding to a given price, as soon as there are two rationed agents, or more, on one side of a market.

As we noted in the preceding subsections the two concepts are, implicitly or explicitly, based on a representation of markets under the form of rationing schemes satisfying voluntary exchange and nonmanipulability. This suggests that if, in the first definition, we further assume that all rationing schemes are frictionless, the two definitions should yield similar sets of equilibrium allocations for a given price system. This was indeed proved by Silvestre (1982, 1983) for both exchange and production economies.

3.5 Price Setting and General Equilibrium

We now describe a general equilibrium concept integrating decentralized price setting by agents internal to the system. As indicated in chapter 1, price setters use their prices so as to "manipulate" the quantity constraints they face (i.e., so as to increase or decrease their possible sales or purchases). As a result our concept of an equilibrium with price setters will be close in spirit to the models of general equilibrium with imperfect competition, notably as developed by Negishi (1961, 1972), Gabszewicz and Vial (1971), and Marschak and Selten (1974).

3.5.1 The General Framework

Consider a framework akin to that of monopolistic competition. An agent i controls the prices of a (possibly empty) subset H_i of the goods. Each good's price is controlled by a single agent so that

$$H_i \cap H_j = \{\emptyset\}, \qquad i \neq j \tag{24}$$

We denote by p_i the set of prices controlled by agent i and by p_{-i} all other prices:

$$p_i = \{p_h \mid h \in H_i\} \tag{25}$$

$$p_{-i} = \{p_h \mid h \notin H_i\} \tag{26}$$

We can further subdivide H_i into H_i^d (goods demanded by i) and H_i^s (goods supplied by i). Agent i appears as a monopolist in markets $h \in H_i^s$ and as a monopsonist in markets $h \in H_i^d$. Since each price setter is alone on his side of the market, his quantity constraints are given simply by

$$\bar{s}_{ih} = \sum_{j \neq i} \tilde{d}_{jh} = \tilde{D}_h, \qquad h \in H_i^s \qquad (27)$$

$$\bar{d}_{ih} = \sum_{j \neq i} \tilde{s}_{jh} = \tilde{S}_h, \qquad h \in H_i^d \qquad (28)$$

Each agent i chooses his price vector p_i taking the other prices p_{-i} as given. The equilibrium structure is thus that of a Nash equilibrium in prices corresponding to the usual framework of monopolistic competition.

In order to be able to pose the problem of the choice of prices by price setters as a standard decision problem, all we now need to know is how the constraints faced by an agent in all markets vary as a function of the prices the agent sets. In other words, we have to construct the *objective demand curves* of the price setter.

3.5.2 Objective Demand Curves

The implicit idea behind the objective demand curve approach is that every price setter knows enough about the economy to be able to compute under all circumstances the actual quantity constraints he would face (i.e., the total demand or supply of the agents facing him). Since we are considering a Nash equilibrium in prices, a price setter must be able to perform this computation for any prices p_i that he sets, and any value p_{-i} of others' prices, that is, he must be able to compute his constraints for any vector of prices p once all quantity feedback effects have been accounted for.

We already know from section 3.4 that for a given organization of the economy (including notably the rationing schemes) and for a given set of prices p, a fixprice equilibrium is characterized by vectors of net demands $\tilde{Z}_i(p)$, transactions $Z_i^*(p)$, and perceived constraints $\bar{D}_i(p)$ and $\bar{S}_i(p)$. If the agent has full knowledge of the parameters of the economy (a strong assumption, of course, but one that is embedded in the notion of an objective demand curve), then he knows this and the objective demand and supply curves in market h will simply be given, respectively, by the function $\bar{S}_{ih}(p)$ if he is a seller, and $\bar{D}_{ih}(p)$ if he is a demander. Moreover, in view of equations (27) and (28), we may note that these objective curves can be expressed under the alternative form:

$$\bar{S}_{ih}(p) = \tilde{D}_h(p), \qquad h \in H_i^s \qquad (29)$$

$$\bar{D}_{ih}(p) = \tilde{S}_h(p), \qquad h \in H_i^d \qquad (30)$$

Now that we have this general definition of the objective demand and supply curves, it is easy to define the best price response of each price setter:

Definition 6 *The optimal price p_i for agent i, given the other prices p_{-i}, is the solution in p_i of the following program:*

$$\max U_i(\omega_i + z_i, m_i) \quad \text{s.t.}$$

$$pz_i + m_i = \bar{m}_i$$

$$-\bar{S}_i(p) \leq z_i \leq \bar{D}_i(p)$$

This yields the optimum price of agent i as a function of the prices of the other agents:

$$p_i = \psi_i(p_{-i}) \tag{31}$$

We can proceed to the definition of an equilibrium:

Definition 7 *An equilibrium with price setters is characterized by a set of prices and quantities $p_i^*, \tilde{z}_i, z_i^*, \bar{d}_i, \bar{s}_i, i = 1, \ldots, n$, such that*

(a) $p_i^* = \psi_i(p_{-i}^*) \quad \forall i$
(b) $\tilde{z}_i, z_i^*, \bar{d}_i$ and $\bar{s}_i$ form a fixprice equilibrium for the price vector p^*, that is, they are equal, respectively, to $\tilde{Z}_i(p^*), Z_i^*(p^*), \bar{D}_i(p^*)$, and $\bar{S}_i(p^*)$ for all i

Further description and conditions for existence can be found in Bénassy (1988), and macroeconomic applications of this concept are found notably in chapters 4 and 5. Before that, let us visualize this concept using again the Edgeworth box already considered earlier (figure 3.3).

Suppose that agent B (the seller) sets the price. The objective demand curve is given by agent A's demand, and thus it corresponds to the locus of tangency points between various budget lines and A's indifference curves. This is depicted as the curved line *OMW* in figure 3.3, where *W* is the Walrasian point. The equilibrium point is then simply point *M*, the tangency point of this curve with B's indifference curve, which yields for agent B the highest possible utility, given A's objective demand behavior. The price chosen by B corresponds, of course, to the slope of the line *OM*.

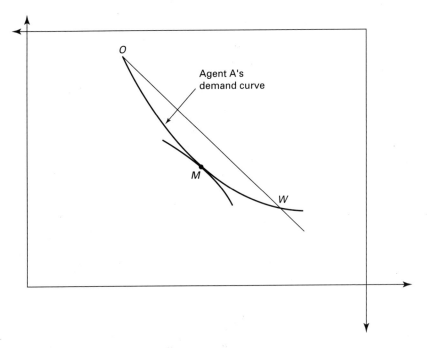

Figure 3.3   Imperfect competition equilibrium

3.6   Optimality

A great virtue of Walrasian equilibrium is the property of Pareto optimality. So
it is quite natural to inquire whether the large class of allocations in our non-
Walrasian equilibria possesses the Pareto-optimality property, or even a weaker
optimality property taking into account the fact that agents trade at "wrong"
prices. As we will see, these two questions are usually answered in the negative.
Before studying in turn these two criteria, we first characterize our equilibria
in a differential way.

3.6.1   A Characterization of Equilibria

Since the largest class of non-Walrasian allocations is that corresponding to
fixprice equilibria (from the previous section, it strictly contains imperfectly
competitive allocations), we will study the optimality properties of fixprice
equilibria. As we saw in section 3.4, transactions in a fixprice equilibrium are

solution in z_i to the program A_0:

$$\max U_i(\omega_i + z_i, m_i) \quad \text{s.t.}$$

$$pz_i + m_i = \bar{m}_i \tag{A_0}$$

$$-\bar{s}_{ih} \leq z_{ih} \leq \bar{d}_{ih} \quad \forall h$$

Call λ_i and δ_{ih} the Kuhn-Tucker multipliers of the constraints above. The Kuhn-Tucker conditions for this program can be written, assuming an interior maximum, as

$$\frac{\partial U_i}{\partial m_i} = \lambda_i \tag{32}$$

$$\frac{\partial U_i}{\partial z_{ih}} = \lambda_i p_h + \delta_{ih} \tag{33}$$

The multiplier λ_i can be interpreted as the marginal utility of income for agent i. δ_{ih} is an index of rationing for agent i in market h:

$\delta_{ih} = 0$ if i is unconstrained on market h $(z_{ih}^* = \tilde{z}_{ih})$

$\delta_{ih} > 0$ if i is constrained in his demand for good h $(0 \leq z_{ih}^* < \tilde{z}_{ih})$

$\delta_{ih} < 0$ if i is constrained in his supply of good h $(\tilde{z}_{ih} < z_{ih}^* \leq 0)$

Let us call the "shadow price" of good h the ratio $(\partial U_i/\partial z_{ih})/(\partial U_i/\partial m_i)$. The relations above allow us to compute the shadow price of good h for agent i as

$$\frac{\partial U_i/\partial z_{ih}}{\partial U_i/\partial m_i} = p_h + \frac{\delta_{ih}}{\lambda_i} \tag{34}$$

We may thus note that the shadow price of good h is greater than, equal to, or smaller than p_h depending on whether agent i is demand constrained, unconstrained, or supply constrained in market h.

We will use the foregoing results to study the optimality properties of fixprice equilibria. Before starting, we must add one more remark and assumption. It is clear that it would be too easy to show that fixprice equilibria are inefficient if some markets were functioning inefficiently themselves. We thus assume in what follows that all markets are frictionless. This immediately implies that the numbers δ_{ih} will be zero for at least all agents on the short side of every market h.

3.6.2 Pareto Optimality

We now inquire whether fixprice allocations have the property of Pareto optimality. From a heuristic point of view, we first note that the constraint of trading at fixed prices does not necessarily rule out Pareto optimality, as figure 3.4 shows. Indeed, there is a point on the budget line, point P, that is a Pareto optimum. But it clearly differs from the fixprice equilibrium A. Continuing with the Edgeworth box example, it is easy to see that this situation is fairly general. Indeed, the set of Pareto optima is the contract curve, whereas the set of fixprice equilibria, when we vary the price, is the lentil-shaped curve (figure 3.5). We see that these two curves intersect only at the Walrasian equilibrium point.

An interesting way to look at this problem is to note (see figure 3.4) that at point P trader A would exchange more than he wants at that price. This leads

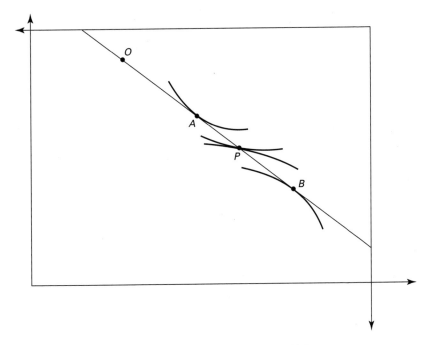

Figure 3.4   Fixprice equilibrium and efficiency

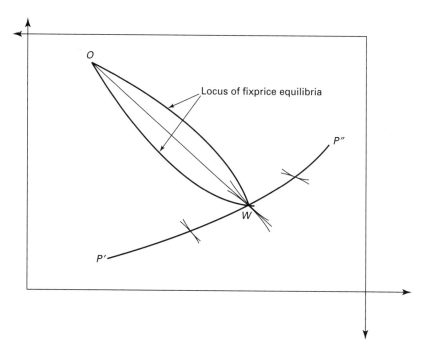

Figure 3.5 Fixprice equilibria and Pareto optima

to the intuition that efficiency would require forced trading and, conversely, that voluntary trading would generally imply inefficiency. This is studied in Silvestre (1985), who showed rigorously that Pareto optimality and voluntary exchange are satisfied together only at the Walrasian allocation.

We can also see in a direct manner why fixprice equilibria generally are not Pareto optima. For that let us first recall the differential characterization of a Pareto optimum. Such an optimum can be obtained by maximizing a weighted sum of agents' utilities, subject to the usual "adding up" constraints:

$$\max \sum_{i=1}^{n} \upsilon_i U_i(\omega_i + z_i, m_i) \quad \text{s.t.}$$

$$\sum_{i=1}^{n} z_{ih} = 0, \qquad h = 1, \dots, \ell$$

$$\sum_{i=1}^{n} m_i = \sum_{i=1}^{n} \bar{m}_i$$

The Kuhn-Tucker conditions for such a program can be rewritten in the traditional form:

$$\frac{\partial U_i / \partial z_{ih}}{\partial U_i / \partial m_i} = \rho_h, \qquad i = 1, \ldots, n \qquad (35)$$

that is, the shadow price of every good h must be the same for all agents.

Now we can see why fixprice equilibria usually are not Pareto optimal: in a market h there are always some agents who are unconstrained (i.e., those on the short side). For these agents, in view of the characterization above (equation 34), the shadow price of good h is equal to p_h. If the allocation is a Pareto optimum, the shadow price must be the same for all agents (equation 35), and thus equal to p_h for all agents. This implies that

$$\delta_{ih} = 0 \qquad \forall i, \forall h \qquad (36)$$

Thus all agents are unconstrained on all markets, meaning that we are in a Walrasian equilibrium.

3.6.3   Constrained Pareto Optimality

Let us investigate a less demanding notion of optimality, due to Uzawa (1962), that takes into account the fact that trades take place at a given price system. We will thus say that an allocation is a constrained Pareto optimum if there is no allocation that (1) satisfies the physical feasibility conditions, (2) satisfies the budget constraints for the given price vector p, and (3) Pareto dominates the allocation considered. In the one-market Edgeworth box example of figure 3.4, we see that the set of constrained Pareto optima is the segment AB, and the fixprice equilibrium A belongs to this set. We will see, however, that this property does not generally extend to the multimarket case.

Indeed, returning to the general framework, we see that a constrained-Pareto-optimal allocation can be obtained as a solution of the following program, where the v_i's are arbitrary positive weights:

$$\max \sum_{i=1}^{n} v_i U_i(\omega_i + z_i, m_i) \quad \text{s.t.}$$

$$\sum_{i=1}^{n} z_{ih} = 0 \qquad \forall h$$

$$p z_i + m_i = \bar{m}_i \qquad \forall i$$

Note that we do not need to write the feasibility constraint for money, since it follows from the other equalities. The Kuhn-Tucker conditions for this program can be written

$$\frac{\partial U_i / \partial z_{ih}}{\partial U_i / \partial m_i} = p_h + \mu_i \delta_h \tag{37}$$

where the μ_i's are positive. The numbers δ_h can have any sign. If we now compare the shadow prices at a constrained Pareto optimum (equation 37) with those in a fixprice equilibrium (equation 34), we see that a constrained Pareto optimum will obtain only under very special circumstances. As formula (37) shows, an agent i should be either constrained in all markets where δ_h is different from zero (if $\mu_i \neq 0$) or constrained in none (if $\mu_i = 0$). A particular case where this occurs is the situation of classical unemployment in the three-goods model (chapter 2, section 2.4), but this type of situation will occur infrequently if many markets do not clear.

There are indeed other cases where constrained optimality structurally cannot hold. Consider, for example, a situation of generalized excess supply where typically each agent is constrained on the goods he sells ($\delta_{ih} < 0$) and unconstrained for the goods he purchases ($\delta_{ih} = 0$). In such a case there is no way the shadow prices at a fixprice equilibrium can be written in the form given by equation (37), and the corresponding equilibrium will be suboptimal, even taking into account the constraint that trades must me made at the given prices. A symmetric situation occurs with generalized excess demand. We already saw striking examples of this suboptimality in chapter 2, section 2.4.

More generally, we may expect suboptimality to occur where there are several markets with excess demands of the same sign (a situation that also leads to multiplier effects; see Bénassy 1975a, 1982, for a study of the relation between the two). As a first example, consider the case, typical in Keynesian theory, of two markets, h and k, both in excess supply. Consider two agents i and j, i being a rationed supplier in k and an unrationed demander in h, j being a rationed supplier in h and an unrationed demander in k. Then the conditions seen above immediately lead to

$$\frac{1}{p_h} \frac{\partial U_i}{\partial z_{ih}} = \frac{\partial U_i}{\partial m_i} > \frac{1}{p_k} \frac{\partial U_i}{\partial z_{ik}} \tag{38}$$

$$\frac{1}{p_k} \frac{\partial U_i}{\partial z_{jk}} = \frac{\partial U_i}{\partial m_j} > \frac{1}{p_h} \frac{\partial U_i}{\partial z_{jh}} \tag{39}$$

One thus sees that i and j would both be interested in exchanging goods h and k directly against each other at the prices p_h and p_k, which suggests a simple Pareto-improving trade. Of course, in general, in the absence of a "double coincidence of wants," such Pareto-improving trades would be much more complex, and therefore more difficult to achieve by decentralized agents.

3.6.4 Multiplier Chains

Generalizing the preceding situation to a more disaggregated level, we can define *multiplier chains* along which a similar phenomenon may occur. Specifically, we define a demand multiplier chain as a set of k traders $(i_1, \ldots, i_k)$ and k goods $(h_1, \ldots, h_k)$ whose markets are all in excess supply, and such that

$$i_1 \text{ is } \begin{cases} \text{constrained in his supply of } h_1 \\ \text{unconstrained in his demand for } h_2 \end{cases}$$

$$i_2 \text{ is } \begin{cases} \text{constrained in his supply of } h_2 \\ \text{unconstrained in his demand for } h_3 \end{cases}$$

$$\cdots\cdots\cdots\cdots\cdots\cdots\cdots\cdots\cdots\cdots\cdots$$

$$i_k \text{ is } \begin{cases} \text{constrained in his supply of } h_k \\ \text{unconstrained in his demand for } h_1 \end{cases}$$

The reason why we call this a multiplier chain is easy to understand if we consider the effect of an exogenous demand shock, say, a fall in the demand of good h_1. Agent i_1, being more constrained in his supply of good h_1, will reduce his demand of good h_2. This will constrain agent i_2 in his supply of h_2, so he will reduce his demand of h_3, and so on. We see that any initial disturbance on the demand side of one of the k markets is transmitted with the same sign to all markets in the chain[4] and returns ultimately to the initial market, launching a new wave of disturbances, and thus yielding a multiplier effect. Generally, many different chains of this type will exist if there is excess supply on many markets. Demand multiplier effects may be observed especially in the case of general excess supply. Of course, the symmetrical (though less observed in reality) case of supply multiplier effects can arise in case of general excess demand (see chapter 2, section 2.4).

---

4 We assume implicitly that a constrained reduction in the sales of one good leads to a reduction in effective demand for other goods, which we take as the "normal" case.

It is also easy to construct for this demand multiplier chain a set of Pareto-improving trades at the given set of prices. The existence of unrealized exchange possibilities at the economy level therefore suggests that in such cases government intervention may improve the situation of the private sector (see chapters 2 and 4 for such an investigation).

3.7 Conclusions

In this chapter we extended the concepts of chapter 1 to a multimarket general equilibrium setting. In doing so, we generalized the usual Walrasian equilibrium to a much richer set of situations, embedding nonclearing markets and imperfect competition.

For the ease and symmetry of the exposition we explicitly described general equilibrium concepts for two extreme cases: one with all prices rigid, another with all prices flexible in a regime of imperfect competition. Clearly, many intermediate concepts with any combination of fixed and flexible prices can be constructed. Also the so-called rigid prices must not be thought of as rigid forever, they may be simply preset for a single period. These possibilities will be explored in the dynamic macromodels of the following parts.

3.8 References

The material in this chapter comes principally from Bénassy (1975a, 1976a, 1977b, 1988, 1990) and Drèze (1975).

The representation of rationing schemes and quantity signals is taken from Bénassy (1975a, 1977b). An alternative approach is in Drèze (1975).

The two concepts of fixprice equilibrium described in this chapter were developed in Bénassy (1975a, 1977b, 1982) and Drèze (1975), respectively. The relations between these concepts have been studied in depth by Silvestre (1982, 1983) and D'Autume (1985).

The issue of uniqueness of a fixprice equilibrium has been studied by Schulz (1983), who derived sufficient conditions for global uniqueness in the Bénassy model. The Drèze equilibrium is usually not unique, but local uniqueness results can be obtained in some specific cases (Laroque 1981).

The concept of equilibrium with imperfect competition described in this chapter is taken from Bénassy (1988, 1990). Studies of general equilibrium under imperfect competition originate in the work of Negishi (1961, 1972), who used the notion of subjective demand curves. The theory of general equilibrium with objective demand curves was first developed in a Cournotian setting by Gabszewicz and Vial (1972), then in some specific models with price setters by Marschak and Selten (1974) and Nikaido (1975).

The suboptimality properties of non-Walrasian equilibria were studied in Bénassy (1975a, 1975b, 1982, 1990), Drèze and Muller (1980), Silvestre (1985), and Younès (1975). The results on the Pareto optimality of non-Walrasian allocations are due to Silvestre (1985). The notion of constrained Pareto optimality is due to Uzawa (1962). Whether fixprice allocations are constrained Pareto optimal was investigated in Bénassy (1975a, 1990) and Younès (1975). Drèze and Muller (1980) showed how constrained optimality may be obtained through "coupon rationing." The inefficiency of multiplier states was discussed in Clower (1965) and Leijonhufvud (1968). This issue was developed more formally in Bénassy (1975a, 1977a, 1982). The role of expectations is discussed in Bénassy (1982, 1986), Neary and Stiglitz (1983), and Persson and Svensson (1983). The properties of monetary and barter economies are compared in Bénassy (1975b, 1982).

Appendix 3.1: Proof of Proposition 1

Let us recall a couple of definitions. The vector of optimal transactions $\zeta_{ih}^*(p, \bar{d}_i, \bar{s}_i)$ is the solution in z_i to the program A_0:

$$\max U_i(\omega_i + z_i, m_i) \quad \text{s.t.}$$

$$pz_i + m_i = \bar{m}_i \tag{A_0}$$

$$-\bar{s}_{ih} \leq z_{ih} \leq \bar{d}_{ih} \quad \forall h$$

The effective demand on market h, $\tilde{\zeta}_{ih}(p, \bar{d}_i, \bar{s}_i)$, is the solution in z_{ih} to the program A_h:

$$\max U_i(\omega_i + z_i, m_i) \quad \text{s.t.}$$

$$pz_i + m_i = \bar{m}_i \tag{A_h}$$

$$-\bar{s}_{ik} \leq z_{ik} \leq \bar{d}_{ik}, \quad k \neq h$$

We can now state and prove proposition 1:

Proposition 1 *The vector of effective demands $\tilde{\zeta}_{ih}(p, \bar{d}_i, \bar{s}_i)$ leads to the best transaction, namely*

$$\min\{\bar{d}_i, \max[\tilde{\zeta}_i(p, \bar{d}_i, \bar{s}_i), -\bar{s}_i]\} = \zeta_i^*(p, \bar{d}_i, \bar{s}_i) \tag{40}$$

Proof Define

$$z_i^* = \min\{\bar{d}_i, \max[\tilde{\zeta}_i(p, \bar{d}_i, \bar{s}_i), -\bar{s}_i]\} \tag{41}$$

The proposition is proved by showing the equality of z_i^* and $\zeta_i^*(p, \bar{d}_i, \bar{s}_i)$ component by component. In effect we must show that $z_{ih}^* = \zeta_{ih}^*$ for all h. Three cases can arise.

First, $-\bar{s}_{ih} \leq \tilde{\zeta}_{ih} \leq \bar{d}_{ih}$. This inequality implies, from the definition of z_i^*, that $z_{ih}^* = \tilde{\zeta}_{ih}$. In this case the constraints in market h are not binding, and the solutions of programs A_0 and A_h are thus the same, which implies $\zeta_{ih}^* = \tilde{\zeta}_{ih}$. The two previous equalities yield

$$z_{ih}^* = \zeta_{ih}^* \tag{42}$$

Second, $\tilde{\zeta}_{ih} > \bar{d}_{ih}$. This inequality implies, in view of the definition of z_i^*, that $z_{ih}^* = \bar{d}_{ih}$. The constraint $\bar{d}_{ih}$ is binding, and because of the strict concavity of the utility function, we have $\zeta_{ih}^* = \bar{d}_{ih}$. Combining the two previous equalities, we obtain

$$z_{ih}^* = \zeta_{ih}^* \tag{43}$$

Third, $\tilde{\zeta}_{ih} < -\bar{s}_{ih}$. This inequality implies, in view of the definition of z_i^*, that $z_{ih}^* = -\bar{s}_{ih}$. The constraint $\bar{s}_{ih}$ is binding, and because of the strict concavity of the utility function, we have $\zeta_{ih}^* = -\bar{s}_{ih}$. Combining the two previous equalities we obtain

$$z_{ih}^* = \zeta_{ih}^* \tag{44}$$

The equality $z_{ih}^* = \zeta_{ih}^*$ holds in the three possible cases, which proves the proposition. ∎

Part III

Imperfect Competition, Underemployment, and Welfare

4

Are Imperfect Competition Models Keynesian?

4.1 Introduction

We are ready to show that the general microeconomic methodology developed in chapters 1 and 3 is fully operational, and that it allows us to build simple non-Walrasian macroeconomic models with rigorous microfoundations. So in this chapter we construct such a macroeconomic model and combine in it a number of elements indicated in the preface, namely imperfect competition, objective demand curves, and rational expectations.

With the help of this model we will notably address a question that has puzzled researchers for some time, namely the relation between imperfect competition and Keynesian theory. Indeed, the macroeconomic debate has been dominated for many years by the "classical versus Keynesian" opposition, and therefore a question most often asked when macroeconomic models with imperfect competition were being developed was whether their properties would be more classical or Keynesian in character. Although the matter is not so ambiguous, as will be seen below, a number of misleading views can be found in the literature, and the purpose of this chapter is to give a few basic clarifications in a simple and pedagogic way. This we will do not by reviewing all contributions to the subject, but rather by constructing a simple prototype model with rigorous microfoundations including notably rational expectations and objective demand curves, and then by examining how the model's properties relate to those of Keynesian and classical models.

4.2   The Model

Because we want a simple intertemporal structure we will use in this part an
overlapping generations model with fiat money. In order to introduce difficulties
progressively, we will consider a deterministic setting and leave the introduction
of stochastic shocks to subsequent parts. Since everything is stationary in what
follows, we will omit the time index altogether in this and the next chapter.

Agents in the economy are households, each living two periods, firms, and
the government. Households are indexed by $i \in [0, 1]$, and firms indexed by
$j \in [0, 1]$. There are four types of goods: money, which is the numéraire,
medium of exchange and unique store of value, a homogeneous consumption good (output), differentiated intermediate goods indexed by $j \in [0, 1]$, and
different types of labor indexed by $i \in [0, 1]$. Household i is the only one to
supply labor of type i (when young) and sets the corresponding wage W_i. Firm
j is the only one to produce intermediate good j and sets its price P_j.

The price of output is P. It is produced by competitive firms endowed with
the following CES production function:

$$Y = \left(\int_0^1 Y_j^\theta \, dj \right)^{1/\theta} \tag{1}$$

Firm j produces intermediate good j using quantities of the various labor types
$N_{ij}, i \in [0, 1]$, with a production function

$$Y_j = F(N_j) \tag{2}$$

where F is a strictly concave function and N_j, a scalar index, is deduced from
the N_{ij}'s via a CES aggregation function:[1]

$$N_j = \left(\int_0^1 N_{ij}^\nu \, di \right)^{1/\nu} \tag{3}$$

Firm j's objective is to maximize its profits Π_j:

$$\Pi_j = P_j Y_j - \int_0^1 W_i N_{ij} \, di \tag{4}$$

---

1 This modeling of the labor market is due to Snower (1983). It enables us to disentangle
in a simple manner the market power in the labor market from that in the goods market.
The more traditional representation, with specific trade-unions within each firm, does

Houschold i lives two periods, consumes quantities of output C_i and C'_i during the first and second period of its life, and is taxed an amount T_i in real terms. During the first period household i sets its wage W_i and supplies a total quantity of labor N_i given by

$$N_i = \int_0^1 N_{ij}\, dj \tag{5}$$

Household i maximizes the utility function

$$\alpha \log C_i + (1 - \alpha) \log C'_i - V(N_i) \tag{6}$$

where V is a convex function. Household i has two budget constraints, one for each period of its life:

$$PC_i + M_i = W_i N_i + \Pi_i - PT_i, \qquad P'C'_i = M_i \tag{7}$$

where M_i is the quantity of money transferred as savings to the second period, P' is the price of output in this future period, T_i is the amount of (lump-sum) real taxes paid to the government, and Π_i is household i's profit income, equal to

$$\Pi_i = \int_0^1 \Pi_j\, dj \tag{8}$$

The two budget constraints in (7) aggregate into the intertemporal budget constraint:

$$PC_i + P'C'_i = W_i N_i + \Pi_i - PT_i \tag{9}$$

Government purchases an amount of goods G. Finally we denote by $\bar{M}_i$ the quantity of money held by old household i at the outset of the period considered (this quantity of money corresponds, of course, to its savings of the previous period). Since the model is totally symmetric so far, we can also assume that

$$T_i = T, \quad \bar{M}_i = \bar{M}, \qquad \forall i \tag{10}$$

---

not separate well the two unless additional features are introduced. This issue will be covered in the next chapter.

Accordingly, the government's budget constraint is

$$M - \bar{M} = P(G - T) \tag{11}$$

where M is the aggregate quantity of money at the end of the period.

4.3 Objective Demand Curves

As we mentioned earlier, firm j sets the price P_j, and the young household i sets the wage W_i. Each does so taking all other prices and wages as given. The equilibrium is thus a Nash equilibrium in prices and wages. A central element in the construction of this equilibrium is the set of objective demand curves faced by price and wage setters, to which we now turn.

When computing the objective demand curve for the product he sells, each price or wage setter has to forecast the demand forthcoming to him for any value of (1) the price or wage he determines and (2) the prices and wages set by all other agents. As we developed more formally in chapter 3, section 3.5, the natural definition of objective demand at a given price–wage vector is simply the demand forthcoming at a fix-price equilibrium corresponding to that vector, which we will compute below.

Before we actually proceed to the computations, we may recall from chapter 1 that each price setter will set the price of the good he controls at a level high enough for him to be willing to meet all demand forthcoming, and actually even more. We are thus, in fixprice terminology, in a situation of generalized excess supply where each agent is both unconstrained in his demands but constrained in his supplies, and thus takes the level of his sales as a constraint.

Proposition 1 *The aggregate output Y, objective demands Y_j and N_i respectively addressed to firm j and household i, are equal to*

$$Y = \frac{1}{1-\alpha}\left(\frac{\bar{M}}{P} + G - \alpha T\right) \tag{12}$$

$$Y_j = \left(\frac{P_j}{P}\right)^{-1/(1-\theta)} Y \tag{13}$$

$$N_i = \left(\frac{W_i}{W}\right)^{-1/(1-\nu)} \int_0^1 F^{-1}(Y_j)\, dj \tag{14}$$

where the aggregate price and wage indexes, P and W, are given by the traditional CES formulas:

$$P = \left(\int_0^1 P_j^{-\theta/(1-\theta)} \, dj \right)^{-(1-\theta)/\theta} \tag{15}$$

$$W = \left(\int_0^1 W_i^{-v/(1-v)} \, di \right)^{-(1-v)/v} \tag{16}$$

Proof Consider first the competitive output producing firms. Their optimization program is

$$\max PY - \int_0^1 P_j Y_j \, dj \quad \text{s.t.}$$

$$Y = \left(\int_0^1 Y_j^{\theta} \, dj \right)^{1/\theta}$$

The solution is

$$Y_j = Y \left(\frac{P_j}{P} \right)^{-1/(1-\theta)} \tag{17}$$

where the aggregate price P is equal to the usual CES index (15) associated to the production function (1).

Consider next firm j. With given wages and prices, its profit maximization program is

$$\max P_j Y_j - \int_0^1 W_i N_{ij} \, di \quad \text{s.t.}$$

$$F(N_j) = F \left[\left(\int_0^1 N_{ij}^v \, di \right)^{1/v} \right] = Y_j$$

where Y_j, the demand addressed to firm j, is exogenous to the firm, and a binding constraint. The solution is

$$N_{ij} = \left(\frac{W_i}{W} \right)^{-1/(1-v)} N_j = \left(\frac{W_i}{W} \right)^{-1/(1-v)} F^{-1}(Y_j) \tag{18}$$

where W is the aggregate wage index (16) associated by duality to function (3). The cost for firm j to produce Y_j is $WN_j = WF^{-1}(Y_j)$. Now aggregating equation (18) across all firms, we find the total demand for labor i:

$$N_i = \int_0^1 N_{ij}\, dj = \left(\frac{W_i}{W}\right)^{-1/(1-\nu)} \int_0^1 F^{-1}(Y_j)\, dj \tag{19}$$

In order to have a self-contained expression of the effective demand for good j, we must now derive the value of Y. Since we are in the demand determined regime, output is equal to total demand:

$$Y = \int_0^1 C_i\, di + \int_0^1 C_i'\, di + G \tag{20}$$

Old household i has a quantity of money $\bar{M}$. Its consumption is thus equal to

$$C_i' = \frac{\bar{M}}{P} \tag{21}$$

Consider finally young household i. Its current consumption C_i is determined through the following maximization program:

$$\max \alpha \log C_i + (1 - \alpha) \log C_i' - V(N_i) \quad \text{s.t.}$$

$$PC_i + P'C_i' = W_i N_i + \Pi - PT$$

where the right-hand side (and notably the quantity N_i of labor sold) is exogenous to household i. The solution is

$$C_i = \alpha \left(\frac{W_i N_i + \Pi - PT}{P}\right) \tag{22}$$

Combining equations (20), (21), and (22), we obtain

$$Y = \frac{\bar{M}}{P} + G - \alpha T + \alpha \int_0^1 \frac{W_i N_i + \Pi}{P}\, di \tag{23}$$

Now, by the aggregate incomes identity, we have

$$\int_0^1 (W_i N_i + \Pi)\, di = \int_0^1 P_j Y_j\, dj = PY \tag{24}$$

Next we combine (23) and (24) and obtain expression (12) for aggregate output. Then we combine this with (17) and (18) and obtain expressions (13) and (14) for the objective demands addressed to firm j and household i. ∎

4.4 The Imperfect Competition Equilibrium

Having derived the objective demand curves, we can proceed to compute the imperfectly competitive equilibrium along familiar lines.

4.4.1 Price Setting

Knowing the demand curve for good j (13), we can write the program of firm j, which sets the price P_j, as

$$\max P_j Y_j - W N_j \quad \text{s.t.}$$

$$Y_j = F(N_j)$$

$$Y_j \leq \left(\frac{P_j}{P}\right)^{-1/(1-\theta)} Y$$

The solution is characterized by the usual "marginal cost equals marginal revenue" equality

$$\frac{W}{P_j} = \theta F'(N_j) \tag{25}$$

We see that compared to the competitive pricing equation, which here would be $W/P_j = F'(N_j)$, we have a multiplicative "markup." This markup is, of course, lowest when θ is closest to 1, meaning the goods are more substitutable and therefore the demand curve is more elastic.

4.4.2 Wage Setting

Let us now consider the young household i. It will choose its wage W_i and its consumptions and labor supply so as to solve the following maximization program:

$$\max \alpha \log C_i + (1 - \alpha) \log C_i' - V(N_i) \quad \text{s.t.}$$

$$PC_i + P'C_i' = W_i N_i + \Pi - PT$$

$$N_i \leq \left(\frac{W_i}{W}\right)^{-1/(1-\nu)} \int_0^1 F^{-1}(Y_j) \, dj$$

The first-order conditions for this program are

$$C_i = \alpha \frac{W_i N_i + \Pi - PT}{P} \tag{26}$$

$$\frac{\alpha \nu}{PC_i} = \frac{V'(N_i)}{W_i} \tag{27}$$

Equation (26) is the consumption function, which we already saw. Equation (27) is the wage-setting equation; it adds to the competitive equation a markup related to ν, the parameter depicting the substitutability between various types of work, and therefore the market power of wage setters. The closer ν is to 1, the lower this market power is.

4.4.3 Symmetric Equilibrium

We assume that the equilibrium is unique. Since everything is symmetric, prices and quantities will be symmetric in equilibrium:

$$N_j = N, \quad Y_j = Y, \quad P_j = P, \qquad \forall j$$

$$N_i = N, \quad C_i = C, \quad C_i' = C', \quad W_i = W, \qquad \forall i$$

$$N_{ij} = N, \qquad \forall i, j$$

To compute all equilibrium values, we rewrite the three first-order conditions (25), (26) and (27) in symmetric form:

$$\frac{W}{P} = \theta F'(N) \tag{28}$$

$$C = \alpha \frac{WN + \Pi - PT}{P} = \alpha(Y - T) \tag{29}$$

$$\frac{\alpha v}{PC} = \frac{V'(N)}{W} \tag{30}$$

To these we add the equations corresponding, respectively, to the production function, the household's intertemporal budget constraint, the equation of physical balance on the goods market, and the budget constraint of the old household:

$$Y = F(N) \tag{31}$$

$$PC + P'C' = WN + \Pi - PT = P(Y - T) \tag{32}$$

$$C + C' + G = Y \tag{33}$$

$$PC' = \bar{M} \tag{34}$$

Combining first (28), (29), (30), and (31), we find that the equilibrium level of employment is given by

$$[F(N) - T]V'(N) = \theta v F'(N) \tag{35}$$

Once N is known, all other values can be deduced easily:

$$Y = F(N) \tag{36}$$

$$\frac{W}{P} = \theta F'(N) \tag{37}$$

$$C = \alpha(Y - T) \tag{38}$$

$$C' = (1 - \alpha)Y + \alpha T - G \tag{39}$$

$$P = \frac{\bar{M}}{(1 - \alpha)Y + \alpha T - G} \tag{40}$$

$$\frac{P'}{P} = \frac{(1 - \alpha)(Y - T)}{(1 - \alpha)Y + \alpha T - G} \tag{41}$$

Now that we have fully characterized the equilibrium, we can investigate whether it has more Keynesian or classical properties.

4.5   Apparent Keynesian Inefficiencies

Obviously the equilibrium we have just obtained is not a Pareto optimum. We will see further that the nature of the allocation and its inefficiency properties resemble some of those encountered in traditional Keynesian equilibria.

The first common point we observe is that in our equilibrium there is a potential excess supply of both goods and labor. Equation (25) shows that marginal cost is strictly below price for every firm, and thus that firms would be willing to produce and sell more at the equilibrium price and wage if the demand was forthcoming. Similarly (27) shows that the households would be willing to sell more labour at the given price and wage if there was more demand for it. We are thus, in terms of the terminology of fixprice equilibria, in the general excess supply zone.

Second the determination of output for *given* prices and wages is very similar to that found in the traditional Keynesian fixprice-fixwage model. Let us recall formula (12) giving the level of output:

$$Y = \frac{1}{1 - \alpha} \left(\frac{\bar{M}}{P} + G - \alpha T \right) \tag{42}$$

This is a very traditional Keynesian multiplier formula whose multiplier is equal to $1/(1 - \alpha)$.

We finally see that our equilibrium has a strong inefficiency property, which is characteristic of multiplier equilibria (e.g., chapters 2 and 3), specifically that it is possible to find additional transactions that, at the given prices and wages, would increase all firms' profits and all consumers' utilities.

To be more precise, let us imagine that all young households work an extra amount dN, which is equally shared among all firms. The extra production is shared equally among all these young households so that each one sees its current consumption index increase by

$$dC = dY = F'(N)\, dN \tag{43}$$

Consider first the representative firm. Using equation (28), we find that its profits in real terms increase by

$$d\left(\frac{\Pi}{P}\right) = (1-\theta)F'(N)\,dN > 0 \tag{44}$$

Consider now the representative young household. The net increment in its utility is:

$$dU = \frac{\partial U}{\partial C}\,dC + \frac{\partial U}{\partial N}\,dN \tag{45}$$

Using equations (28) and (30), this yields

$$dU = (1-\theta v)\frac{\partial U}{\partial C}F'(N)\,dN > 0 \tag{46}$$

Equations (44) and (46) show that the increment in activity clearly leads to a Pareto improvement.

All the characterizations above point in the same direction: in our equilibrium, activity is blocked at too low a level, and it would be desirable to implement policies that increase this level of activity. The traditional Keynesian prescription is to use expansionary demand policies, such as monetary or fiscal expansions. Equation (42) shows us that if prices and wages remained fixed, these expansionary policies would indeed be successful in increasing output and employment. But, and this is where resemblance to Keynesian theory stops, government policies will bring about price and wage changes which will completely change their impact. To this we now turn.

4.6   The Impact of Government Policies

We will study here the impact of two traditional Keynesian expansionary policies. We want to show that because of the price and wage movements that they induce, these expansionary policies will have "classical" effects quite similar to those that would occur in the corresponding Walrasian model. We may readily acquire a quick intuitive understanding of such results from equations (35) through (41), which define the equilibrium. It is easy to see that the corresponding Walrasian equilibrium would be defined by exactly the same equations, with

θ and v both equal to 1. The closeness of the first-order conditions explains why policy responses will be similar.

4.6.1   The Neutrality of Money

Consider the first type of expansionary policy, a proportional expansion of the money stock that is multiplied by a quantity $\mu > 1$. This is implemented by endowing all old households with a quantity of money $\mu \bar{M}$ instead of $\bar{M}$, a kind of Friedmanian "helicopter" monetary policy.

The response to such a policy is particularly easy to compute: we may note indeed that all equations (35) to (41) are homogeneous of degree zero in the "nominal" variables $\bar{M}$, P, P', and W. So an expansion of $\bar{M}$ by a factor μ will multiply P, W and P' by the same factor μ, leaving all quantities unchanged. Money is thus neutral in this case, as it would be in the corresponding Walrasian model.

4.6.2   Fiscal Policy and Crowding-Out

Let us also take a look at the effects of other traditional Keynesian policies, namely government spending G and taxes T. Recall equation (35), which gives the equilibrium level of employment:

$$[F(N) - T]V'(N) = \theta v F'(N) \tag{47}$$

After differentiating with respect to G and T, we obtain

$$\frac{\partial Y}{\partial G} = 0, \quad \frac{\partial C}{\partial G} = -1 \tag{48}$$

$$\frac{\partial Y}{\partial T} > 0 \tag{49}$$

We see that the results have nothing Keynesian: equation (48) indicates no effect of public spending on output, and therefore there is 100 percent crowding-out. Equation (49) indicates that an *increase* in taxes, and not a decrease, as in Keynesian models, will increase output. The mechanism is nevertheless intuitive, and goes through the labor supply behavior of the household: a tax increase makes young households poorer, and since leisure is a normal good here, the income effect will naturally lead the household, other things being equal, to work more, thus increasing labor supply and activity. We should note that this effect is present as well in the corresponding Walrasian model and is thus fully "classical."

So one wonders how with models of similar inspiration some authors may have thought to have found there the foundations of the Keynesian multiplier.[2] A potential confusion may arise if one studies only balanced budgets ($G = T$). In that case, differentiating relation (47), one finds that

$$0 < \frac{\partial Y}{\partial G} < 1 \qquad (50)$$

which might create the illusion of a "Keynesian" effect. But clearly the mechanism at work here has nothing to do with a Keynesian demand multiplier, but goes through the labor supply behavior of the household, as explained above.

We should at this point also note that whereas the crowding-out effect is fairly robust,[3] the output expansion effect (49) is more fragile, and notably depends very much on the method of taxation. To see this, let us assume that taxes are not levied in a lump sum fashion, but proportionally on all incomes (profits and wages). In that case it is easy to compute that equation (47) becomes

$$F(N)V'(N) = \theta v F'(N) \qquad (51)$$

with all other equations remaining the same. In this case employment and output are entirely unaffected by the level of taxes. The reasoning behind this is intuitively simple: while the income effect of taxes continues to induce more work effort, inversely the proportional taxation of labor income discourages additional work. In this particular instance, the two effects cancel out exactly.

4.7   Conclusions

We constructed in this chapter a simple prototype model of imperfect competition with rational expectations and objective demand curves, studied its various properties, and compared them with those of the basic classical and Keynesian models.

2 Such a thesis is presented, for example, by Mankiw (1988).

3 What is robust is, of course, that there is crowding-out, and *not* that this crowding-out is exactly 100 percent.

The first thing that appears most clearly is that the introduction of imperfect competition yields a much richer framework than the Walrasian one. Indeed, the corresponding Walrasian model can be obtained as a limit case by making the parameters θ and ν go to one. This added generality is not acquired at the cost of rigor, since notably prices and wages result from explicit maximization, unlike in the Walrasian model where the equality between supply and demand is simply postulated.

As to settling the question posed in the introduction on whether such models are Keynesian, we must admit that the answer is rather on the negative side, and that these models behave more in a classical way. It is true that the inefficiency properties of the equilibria closely resemble those of the Keynesian fixprice-fixwage model. But what economists usually mean by classical or Keynesian concerns the response to government policy. We saw that the response to such policies, fiscal or monetary, is in fact of a classical nature. In a nutshell, the intuitive reason is that imperfectly competitive models generate real rigidities, whereas Keynesian features are usually associated with nominal rigidities.

Should we conclude that there is a fundamental break between imperfect competition and Keynesianism? The answer is actually no. We have seen that imperfect competition per se does not create any Keynesian effects. But we also noted that imperfectly competitive models provide a richer framework of analysis than the traditional market-clearing one. It is thus quite possible to add to this framework additional hypotheses that introduce nominal rigidities and Keynesian features, as will be demonstrated later in parts V and VI.

4.8   References

This chapter is based on Bénassy (1991a, 1995c). The reader who desires a more complete perspective on the macroeconomics of imperfect competition should also read the excellent survey articles by Silvestre (1993, 1995) and Dixon and Rankin (1994).

Imperfectly competitive macroeconomic models were developed in Bénassy (1977a) and Negishi (1977), who showed, among other things, how equilibria displaying notably inefficient underemployment of resources could be obtained as imperfect competition equilibria. Policy issues were introduced in Hart (1982), who constructed a model responding in a "Keynesian" manner to some policy experiments. Soon after, it was realized that the most Keynesian results were due to peculiar assumptions, and the next generation of articles obtained much more "classical" results: Snower (1983) and Dixon (1987) showed that fiscal policies have crowding-out effects very similar to those of Walrasian "classical" models. Bénassy (1987), Blanchard and Kiyotaki (1987), and Dixon (1987) showed that money has neutrality properties similar to those of Walrasian models. The sensitivity to the method of taxation was studied by Molana and Moutos (1992). Finally normative policy prescriptions were studied in Bénassy (1991a, c), and they appear to be neither classical nor Keynesian.

Appendix 4.1: A Welfare Paradox

We describe in this appendix an apparent paradox of the model developed in this chapter, namely that the welfare of households is, in general, negatively related to their market power, whereas intuition tells us that these should be positively related. More precisely we show that while the market power of the households is negatively related to the parameter v, household welfare depends positively on it. We begin by first recalling the household's utility:

$$U = \alpha \log C + (1 - \alpha) \log C' - V(N) \tag{52}$$

The values of consumptions and employment at equilibrium are given by (see equations 35, 36, 38, and 39)

$$C = \alpha(Y - T) \tag{53}$$

$$C' = (1 - \alpha)Y + \alpha T - G \tag{54}$$

$$Y = F(N) \tag{55}$$

$$[F(N) - T]V'(N) = \theta v F'(N) \tag{56}$$

Differentiating first (56), we find that

$$\frac{\partial N}{\partial v} > 0 \tag{57}$$

Now differentiating (52) and using (53), (54), and (55), we obtain

$$\frac{\partial U}{\partial N} = \frac{\alpha F'(N)}{F(N) - T} + \frac{(1 - \alpha)^2 F'(N)}{(1 - \alpha)F(N) + \alpha T - G} - V'(N) \tag{58}$$

To make the discussion more transparent, we consider the balanced budget case:

$$G = T \tag{59}$$

Combining (56), (58), and (59), we obtain

$$\frac{\partial U}{\partial N} = (1 - \theta v)\frac{F'(N)}{F(N) - T} > 0 \tag{60}$$

Then combining (57) and (60), we have

$$\frac{\partial U}{\partial v} = \frac{\partial U}{\partial N}\frac{\partial N}{\partial v} > 0 \tag{61}$$

So we see that household utility depends positively on v, and therefore negatively on the households' market power. Of course, this is only an apparent paradox, as will become clear in chapter 5.

5

Bargaining Power, Underemployment, and Welfare

5.1 Introduction

We build in this chapter another model studying the effects of imperfect competition on employment and welfare. As in the preceding chapter the model combines rational expectations and objective demand curves. This time the emphasis will be placed on disentangling the effects of market power at the microeconomic and macroeconomic levels.

This differentiation of the micro and macro levels will enable us to see, for example, whether prices, wages, and employment in various sectors are more influenced by sectoral or global parameters. It will also allow us, among other results, to dispel a paradox that sometimes arises when scrutinizing various macroeconomic models of imperfect competition in the literature, a paradox that we encountered in the model we studied in chapter 4 (see appendix 4.1). In these models the market power of agents is represented by a small number of macroeconomic parameters, each representing the market power of a whole class of agents. As a consequence it is difficult to disentangle micro from macro effects, which sometimes gives rise to paradoxical results. For example, in the model of the preceding chapter, the welfare of the representative household is generally a decreasing function of the market power it has in the labor markets. So one could ask, why should a household bother to exert its market power if, in the end, this woul be detrimental to its well-being? To answer this question, we have to build a model where bargaining powers at the local and the global level can be clearly separated. So in this chapter we develop a model where the equilibrium can be computed even when market powers are different for all agents. As a consequence we are able to see that the effects on individual welfare are completely different depending on whether one considers market power at the microeconomic or macroeconomic level.

The process of wage setting we use in this chapter is a standard one, since we will consider firm-specific trade unions. A possible limitation of this traditional modeling is that market powers of firms and trade unions cannot be easily separated: indeed the elasticity of the demand curve for a firm's labor is mechanically tied to that of the demand curve for the good sold by this firm, so a trade union has market power in its internal labor market inasmuch as, and only inasmuch as, the firm it is active in has power in its goods market.

For this reason we will introduce a second feature that will enable us to disentangle these two market powers: instead of having wages set unilaterally by the trade union, we will assume that wages are bilaterally bargained between the firm and the trade union. This will introduce a new parameter, the bargaining power of workers within each firm.

Although, in general, such models can only be solved explicitly in fully symmetrical cases, we will be able to solve the model for different values across sectors of both the productivity within the firm and the bargaining power within each firm. As a result we will obtain a richer and sometimes surprising set of results.

First, we have the traditional result that more bargaining power on the side of workers in a firm results in less employment within that firm. But we will also find that the utility of workers in that firm actually increases continuously as bargaining power increases and employment decreases. So it appears that measuring employment effects only, as some authors do, can be misleading in terms of welfare.

That result is valid at the level of a single firm, taking everything else as given. If we take a more "macroeconomic" view, we find that more bargaining power is profitable to workers as a group only up to a certain point. Beyond that threshold level of the bargaining power, more power is actually detrimental to workers in the aggregate. The "local" effects of bargaining power can be completely different from the "global" effects. This is why, as we saw in the previous chapter, an increase in market power of all workers taken together can be detrimental to them, whereas such an increase is positive at the microeconomic level.

5.2 The Model

As in chapter 4 we study here an intertemporal model with overlapping generations and fiat money. The agents are households living two periods each, and firms.

5.2.1 The Agents

Final output is produced from intermediate inputs, indexed by $j \in [0, 1]$, by competitive firms endowed with a technology

$$Y = \left(\int_0^1 Y_j^\theta \, dj \right)^{1/\theta} \tag{1}$$

Intermediate inputs are produced by firms indexed by $j \in [0, 1]$, with production functions

$$Y_j = Z_j N_j^\nu \tag{2}$$

where N_j is the quantity of labor used in firm j and Z_j is a productivity index specific to firm j. The firm sets the price P_j of good j and maximizes its profit $\Pi_j = P_j Y_j - W_j N_j$, where W_j is the wage negotiated in firm j.

Households, indexed by i, live two periods. They belong to two categories: workers and capitalists.[1] Worker i works during the first period of his life an amount N_i at a wage W_i. His budget constraints for the two periods are

$$PC_i + M_i = W_i N_i, \tag{3}$$

$$P'C_i' = M_i, \tag{4}$$

where M_i is the quantity of money saved, C_i and C_i' are agent i's consumptions in the current and future period, and P and P' are the current and future prices of output. Worker i has a utility function U_i given by

$$\log U_i = \alpha \log C_i + (1 - \alpha) \log C_i' - V(N_i), \tag{5}$$

where $V(N_i)$, the disutility of labor, is a convex function.

---

1 Our separating workers and capitalists is not meant to have any kind of socio-political meaning. We do so only to simplify some calculations.

Capitalist i receives in the first part of his life a share of profits given by

$$\Pi_i = \int_0^1 \vartheta_{ij} \Pi_j \, dj, \tag{6}$$

where ϑ_{ij} is capitalist i's share in firm j. His budget constraints are thus

$$PC_i + M_i = \Pi_i \tag{7}$$

$$P'C_i' = M_i \tag{8}$$

and his utility function is given by

$$\log U_i = \alpha \log C_i + (1 - \alpha) \log C_i' \tag{9}$$

5.2.2   The Structure of Equilibria

In each period the equilibrium is determined in two steps:

1. In each firm j a wage W_j is negotiated between the managers, representing shareholders, and a trade union, representing the workers of the firm.
2. Each firm j chooses its price P_j. Transactions occur on all markets.

As is usual, we will solve the model by considering these two steps in an order inverse of the chronological order.

5.3   Price Setting and Equilibrium

Consider a firm j where a wage W_j has been negotiated. A fundamental element in determining firm j's behavior in terms of prices and production is the objective demand curve for good j. We call $\bar{M}$ the total quantity of money in the economy, which is in the hands of the old households. Using the same methodology as in chapters 3 and 4, we characterize this objective demand curve through the following proposition:

Proposition 1   *The objective demand curve for good j is given by*

$$Y_j = \frac{1}{1 - \alpha} \frac{\bar{M}}{P} \left(\frac{P_j}{P} \right)^{-1/(1-\theta)} \tag{10}$$

with

$$P = \left(\int_0^1 P_j^{-\theta/(1-\theta)} \, dj \right)^{-(1-\theta)/\theta} \tag{11}$$

Proof As we saw in chapter 3, the objective demand for good j is given by the effective demand for good j at a fixprice equilibrium corresponding to the prices and wages P_j and W_j, $j \in [0, 1]$. Since firm j sets the price of good j, we further know that it will choose a price level such that households are not rationed on their demands for this good.

Let us begin with the final output firms. They maximize their profits

$$PY - \int_0^1 P_j Y_j \, dj = P \left(\int_0^1 Y_j^\theta \, dj \right)^{1/\theta} - \int_0^1 P_j Y_j \, dj \tag{12}$$

which yields a demand for intermediate good j:

$$Y_j = Y \left(\frac{P_j}{P} \right)^{-1/(1-\theta)} \tag{13}$$

Moreover, since this sector is competitive, the price P is equal to the cost index associated with the CES function (11).

Old households have all the money in the economy $\bar{M}$, which they spend totally, so their consumption demand is $\bar{M}/P$.

In view of utility functions (5) and (9), young consumers, whether workers or capitalists, will consume exactly a fraction α of their incomes. So the total consumption of young consumers is equal to

$$\frac{\alpha}{P} \left(\int_i W_i N_i \, di + \int_i \Pi_i \, di \right) \tag{14}$$

The total production is equal to the consumption of the young plus the consumption of the old:

$$Y = \frac{\alpha}{P} \left(\int_i W_i N_i \, di + \int_i \Pi_i \, di \right) + \frac{\bar{M}}{P} \tag{15}$$

Now let us use the global incomes identity:

$$\int_i W_i N_i \, di + \int_i \Pi_i \, di = \int_j P_j Y_j \, dj = PY \tag{16}$$

Combining (15) and (16), we obtain

$$Y = \frac{1}{1-\alpha} \frac{\bar{M}}{P} \tag{17}$$

Then combining (17) and (13), we obtain the objective demand (10). ∎

So the objective demand for goods is given by proposition 1. On the other hand, on the labor market the firm cannot obtain more than what is supplied by the workers. It is easy to compute, using utility function (5), that whatever the vectors of prices and wages, each worker supplies exactly a fixed quantity N_0 given by the equation

$$N_0 V'(N_0) = 1 \tag{18}$$

Employment N_j in firm j is thus constrained by

$$N_j \leq N_0 \tag{19}$$

Combining the various constraints to which the firm is submitted, we see that the price P_j, employment N_j, and production Y_j in firm j are given by

$$\max P_j Y_j - W_j N_j \quad \text{s.t.}$$

$$Y_j = Z_j N_j^v$$

$$Y_j \leq \frac{1}{1-\alpha} \frac{\bar{M}}{P} \left(\frac{P_j}{P} \right)^{-1/(1-\theta)}$$

$$N_j \leq N_0$$

The solution to this program can take two forms, depending on whether excess supply or excess demand prevails on the labor side. In both cases the production function and demand equation hold:

$$Y_j = Z_j N_j^v \tag{20}$$

$$Y_j = \frac{1}{1-\alpha} \frac{\bar{M}}{P} \left(\frac{P_j}{P} \right)^{-1/(1-\theta)} \tag{21}$$

If there is excess demand for labor in firm j, then employment in this firm is determined by the supply of labor:

$$N_j = N_0 \qquad (22)$$

If, on the contrary, labor is in excess supply, the employment level is determined by the traditional "marginal revenue equals marginal cost" equality. This equality can be written in the following form, where the distribution of income appears particularly well:

$$W_j N_j = \theta v P_j Y_j \qquad (23)$$

As a useful reference, we can compute the wage level W_j^*, which balances supply and demand of labor within firm j. This wage W_j^* is naturally the solution in W_j of the system of four equations (20) to (23), which yields

$$W_j^* = \theta v \left(\frac{\bar{M}}{1 - \alpha} \right)^{1-\theta} (P Z_j)^\theta N_0^{\theta v - 1} \qquad (24)$$

For given W_j there are two possible regimes for firm j, excess demand or excess supply of labor. N_j will be equal to the minimum of demand and supply. So the values of Y_j, P_j, and N_j will be determined by the system of equations (20), (21), and (22) in case of excess demand, or (20), (21), and (23) in case of excess supply.

5.4 Wage Negotiations

The wage in firm j, W_j, is determined by negotiation between firm j's management and a trade union specific to that firm. We will assume that the negotiated wage is determined by the Nash asymmetric solution (e.g., see Binmore, Rubinstein, and Wolinsky 1986), which corresponds to the maximum of the quantity Δ_j defined by

$$\log \Delta_j = \delta_j \log(U_{tj} - \bar{U}_{tj}) + (1 - \delta_j) \log(U_{mj} - \bar{U}_{mj}) \qquad (25)$$

where δ_j, a central parameter in all that follows, is the bargaining power of workers within firm j. U_{mj} and U_{tj} are the utilities of management and trade union in case of agreement and $\bar{U}_{mj}$ and $\bar{U}_{tj}$ are these same utilities in case of disagreement. To evaluate these various quantities, let us first consider a worker i

working in a firm j. In case of disagreement, this worker has no income and cannot consume, so $\bar{U}_i = 0$. In case of agreement it is easily computed that

$$C_i = \alpha \frac{W_j N_j}{P}, \quad C_i' = (1 - \alpha) \frac{W_j N_j}{P'} \tag{26}$$

The price indexes P and P' are exogenous for the worker, and therefore up to an additive constant

$$\log(U_{tj} - \bar{U}_{tj}) = \log W_j N_j - V(N_j) \tag{27}$$

Consider now a shareholder i receiving profits Π_i. Again, we easily compute

$$C_i = \alpha \frac{\Pi_i}{P}, \quad C_i' = (1 - \alpha) \frac{\Pi_i}{P'} \tag{28}$$

and thus up to a constant, the shareholder's utility is equal to Π_i. Consider now the point of view of firm j's management. If negotiations fail, a capitalist i who has shares ϑ_{ij} in firm j loses his share of firm j's profits, so $U_i - \bar{U}_i = \vartheta_{ij} \Pi_j$. Thus, up to a multiplicative constant, all capitalists unanimously share the same objective Π_j, and we will take naturally

$$\log(U_{mj} - \bar{U}_{mj}) = \log \Pi_j = \log(P_j Y_j - W_j N_j) \tag{29}$$

Combining (25), (27), and (29), we see that the wage W_j will be determined by the maximization of

$$\log \Delta_j = \delta_j \log(W_j N_j) - \delta_j V(N_j) + (1 - \delta_j) \log(P_j Y_j - W_j N_j) \tag{30}$$

We will study in turn situations of excess supply and excess demand of labor.

5.4.1 Excess Supply of Labor

In that case equations (20), (21), and (23) are valid. Differentiating these equations as well as (30), we find that

$$\frac{\partial \log \Delta_j}{\partial \log W_j} = \frac{1}{1 - \theta v} [\delta_j N_j V'(N_j) - \theta v] \tag{31}$$

Since N_j is a decreasing function of W_j, $\log \Delta_j$ is concave in $\log W_j$ and its maximum is found by equating to zero the derivative above, which yields

$$N_j V'(N_j) = \frac{\theta v}{\delta_j} \tag{32}$$

We can denote the solution in N_j to this equation as

$$N_j = \Lambda \left(\frac{\theta v}{\delta_j} \right), \qquad \Lambda' > 0 \tag{33}$$

We thus find the traditional result that the employment level is a decreasing function of the bargaining power δ_j. We must still check that we are in the regime of an excess supply of labor, which will be the case if the quantity given by (32) is inferior to the supply N_0 defined in equation (18). This gives the condition

$$\delta_j \geq \theta v \tag{34}$$

So there will be underemployment in firm j if condition (34) is satisfied with strict inequality. Note that this underemployment is fully "voluntary" from the workers' side. Combining (20), (21), (23), and (33), we compute the wage W_j in sector j as

$$W_j = \theta v \left(\frac{\bar{M}}{1-\alpha} \right)^{1-\theta} (PZ_j)^\theta \left[\Lambda \left(\frac{\theta v}{\delta_j} \right) \right]^{\theta v - 1} \tag{35}$$

We compute also the utility U_j of a worker in firm j which, up to a constant, is equal to

$$\log U_j = \log \theta v + \theta \log Z_j + \theta v \log \left[\Lambda \left(\frac{\theta v}{\delta_j} \right) \right] - V \left[\Lambda \left(\frac{\theta v}{\delta_j} \right) \right] \tag{36}$$

The utility of workers in firm j is strictly increasing in Z_j. Considering now the effect of bargaining power, we see that although employment is a decreasing function of δ_j (33), the utility of each worker is strictly increasing in δ_j as long as $\delta_j < 1$. Indeed, differentiating (36) and using the definition of Λ (32), we find that

$$\frac{\partial \log U_j}{\partial \log \delta_j} = \theta v \left(1 - \frac{1}{\delta_j} \right) \frac{\partial \log \Lambda}{\partial \log \delta_j} > 0 \tag{37}$$

Notice that the macroeconomic paradox of the previous chapter disappears completely at the microeconomic level. As (37) shows, in every firm j the welfare of workers is increasing in their bargaining power. As a result workers in a firm will want to fully exert their local bargaining power simply because, other things equal, and although this decreases employment, bargaining power is beneficial to their welfare at the microeconomic level.

5.4.2 Excess Demand for Labor

We have the case where N_j is equal to N_0 (equation 22). Differentiating (30), we find that

$$\frac{\partial \log \Delta_j}{\partial \log W_j} = \delta_j - (1 - \delta_j)\frac{W_j N_j}{P_j Y_j - W_j N_j} \tag{38}$$

which is decreasing in W_j, so $\log \Delta_j$ is concave in $\log W_j$. The maximum is found by equating the derivative above to zero, which yields

$$W_j = \frac{\delta_j P_j Y_j}{N_j} \tag{39}$$

where Y_j, P_j, and N_j are given by equations (20), (21), and (22). We must still check that we are in the zone of excess demand for labor. For that the derivative (38) at the point of labor market equilibrium ($W_j = W_j^*$) must be negative, which yields, taking into account that at this point equation (23) holds

$$\delta_j \leq \theta\nu \tag{40}$$

We can compute, using (39) and equations (20), (21), and (22), the negotiated wage W_j as a function of the parameters exogenous to the firm j

$$W_j = \delta_j \left(\frac{\bar{M}}{1 - \alpha}\right)^{1-\theta} (PZ_j)^\theta N_0^{\theta\nu - 1} \tag{41}$$

We see that the wage W_j is an increasing function of the productivity Z_j and bargaining power δ_j. We can also compute the utility of the representative worker in firm j, which is equal, up to a constant, to

$$\log U_j = \log \delta_j + \theta \log Z_j + \theta\nu \log N_0 - V(N_0) \tag{42}$$

Again, note that as in the excess supply case, the utility of a worker in firm j is strictly increasing in the bargaining power δ_j, so that workers will want to fully exercise their bargaining power.

In order to see how the picture may change at the macro level, we now move to the general equilibrium of the model.

5.5 General Equilibrium

Many of the sectoral values we computed above, including the levels of wages negotiated in each sector (equations 35 and 41), depend on the general price level P, given by equation (11):

$$P = \left(\int_0^1 P_j^{-\theta/(1-\theta)} \, dj \right)^{-(1-\theta)/\theta} \tag{43}$$

In order to describe fully the general equilibrium, we will compute this aggregate price level. Let us first invert equation (10) to obtain the local price level P_j as a function of Y_j and P:

$$P_j = P^\theta \left[\frac{\bar{M}}{(1-\alpha)Y_j} \right]^{1-\theta} \tag{44}$$

Combining (43) and (44), we obtain the general price level as a function of the production levels in all sectors:

$$P = \frac{\bar{M}}{1-\alpha} \left(\int_0^1 Y_j^\theta \, dj \right)^{-1/\theta} = \frac{\bar{M}}{(1-\alpha)Y} \tag{45}$$

Next, combining equations (20), (22), (23), (33), (39), and (45), we have equilibrium prices and quantities given by the following formulas:

$$N_j = \min \left\{ N_0, \Lambda \left(\frac{\theta v}{\delta_j} \right) \right\} \tag{46}$$

$$Y_j = Z_j N_j^v \tag{47}$$

$$Y = \left(\int_0^1 Y_j^\theta \, dj \right)^{1/\theta} \tag{48}$$

$$P = \frac{\bar{M}}{(1-\alpha)Y} \qquad (49)$$

$$P_j = P \left(\frac{Y}{Y_j}\right)^{1-\theta} \qquad (50)$$

$$W_j = \frac{P_j Y_j}{N_j} \min(\delta_j, \theta v) \qquad (51)$$

Equations (46) to (51) completely describe the general equilibrium. As indicated earlier, this equilibrium can be computed for asymmetric values of productivity and bargaining powers. These computations will enable us to see how the microeconomic and macroeconomic effects of bargaining power may end up being almost opposite.

5.6 Bargaining Power and Global Efficiency

Bruno and Sachs (1985), Calmfors and Driffill (1988), and Cahuc and Zylberberg (1991) have shown that decentralized wage negotiations, like those we consider here, could create more unemployment than, for example, negotiations through a centralized trade union.

As we saw earlier, employment is only one part of the problem, however, since lower employment levels can be accompanied by higher real wages and higher utility. In the end what we need to scrutinize is the welfare of the workers concerned.

In our model it is clear that the high bargaining power of a trade union in one firm (i.e., a high δ_j) increases underemployment in the corresponding firm (see formula 33). This underemployment, however, is beneficial for the concerned workers since we saw that, others things equal, the utility of workers in firm j is strictly increasing in δ_j.

We will now show that if one takes a global perspective, as would be that of a centralized trade union representing all workers, too much bargaining power at the level of all firms can be bad for workers as a whole. This apparently paradoxical effect is much like that which we observed in the previous chapter.

To demonstrate this effect, we will consider a symmetrical equilibrium, where $Z_j = Z$ and $\delta_j = \delta$. In this case the real wage W/P and employment per worker N are the same in all firms, and the central trade union's objective is to maximize

$$\log\left(\frac{WN}{P}\right) - V(N) \qquad (52)$$

Clearly, the maximum of this quantity cannot be in the excess demand zone since, for given N, it will always be in the workers' interest to obtain a higher real wage. This means that we are in the excess supply zone where (from formulas 20 and 23)

$$\frac{W}{P} = \theta v Z N^{v-1} \qquad (53)$$

Maximization of (52) under constraint (53) gives us immediately the optimum level of N from the point of view of workers, N^*:

$$N^* V'(N^*) = v \qquad (54)$$

The optimum real wage is deduced from it through formula (53). Now let us consider again formula (32), giving N as a function of a uniform bargaining power δ:

$$NV'(N) = \frac{\theta v}{\delta} \qquad (55)$$

Comparing (54) and (55), we see that the optimum corresponds to an index of bargaining power for the workers, which is equal to

$$\delta^* = \theta < 1 \qquad (56)$$

Any bargaining power beyond this level is detrimental to workers as a group. The explanation for this result is intuitive: we have seen that other things equal, an increase in the workers' bargaining power within firm j strictly increases their welfare. But at the same time it increases the general price level, which *decreases* the welfare of workers in other firms. When all bargaining powers increase, at some point this negative "Nash externality" outweighs the positive effect and the paradoxical result occurs.[2]

5.7   Conclusions

In order to investigate the role of market power at the micro- and macroeconomic levels, we constructed in this chapter a model where the trade unions' bargaining power can differ across all firms, and nevertheless an explicit closed form solution can be found. This enabled us to clarify some apparently paradoxical issues.

We first found that although employment in a particular firm is a nonincreasing function of the workers' bargaining power in that firm, the welfare of these workers is a strictly increasing function of their bargaining power. This explains why workers will always find it beneficial to fully use their bargaining power, though this might result in their underemployment.

Going to the macroeconomic level, we saw that macroeconomic effects can be very different from the microeconomic ones. Notably we found that a *uniform* increase in the bargaining power of workers beyond a certain level can be detrimental to all workers.

5.8   References

This chapter is based on Bénassy (1994). Rigorous general equilibrium models with wage bargaining are found, for example, in Arnsperger and de la Croix (1993), Jacobsen and Schultz (1990, 1994), and Licandro (1995).

The relation between the level at which wages are bargained and overall macroeconomic performance has been studied notably by Bruno and Sachs (1985), Calmfors and Driffill (1988), and Cahuc and Zylberberg (1991). The relations between the functioning of labor markets and the macroeconomy are notably investigated in Layard, Nickell, and Jackman (1991) and Cahuc and Zylberberg (1996).

2 The reader may wonder why this negative effect occurs here only for $\delta > \theta$, and not for all values as in the previous chapter. This is because, unlike the present case, in the previous chapter workers and capitalists were not separated. As a consequence, an increase in workers' bargaining power hurts profits, which creates an additional negative effect in the model of the previous chapter, and therefore broadens the reach of the paradoxical effect.

Part IV

Imperfect Competition, Fluctuations, and Growth

6

Fluctuations and Imperfect Competition

6.1 Introduction

So far, for simplicity, we have treated the imperfectly competitive models of the previous part in a deterministic framework. Here we begin to introduce stochastic shocks and construct various models of fluctuations embedding imperfect competition.

Dynamic general equilibrium models with stochastic shocks have become extremely popular in recent years under the generic name of real business cycles (RBC). A strong point of this methodology is that, unlike deterministic models, these models immediately deliver relative variances and correlations between economic variables that can be compared to real world data.

Following the initial contributions by Kydland and Prescott (1982) and Long and Plosser (1983), this line of analysis remained for some time confined to pure Walrasian environments. This proved to be too restrictive, as several important real world features remained unexplained. So in the chapters that follow we will see that this methodology can be fruitfully extended to a nonmarket-clearing imperfectly competitive framework. Our plan is to consider imperfect competition without nominal rigidities in the three chapters of this part, and nominal rigidities in the three chapters of the following part.

A common characteristic of most RBC analyses is that they perform essentially numerical calibrations. This has the obvious advantage of allowing immediate comparison with real world data. However, for the average economist, this may make a little obscure the specific contribution of each assumption and parameterization to the results obtained. For this reason our purpose is to construct simple models with explicit solutions, which will make more transparent the basic properties and economic mechanisms at work.[1]

Following Long-Plosser (1983), such a benchmark model was already constructed for the traditional RBC framework by McCallum (1989). As compared to this early contribution, we will add a few important and realistic features. The economy we consider is a monetary one, subject to monetary shocks as well as to the "usual" technology shocks. There will be imperfect competition in both goods and labor markets, as well as inefficient underemployment.

We now turn to a more detailed description of this economy.

6.2   The Model

The economy studied is an infinite-horizon monetary economy. It includes households and a production sector, which we describe in turn.

6.2.1   Households

The households are atomistic. Their population size is normalized to 1. In period t the representative household works N_t, consumes C_t, and ends the period with a quantity of money M_t. It maximizes the expected value of discounted utilities with the following utility:

$$U = E_0 \sum_{t=0}^{\infty} \beta^t \left[\log C_t + \omega \log \frac{M_t}{P_t} - V(N_t) \right] \qquad (1)$$

where V is a convex function. Households can accumulate under the form of money holdings M_t, or invest I_t in capital, which they rent to firms. To obtain closed-form solutions, we will assume that this capital depreciates fully in one period:[2]

$$K_{t+1} = I_t \qquad (2)$$

---

1 This is, of course, a "complementary good" to the numerical simulations, not a substitute.

2 The model can also be solved using a more general loglinear depreciation function (see the appendix at the end of chapter 9, where this is done for a relatively similar model).

The budget constraint of the representative household is thus

$$C_t + \frac{M_t}{P_t} + I_t = \frac{W_t}{P_t} N_t + \kappa_t I_{t-1} + \frac{\mu_t M_{t-1}}{P_t} \tag{3}$$

where κ_t is the real rate of return in t on investments made in $t-1$. The multiplicative factor μ_t is a money shock as in Lucas (1972), whereby money holdings M_{t-1} carried from $t-1$ are multiplied by μ_t, so that the household starts period t with money holdings $\mu_t M_{t-1}$.

6.2.2 The Production Sector

There are two types of goods in the economy: homogeneous final goods, or output, used for both consumption and investment, and differentiated intermediate inputs indexed by j. The final good is produced by competitive firms according to a CES production function:

$$Y_t = \left(\int_0^1 Y_{jt}^\theta dj \right)^{1/\theta}, \qquad 0 < \theta < 1 \tag{4}$$

where Y_t is the quantity of total output and Y_{jt} intermediate input j, with $j \in [0, 1]$. Call P_t the price of output and P_{jt} the price of intermediate input j. Output firms competitively maximize profits:

$$P_t Y_t - \int_0^1 P_{jt} Y_{jt} dj \tag{5}$$

Firms producing intermediate inputs are indexed by j. The production function of firm j is

$$Y_{jt} = Z_t K_{jt}^\gamma N_{jt}^{1-\gamma} \tag{6}$$

where K_{jt} is capital rented by firm j, N_{jt} labor used by firm j, and Z_t a stochastic technological shock common to all intermediate firms. Firm j sets the price P_{jt} in a framework of monopolistic competition, as we will see in more detail below.

As for wages, they are also firm specific. We assume that all workers in a firm j form a union and choose their wage W_{jt} so as to maximize the utility of the representative worker in the firm.

6.3   Resolution

The dynamic equilibrium solution will take a few steps.

6.3.1   Output Firms

Since the output firms are competitive, we have

$$\frac{P_{jt}}{P_t} = \frac{\partial Y_t}{\partial Y_{jt}} \tag{7}$$

This immediately yields the demand for intermediate output j corresponding to an output level Y_t:

$$Y_{jt} = Y_t \left(\frac{P_{jt}}{P_t} \right)^{-1/(1-\theta)} \tag{8}$$

Furthermore, because of the competitiveness of the output industry, output price P_t is equal to the cost index associated to production function (4), namely

$$P_t = \left(\int_0^1 P_{jt}^{-\theta/(1-\theta)} \, dj \right)^{-(1-\theta)/\theta} \tag{9}$$

6.3.2   Intermediate Inputs Firms

Intermediate firm j maximizes its profits Π_{jt},

$$\Pi_{jt} = P_{jt} Y_{jt} - R_t K_{jt} - W_{jt} N_{jt} \tag{10}$$

subject to production function (6) and the demand function for intermediate input j (equation 8). $R_t = \kappa_t P_t$ is the money rental of capital. The first-order conditions can be written in the following form, which shows clearly the distribution of incomes:

$$W_{jt} N_{jt} = (1 - \gamma)\theta \, P_{jt} Y_{jt} \tag{11}$$

$$R_t K_{jt} = \gamma \theta \, P_{jt} Y_{jt} \tag{12}$$

The values of P_{jt}, Y_{jt}, N_{jt}, and K_{jt} are solutions of the system of equations (6), (8), (11), and (12). Solving in N_{jt}, we obtain the demand for labor in firm j:

$$N_{jt} = \Omega_{jt} W_{jt}^{-(1-\gamma\theta)/(1-\theta)} \qquad (13)$$

with

$$\Omega_{jt} = \left[\theta\gamma^{\gamma\theta}(1-\gamma)^{1-\gamma\theta} P_t Z_t^\theta Y_t^{1-\theta} R_t^{-\gamma\theta}\right]^{1/(1-\theta)} = \Omega_t \qquad (14)$$

Note that because of the model's symmetry, Ω_{jt} and the elasticity of the demand curve curve for labor do not depend on j.

6.3.3 Households

The program of a household working in a particular firm j is simply to maximize the expected value of its utility (1), subject to the sequence of its budget constraints (3) and the demand functions for the type of labor it supplies (13). That is to say, the household indexed j will solve the following program:

$$\max E_0 \sum_{t=0}^{\infty} \beta^t \left[\log C_{jt} + \omega \log \frac{M_{jt}}{P_t} - V(N_{jt})\right] \quad \text{s.t.}$$

$$C_{jt} + \frac{M_{jt}}{P_t} + I_{jt} = \frac{W_{jt}}{P_t} N_{jt} + \kappa_t I_{jt-1} + \frac{\mu_t M_{jt-1}}{P_t}$$

$$N_{jt} = \Omega_t W_{jt}^{-(1-\gamma\theta)/(1-\theta)}$$

The first thing to note is that since the demands for labor are symmetrical, the programs are the same for all households despite the different firms in which they work. All households thus make exactly the same decisions. So we can omit the index j pertaining to the firm with which a household is affiliated.

Call $\beta^t \lambda_t$ the marginal utility of real wealth in t, that is, the Lagrange multiplier associated with the budget constraint. Then the first-order conditions for the consumer's intertemporal utility maximization are written

$$\frac{1}{C_t} = \lambda_t \qquad (15)$$

$$V'(N_t) = \lambda_t \frac{(1-\gamma)\theta}{1-\gamma\theta} \frac{W_t}{P_t} \qquad (16)$$

$$\lambda_t = \beta E_t \left(\lambda_{t+1} \kappa_{t+1} \right) \tag{17}$$

$$\frac{\lambda_t}{P_t} = \frac{\omega}{M_t} + \beta E_t \left(\frac{\lambda_{t+1} \mu_{t+1}}{P_{t+1}} \right) \tag{18}$$

6.3.4 Equilibrium

In order to solve the system above, we need an expression for the real rate of return on investment κ_t. Since the equilibrium is fully symmetrical,

$$P_{jt} = P_t, \quad Y_{jt} = Y_t, \quad K_{jt} = K_t, \quad N_{jt} = N_t \tag{19}$$

Combining (19) with (12) and $R_t = \kappa_t P_t$, we find that

$$\kappa_t = \frac{\gamma \theta Y_t}{K_t} \tag{20}$$

Now, combining (15), (17), and (20), we obtain

$$\frac{1}{C_t} = \beta E_t \left(\frac{\gamma \theta Y_{t+1}}{C_{t+1} K_{t+1}} \right) \tag{21}$$

Because of full capital depreciation $K_{t+1} = I_t$. Moreover we have the equality $Y_t = C_t + I_t$, so (21) is rewritten as

$$\frac{I_t}{C_t} = \beta \gamma \theta + \beta \gamma \theta E_t \left(\frac{I_{t+1}}{C_{t+1}} \right) \tag{22}$$

It is solved, using the usual transversality condition, as

$$\frac{I_t}{C_t} = \frac{\beta \gamma \theta}{1 - \beta \gamma \theta} \tag{23}$$

and therefore

$$C_t = (1 - \beta \gamma \theta) Y_t \tag{24}$$

$$I_t = K_{t+1} = \beta \gamma \theta Y_t \tag{25}$$

The equilibrium condition for money is that money demanded by households M_t is equal to the available money holdings in that period, namely $\mu_t M_{t-1}$, which yields

$$M_t = \mu_t M_{t-1} \qquad (26)$$

Combining (15), (18), and (26), we obtain

$$\frac{M_t}{P_t C_t} = \omega + \beta E_t \left(\frac{M_{t+1}}{P_{t+1} C_{t+1}} \right) \qquad (27)$$

whose solution is

$$\frac{M_t}{P_t C_t} = \frac{\omega}{1 - \beta} \qquad (28)$$

Combining (28) with the equation giving consumption (24), we obtain the level of real money balances:

$$\frac{M_t}{P_t} = \frac{\omega(1 - \beta \gamma \theta)}{1 - \beta} Y_t \qquad (29)$$

Note that this equation is reminiscent of the traditional "quantity of money" equation. Finally we want to determine the quantity of labor N_t. Combining (11) and (19), we obtain the expression for the real wage:

$$\frac{W_t}{P_t} = \theta(1 - \gamma) \frac{Y_t}{N_t} \qquad (30)$$

Then, combining (15), (16), (24), and (30), we see that N_t is constant and equal to N, which is given by

$$N V'(N) = \frac{(1 - \gamma)^2 \theta^2}{(1 - \gamma\theta)(1 - \beta\gamma\theta)} \qquad (31)$$

6.4 Properties of the Dynamic Equilibrium

Let us now look at a few properties of this dynamic imperfectly competitive model.

6.4.1   Real and Monetary Variables

First, from the preceding equations defining the dynamic equilibrium, we see that the model somehow "dichotomizes," as the central real variables are unaffected by the evolution of money.[3] The dynamics of the real core of the model are described by the following equations:

$$N V'(N) = \frac{(1 - \gamma)^2 \theta^2}{(1 - \gamma\theta)(1 - \beta\gamma\theta)} \tag{32}$$

$$Y_t = Z_t K_t^\gamma N^{1-\gamma} \tag{33}$$

$$\frac{W_t}{P_t} = \theta(1 - \gamma)\frac{Y_t}{N} \tag{34}$$

$$C_t = (1 - \beta\gamma\theta)Y_t \tag{35}$$

$$K_{t+1} = \beta\gamma\theta Y_t \tag{36}$$

The values of the nominal wage and price are given by

$$W_t = \frac{\theta(1 - \beta)(1 - \gamma)}{\omega(1 - \beta\gamma\theta)}\frac{M_t}{N} \tag{37}$$

$$P_t = \frac{1 - \beta}{(1 - \beta\gamma\theta)\omega}\frac{M_t}{Y_t} \tag{38}$$

We further note that we can obtain very simply a Walrasian version of this model by setting $\theta = 1$. In comparing the two, it appears that fluctuations in our imperfectly competitive model are very similar to those in the corresponding Walrasian model. However, this similarity will completely disappear when nominal rigidities are introduced, as we will later see notably in parts V and VI.

---

3 Of course, the total absence of effects of monetary shocks on real variables is due to our specific model, notably the utility of money and the "Lucas" money shocks. Usually these effects are not quantitatively important in standard dynamic monetary Walrasian models.

6.4.2 Underemployment and Growth

There are, however, a number of aspects for which imperfect competition does matter. The first is capital accumulation, as given by equation (25):

$$K_{t+1} = \beta \gamma \theta Y_t \qquad (39)$$

We see that high market power, namely a low θ, decreases the fraction of output devoted to capital accumulation. Since we are here in a model of "exogenous growth," this lower rate of capital accumulation will not harm the long-term growth of the economy. In chapter 8 we will see that when elements of endogenous growth are introduced, changes in market power can affect the long-term rate of growth as well.

The second point where market power matters is in the determination of employment, given by

$$N V'(N) = \frac{(1 - \gamma)^2 \theta^2}{(1 - \gamma\theta)(1 - \beta\gamma\theta)} \qquad (40)$$

As (40) shows, the level of employment depends positively on the parameter θ. The value $\theta = 1$ corresponds to perfect competition in the goods market, whereas $\theta < 1$ indicates market power, this market power being inversely related to θ. Clearly, market power leads to underemployment (we do not speak of unemployment here as the level of employment is voluntarily chosen by workers in order to maximize their utility).

We may note that in this model it is not clear whose market power—the firms' or the workers'—is conducive to underemployment, because both market powers are related to the parameter θ, and both disappear if $\theta = 1$. The same exercise can actually be performed with models where the two market powers are separated, as in the models of chapters 4 and 5.[4]

6.5 Conclusions

We constructed in this chapter a benchmark model that broadens the scope of traditional "real" Walrasian models, since we introduced money and monetary shocks as well as imperfect competition on goods and labor markets. We saw that

4 See, for example, Bénassy (1996), which studies a model similar to that of this chapter, but where the labor market is modeled as in chapter 4.

the respective responses of our imperfectly competitive economy to technology and monetary shocks have strong similarities to those of a Walrasian economy. We also saw that market power substantially affects both employment and the rate of capital accumulation.

One possible cause of disappointment for the reader at the end of this chapter might be that, although we found some underemployment, the level of employment stayed constant in the cycle. This is clearly due to some simplifying assumptions. As we will see in the next chapter, by changing one assumption it is possible to obtain a variable and persistent level of underemployment.

6.6   References

This model is based on Bénassy (1996). Early calibrated dynamic models with imperfect competition are found, among others, in Danthine and Donaldson (1990, 1992), Devereux, Head, and Lapham (1993), Hairault and Portier (1993), Hornstein (1993), and Rotemberg and Woodford (1992). Many aspects of such dynamic imperfectly competitive economies are surveyed in Silvestre (1995).

7

Unemployment Persistence

7.1 Introduction

In the preceding chapter we showed that money and imperfect competition can be introduced in a fully computable model of business cycles. We saw that a notable consequence of imperfect competition is that the dynamic equilibrium displays inefficient underemployment. The level of employment, however, was constant throughout the cycle. This clearly does not mesh with reality where we often observe large fluctuations and persistence in unemployment, or persistence in output beyond that deriving from persistence in the shocks.

Our purpose in this chapter is to show that we can actually generate these missing features within an imperfectly competitive dynamic model. More precisely we will see that the combination of some degree of capital-labor complementarity with imperfect competition in the labor market can lead to persistent unemployment.

Imperfect competition in the labor market is introduced through the usual assumption that wages are set in each firm by a "monopoly union." Capital–labor complementarity will mean an elasticity of substitution between capital and labor lower than 1. The persistence mechanism goes through recurrent "capital shortages" and can be intuitively described as follows: under limited capital–labor substitutability and wage setting by a monopoly union, insufficient capital leads to low employment. Low capital combined to this low employment leads to low production and low accumulation, hence low capital and low employment in the next period. The mechanism therefore produces persistence in all variables, including unemployment.

An important feature of the model we develop is that although the maximization problems are stochastic and nonlinear, we are able, as in the previous chapter, to derive closed-form solutions for the behavior of households, firms, and trade unions. This helps make the analysis and results more transparent than in purely numerically calibrated models.

7.2   The Model

We consider a dynamic model with firms and overlapping generations of households with stochastic lives. The economy is a continuum of representative firms and households which we now describe.

7.2.1   Firms

The production sector consists of two types of firms. Final output is produced by competitive firms with the production function

$$Y_t = \left(\int_0^1 Y_{jt}^\theta \, dj \right)^{1/\theta}, \qquad 0 < \theta < 1 \tag{1}$$

The intermediate inputs are produced by firms indexed by $j \in [0, 1]$ with production functions

$$Y_{jt} = Z_t \, F(K_{jt}, N_{jt}) \tag{2}$$

where Y_{jt} is intermediate output, K_{jt} is the capital available to the firm in period t, N_{jt} is the quantity of labor used, and Z_t is a common technological shock. We will work below with a CES production function

$$Y_{jt} = Z_t \left(a K_{jt}^\chi + b N_{jt}^\chi \right)^{1/\chi} \tag{3}$$

The elasticity of substitution is constant and equal to σ, where

$$\sigma = \frac{1}{1 - \chi} \tag{4}$$

As indicated above, we will assume limited substitutability between capital and labor, more specifically $\sigma < 1$ and thus $\chi < 0$. Capital depreciates at the rate δ, so the evolution of aggregate capital is given by

$$K_{t+1} = (1 - \delta) K_t + I_t \tag{5}$$

Since we want to focus on imperfect competition in the labor markets, we will assume that intermediate firms j behave competitively on all markets. It is actually trivial to adapt the argument to the case where each firm j is a monopolistic competitor and sets the corresponding price P_{jt}.

7.2.2 Households

We will use a model of households with stochastic lives due to Huffman (1993). There is a continuum of households. The preferences of all households alive at date t are represented by the utility function

$$E_t \left[\sum_{s=t}^{\infty} \beta^{s-t} \log C_s \right], \qquad 0 < \beta < 1 \tag{6}$$

We assume a constant population whose size is normalized to 1. At each date all alive households have a uniform probability of dying ϕ, so ϕ households disappear each period and ϕ new ones enter the economy. New entrants in the economy are endowed in the first period of their life with a fixed quantity of labor, which they supply inelastically. We denote by N_0 the aggregate labor supply. Households will thus receive labor income in the first period of their life, and will thereafter save under the form of capital for future consumptions. We assume that households learn at the beginning of each period whether they will be alive next period, so that only "survivors" will actually save and carry capital to the next period.

7.2.3 Trade Unions

Every period households working in a sector j form a trade union, which aims at maximizing the expected utility of the representative worker in the sector. This is a traditional "monopolistic" trade union that sets unilaterally the wage, leaving to the firm the right to choose the level of employment. Then, since labor yields no disutility, and the utility of consumption is logarithmic, the trade union will be led quite naturally to maximize the expected value of the logarithm of real labor income in period t, that is, to maximize the expected value of $\log(W_{jt} N_{jt} / P_t)$.

7.3   Resolution

We first characterize the aggregate consumption and accumulation behavior of households through the following proposition:

Proposition 1   *Households' aggregate consumption and accumulation behavior is given by*

$$K_{t+1} = \frac{\beta(1-\phi)}{1+\beta\phi} [Y_t + (1-\delta)K_t] \qquad (7)$$

$$C_t = \frac{1-\beta+2\beta\phi}{1+\beta\phi} [Y_t + (1-\delta)K_t] \qquad (8)$$

Proof   Consider a household in period t, and looking ahead to period $s \geq t$. With a probability of death ϕ in each period, this household has a probability $(1-\phi)^{s-t}$ to be still alive in period s, and to be announced that it is going to survive at least one more period, while it has a probability $\phi(1-\phi)^{s-t-1}$ to be still alive in period s, and to be announced it will die then.

As a consequence the maximization of expected utility (6) is equivalent (for a surviving household) to solving the following program:

$$\max E_t \left[\sum_{s=t}^{\infty} \beta^{s-t}(1-\phi)^{s-t} \log c_s + \sum_{s=t+1}^{\infty} \beta^{s-t}\phi(1-\phi)^{s-t-1} \log c'_s \right] \quad \text{s.t.}$$

$$c_s + i_s = \kappa_s i_{s-1}, \qquad s \geq t$$

$$c'_s = \kappa_s i_{s-1}, \qquad s \geq t+1$$

where κ_s is the real return in period s on capital invested the previous period i_{s-1}, c_s is consumption in s for a household that will survive, c'_s is consumption for a household that will disappear at the end of the period.[1] The first-order

1 Note that, if t is the first period of the agent's life, the right-hand side of the first constraint should be replaced by labor income for $s = t$, since in the first period of their life agents work and do not have capital. To keep the exposition concise, we omit this constraint, as it does not affect the solution.

conditions for this dynamic program yield

$$\frac{i_s}{c_s} = \beta\phi + \beta(1-\phi)E_s\left(\frac{c_{s+1} + i_{s+1}}{c_{s+1}}\right) \qquad (9)$$

whose solution is a constant consumption investment ratio in all periods:

$$\frac{i_s}{c_s} = \frac{\beta}{1 - \beta + \beta\phi}, \qquad s \geq t \qquad (10)$$

This means that "survivors" invest a fraction $\beta/(1+\beta\phi)$ of their real income. These survivors are in proportion $1 - \phi$ in the population. Since the proportion ϕ of households that will disappear invest nothing, the aggregate propensity to invest is $\beta(1-\phi)/(1+\beta\phi)$.

Since a fraction δ of capital depreciates each period, total income is equal to $Y_t + (1-\delta)K_t$ (wages plus profits plus undepreciated capital), which, multiplied by the above-noted propensity to invest, yields formula (7). ∎

We now move to the determination of employment. This is characterized through the following proposition:

Proposition 2 *Employment at the economy level is determined by*

$$N_t = \min(\mu K_t, N_0) \qquad (11)$$

with

$$\mu = \left[\frac{\chi(1-\theta)a}{\theta(\chi-1)b}\right]^{1/\chi} \qquad (12)$$

Proof Let us start with final output firms. Since they are competitive, we have, calling P_{jt} the price of intermediate output j,

$$\frac{P_{jt}}{P_t} = \frac{\partial Y_t}{\partial Y_{jt}} \qquad (13)$$

This immediately yields the demand for intermediate output j corresponding to an output level Y_t:

$$Y_{jt} = Y_t \left(\frac{P_{jt}}{P_t} \right)^{-1/(1-\theta)} \tag{14}$$

Furthermore, because of the competitiveness of the output industry, output price P_t is equal to the cost index associated to production function (1), that is,

$$P_t = \left(\int_0^1 P_{jt}^{-\theta/(1-\theta)} \, dj \right)^{-(1-\theta)/\theta} \tag{15}$$

Let us now consider intermediate inputs firms. Firm j competitively maximizes profits

$$\Pi_{jt} = P_{jt} Y_{jt} - R_t K_{jt} - W_{jt} N_{jt} \tag{16}$$

subject to production function (3). To characterize the solution, it is convenient to define ζ_{jt}, the cost index associated to the CES production function (3):

$$\zeta_{jt} = \frac{1}{Z_t} \left[a^{1/(1-\chi)} R_t^{-\chi/(1-\chi)} + b^{1/(1-\chi)} W_{jt}^{-\chi/(1-\chi)} \right]^{-(1-\chi)/\chi} \tag{17}$$

Competitive profit maximization yields the usual formulas:

$$P_{jt} = \zeta_{jt} \tag{18}$$

$$N_{jt} = \left(\frac{b \zeta_{jt} Z_t^{\chi}}{W_{jt}} \right)^{1/(1-\chi)} Y_{jt} \tag{19}$$

$$K_{jt} = \left(\frac{a \zeta_{jt} Z_t^{\chi}}{R_t} \right)^{1/(1-\chi)} Y_{jt} \tag{20}$$

Let us finally consider the trade union in firm j. As we indicated above, its objective will be to maximize $\log(W_{jt} N_{jt}/P_t)$. Now, combining equations (14), (18), and (19), we obtain

$$\frac{W_{jt} N_{jt}}{P_t} = \frac{W_{jt} Y_t}{P_t} \left(\frac{b \zeta_{jt} Z_t^{\chi}}{W_{jt}} \right)^{1/(1-\chi)} \left(\frac{P_t}{\zeta_{jt}} \right)^{1/1-\theta} \tag{21}$$

We note that the stochastic term in Z_t enters multiplicatively, so that the trade union will choose the wage W_{jt} in order to maximize the following deterministic quantity:

$$W_{jt} \left(\frac{1}{\zeta_{jt}} \right)^{1/1-\theta} \left(\frac{\zeta_{jt}}{W_{jt}} \right)^{1/1-\chi} = \left[W_{jt}^{-\chi} \zeta_{jt}^{(\chi-\theta)/(1-\theta)} \right]^{1/1-\chi} \tag{22}$$

Using (17), we have in logarithms, up to a constant,

$$\frac{(\chi - \theta)(\chi - 1)}{\chi(1 - \theta)} \log \left[a^{1/(1-\chi)} R_t^{\chi/(1-\chi)} + b^{1/(1-\chi)} W_{jt}^{\chi/(1-\chi)} \right] - \chi \log W_{jt} \tag{23}$$

Let us differentiate (23) with respect to W_{jt}. We obtain the first-order condition:

$$\frac{b^{1/(1-\chi)} R_t^{\chi/(1-\chi)}}{a^{1/(1-\chi)} W_{jt}^{\chi/(1-\chi)}} = \frac{\chi(1-\theta)}{\theta(\chi-1)} \tag{24}$$

But we had from equations (19) and (20),

$$\frac{N_{jt}}{K_{jt}} = \left(\frac{bR_t}{aW_{jt}} \right)^{1/(1-\chi)} \tag{25}$$

So, combining (24) and (25), we obtain

$$\frac{N_{jt}}{K_{jt}} = \left[\frac{\chi(1-\theta)a}{\theta(\chi-1)b} \right]^{1/\chi} = \mu \tag{26}$$

The derivation above implicitly assumes an interior solution for N_{jt}. In fact, employment in the firm cannot be more than the supply N_0. So employment within firm j is finally given by

$$N_{jt} = \min(\mu K_{jt}, N_0) \tag{27}$$

Since all sectors are symmetrical, equation (27) aggregates at the global level as (11).   ∎

Condition (11) shows that when capital is "too low," in the sense that K_t is lower than N_0/μ, then trade unions will voluntarily choose a wage level high enough to create unemployment. The intuitive reason why they choose unemployment is that because of limited substitutability between labor and capital, they would have to reduce the wage tremendously in order to have full employment. For the trade union it is preferable then that fewer workers be employed at a substantially higher wage level.

7.4   The Two Regimes: Dynamics and Persistence

The dynamics of the model can be briefly summarized by putting together equations (1), (2), (7), and (11):

$$N_t = \min(\mu K_t, N_0) \tag{28}$$

$$Y_t = Z_t\, F(K_t, N_t) \tag{29}$$

$$K_{t+1} = \frac{\beta(1-\phi)}{1+\beta\phi}[Y_t + (1-\delta)K_t] \tag{30}$$

with

$$F(K_t, N_t) = \left(aK_t^\chi + bN_t^\chi\right)^{1/\chi} \tag{31}$$

The variables K_t, N_t, and Y_t evolve according to nonlinear stochastic dynamic equations. To get an intuitive grasp of this, we can picture the evolution of capital (which is the state variable) for a constant value of the technological parameter Z, as is done in figure 7.1 for the value $Z = 1$.

Equation (28) tells us that the dynamics involve two clear-cut regimes with markedly different properties. The first regime corresponds to full employment ($N_t = N_0$). There the model behaves as its Walrasian counterpart, which not only produces no unemployment but also relatively little persistence in output, as will appear below in the simulations. In the unemployment regime ($N_t = \mu K_t < N_0$), things change drastically. Indeed, combining the three equations above, we obtain

$$K_{t+1} = \frac{\beta(1-\phi)}{1+\beta\phi}[1 - \delta + Z_t F(1, \mu)]K_t \tag{32}$$

$$N_t = \mu K_t \tag{33}$$

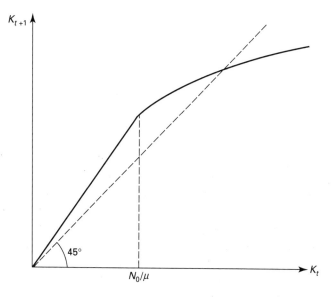

Figure 7.1   Capital dynamics

Call k_t, n_t, and z_t the logarithms of K_t, N_t, and Z_t. Loglinearizing the first equation around the value $z_t = 0$, we obtain the following dynamics in k_t and n_t:

$$k_{t+1} = k_t + \psi z_t + \xi \tag{34}$$

$$n_t = k_t + \log \mu \tag{35}$$

with

$$\psi = \frac{F(1, \mu)}{1 - \delta + F(1, \mu)} \tag{36}$$

$$\xi = \log \left[\frac{\beta(1 - \phi)}{1 + \beta\phi} \right] + \log \left[1 - \delta + F(1, \mu) \right] \tag{37}$$

$$F(1, \mu) = \left[\frac{a\,(\chi - \theta)}{\theta\,(\chi - 1)} \right]^{1/\chi} \tag{38}$$

We see that there is a large amount of persistence. Indeed, if z_t is white noise, then k_t and n_t follow a random walk with drift in that regime!

Of course, the system will switch from one regime to the other, and the actual dynamics will be some complex combination of the "Walrasian" and "unemployment" dynamics. The calculations above suggest that as soon as shocks are strong enough to bring the economy into the unemployment regime,[2] there will be observed much more persistence than in the corresponding Walrasian economy. This cannot be studied analytically because of the nonlinearities, so we will use simulations based on a simple example.

7.5   Numerical Simulations

We will simulate the dynamic effects of simple autoregressive technological shocks of the form

$$z_t = \rho z_{t-1} + \varepsilon_t \tag{39}$$

where the variables ε_t are iid. The model has not been subject to any kind of "calibration" or estimation, so the results that follow are simply meant to show that the intuitions about persistence that can be derived from equations such as (34) and (35) are actually supported by numerical experiments.[3]

7.5.1   Impulse Response Functions

A first exercise consists in studying the impulse response functions of shocks, namely the dynamic response to a one time shock on ε_t. An example of such response functions for output is depicted in figure 7.2, which corresponds to full depreciation ($\delta = 1$) and an autoregressive shock ($\rho = 0.5$). Two things appear quite clearly on this graph (the upper curve corresponds to a positive shock, the lower one to a negative shock of the same magnitude):

The first obvious thing is the asymmetry between the effects of positive and negative shocks: negative shocks yield "stronger" effects than positive ones, since unemployment occurs. Second, when there is a large enough negative

2 Note that this requires shocks of some minimal amplitude since, in the absence of shocks, the long-term equilibrium would be in the *interior* of the Walrasian regime (see figure 7.1).

3 The simulations below were carried with the following parameter values: $\delta = 1$, $\chi = -2$, $\theta = 0.25$, $\xi = 0.01$, and $b/a = 2$. These values are notably such that the ratio of labor income to total income is equal to 2/3, a traditional value, and $\mu = 1$, a convenient normalization.

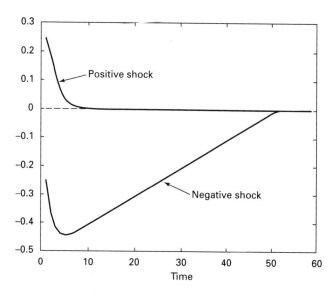

Figure 7.2   Output IRF to a technology shock

shock, we observe some kind of "persistence," in the sense that unemployment decreases slowly. As a consequence the return of output to its steady state value is delayed as compared to the full-employment case.

7.5.2   Fluctuations and Persistence

To show the potentiality of this imperfectly competitive model to generate actual persistence (i.e., persistence in some statistical sense) in unemployment and other variables, simulations have been run in the case least likely to produce persistence in capital (and therefore employment), that where capital fully depreciates in each period ($\delta = 1$). Then, while equation (35) remains valid, the loglinear approximation (34) becomes the *exact* formula

$$k_{t+1} = k_t + z_t + \xi \qquad (40)$$

Some of the various simulation results are depicted in figures 7.3, 7.4, and 7.5. These simulations tell us a number of important things.

First, from the autocorrelations for unemployment displayed in figure 7.3 in the case of iid shocks ($\rho = 0$), we see that the mechanism we studied produces a large persistence in unemployment even though the underlying shocks are totally uncorrelated. This is something that most traditional RBC models fail

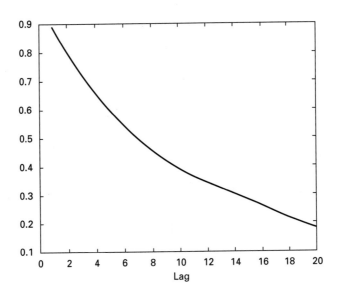

Figure 7.3   Unemployment serial correlations

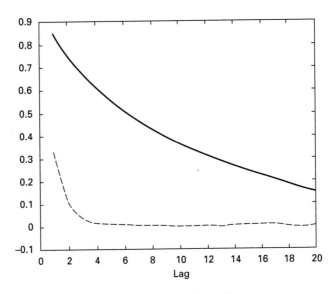

Figure 7.4   Output serial correlations

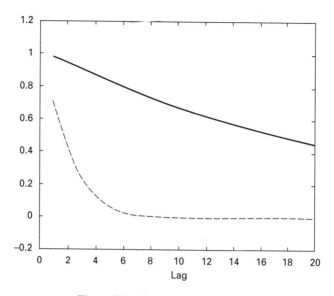

Figure 7.5 Output serial correlations

to obtain. Other simulations show that these autocorrelations still increase as shocks become more persistent.

Figures 7.4 and 7.5 display the output autocorrelations (in logarithms) for both our imperfectly competitive model (continuous lines) and the corresponding Walrasian model (dotted lines). Figure 7.4 corresponds to iid shocks ($\rho = 0$), and figure 7.5 to autocorrelated shocks ($\rho = 0.5$). In both cases it clearly appears that the introduction of imperfect competition dramatically increases the persistence of output, whether the underlying shocks are correlated or not.

7.6 Conclusions

We constructed in this chapter a rigorous dynamic model of an imperfectly competitive economy subject to technology shocks. A closed-form solution was obtained, yielding nonlinear stochastic evolutions. A study of this dynamic system showed that low capital–labor substitutability combined with imperfect competition in the labor market can yield unemployment, and that this unemployment can be highly persistent, even if the underlying shocks are not. Output is similarly found to be much more persistent than in the corresponding Walrasian economy. Finally the system displays an interesting asymmetry due to the existence of two well distinct regimes.

7.7   References

This chapter is based on Bénassy (1997a). The idea that insufficient capital accumulation combined with imperfect competition in the labor market might be the cause of high and persistent unemployment, particularly in Europe, is found notably in Burda (1988). Similar ideas have been explored under various forms by numerous authors (Bean 1989; Hénin and Jobert 1993; Sneessens 1987; Van de Klundert and Von Schaik 1990). Drèze and Bean (1990) includes a number of interesting country studies attempting, in particular, to ascertain the role of capital shortages in recent European unemployment.

8

Endogenous Growth

8.1 Introduction

Chapter 6 showed us how we could integrate imperfect competition into the standard dynamic general equilibrium stochastic model, and chapter 7 how we could generate within such a model highly persistent unemployment and output. These models were models of "stochastic exogenous growth" whereby the degree of factor utilization is affected by imperfect competition but average growth is not.

We now show that imperfect competition can affect both the degree of utilization of factors and the growth rate. Several authors have already studied the relations between imperfect competition and growth, notably via the effect on technical progress. For example, Romer (1990) finds a negative effect of competition, because less competition provides more rent to innovators and therefore induces them to invest more in research, which advances technological growth. In contrast, Young (1998) finds a positive effect of competition on technological progress, because with more competition the successful innovator can capture a larger fraction of the market, and thus more innovation is seen as profitable.

Here we will pursue a complementary goal: we assume that basic technological progress is given, but we will inquire whether, with given technological progress, imperfect competition per se has an effect on growth. We will see that it does.

8.2   The Model

The model is similar to that of Lucas (1988), with the addition of imperfect competition. Two goods can be accumulated: physical and human capital. The stock of physical capital in period t is denoted K_t and that of human capital H_t.

The production functions for output Y_t and "human capital goods" X_t are, respectively,

$$Y_t = \left(\int_0^1 Y_{jt}^\theta \, dj \right)^{1/\theta} \tag{1}$$

$$X_t = \left(\int_0^1 X_{it}^\theta \, di \right)^{1/\theta} \tag{2}$$

where the Y_{jt} and X_{it} are intermediate goods. The intermediates Y_{jt}, $j \in [0, 1]$, are produced from physical and human capital:

$$Y_{jt} = Z_t K_{jt}^\gamma H_{jt}^{1-\gamma} \tag{3}$$

Similarly for the intermediates X_{it}, $i \in [0, 1]^1$,

$$X_{it} = A_t K_{it}^\gamma H_{it}^{1-\gamma} \tag{4}$$

Output Y_t is divided between consumption C_t and investment I_t, while the production of human capital goods X_t can only be used to increase the stock of human capital. To simplify the computations, we assume that physical capital fully depreciates in each period, that is,

$$K_{t+1} = I_t \tag{5}$$

and similarly for human capital:

$$H_{t+1} = X_t \tag{6}$$

Equation (6) represents the fundamental departure from the previous models, as the quantity of labor available in a given period does not result from an

---

1 We assume, for the simplicity of the exposition, that the exponents of the two Cobb-Douglas functions in (3) and (4) are the same. The appendix gives the results of calculations with different exponents.

exogenously given endowment but rather from the voluntary accumulation of human capital.

Households maximize the expected value of their discounted intertemporal utility

$$\sum_t \beta^t \left[\log C_t + \omega \log \left(\frac{M_t}{P_t} \right) \right] \tag{7}$$

subject to the budget constraints:

$$C_t + I_t + \frac{M_t}{P_t} + \frac{Q_t H_{t+1}}{P_t} = \frac{R_t K_t}{P_t} + \frac{W_t H_t}{P_t} + \frac{\mu_t M_{t-1}}{P_t} + \frac{\Pi_t}{P_t} \tag{8}$$

where K_t and H_t are accumulated physical and human capital, Q_t is the purchasing price of human capital, R_t is the monetary return on physical capital, and Π_t is profits in nominal terms. To keep the model simple, we assume that the labor market is competitive.

8.3   Dynamic Equilibrium

The dynamic equilibrium of the preceding model can be characterized by the following proposition, proved in section 8.4:

Proposition 1   *Equilibrium quantities are determined by the following relations:*

$$\frac{K_{jt}}{K_t} = \frac{H_{jt}}{H_t} = 1 - \beta\theta + \beta\gamma\theta \tag{9}$$

$$\frac{K_{it}}{K_t} = \frac{H_{it}}{H_t} = \beta\theta(1 - \gamma) \tag{10}$$

$$C_t = \frac{1 - \beta\theta}{1 - \beta\theta + \beta\gamma\theta} Y_t \tag{11}$$

$$K_{t+1} = \frac{\beta\gamma\theta}{1 - \beta\theta + \beta\gamma\theta} Y_t \tag{12}$$

We see that the parameter θ, depicting the degree of substitutability between intermediate goods, and therefore the degree of imperfect competition, influences both the global rate of investment and the amount of resources devoted to each of the accumulated factors.

8.4   Resolution

8.4.1   Final Output Firms

Denote by P_{jt} the price of intermediate j. Since the output producing firms are competitive, the demand for intermediate output j corresponding to an output level Y_t is

$$Y_{jt} = Y_t \left(\frac{P_{jt}}{P_t} \right)^{-1/(1-\theta)} \tag{13}$$

and output price P_t is equal to the cost index associated to the production function (1):

$$P_t = \left(\int_0^1 P_{jt}^{-\theta/(1-\theta)} \, dj \right)^{-(1-\theta)/\theta} \tag{14}$$

Symmetrically we have in the sectors producing human capital:

$$X_{it} = X_t \left(\frac{Q_{it}}{Q_t} \right)^{-1/(1-\theta)} \tag{15}$$

where Q_{it} is the price of intermediate i, and

$$Q_t = \left(\int_0^1 Q_{it}^{-\theta/(1-\theta)} \, di \right)^{-(1-\theta)/\theta} \tag{16}$$

8.4.2   Intermediate Inputs Firms

Intermediate firm j maximizes profits $\Pi_{jt} = P_{jt} Y_{jt} - R_t K_{jt} - W_t H_{jt}$ subject to the production function (3) and the demand function for intermediate input j (equation 13). The first-order conditions can be written in the following form, which makes particularly clear the distribution of incomes:

$$W_t H_{jt} = (1 - \gamma)\theta P_{jt}Y_{jt} \tag{17}$$

$$R_t K_{jt} = \gamma\theta P_{jt}Y_{jt} \tag{18}$$

We will need below a simple expression for the rate of return on investment R_t and the wage W_t. Let us first define a few aggregates:

$$K_{Yt} = \int_0^1 K_{jt}\,dj, \quad K_{Xt} = \int_0^1 K_{it}\,di, \quad K_t = K_{Yt} + K_{Xt} \tag{19}$$

$$H_{Yt} = \int_0^1 H_{jt}\,dj, \quad H_{Xt} = \int_0^1 H_{it}\,di, \quad H_t = H_{Yt} + H_{Xt} \tag{20}$$

From equation (18) we find that the nominal return on capital is equal to

$$R_t = \frac{\gamma\theta P_{jt}Y_{jt}}{K_{jt}} = \frac{\gamma\theta \int P_{jt}Y_{jt}}{\int K_{jt}} = \frac{\gamma\theta P_t Y_t}{K_{Yt}} \tag{21}$$

Similarly, using equation (17), we obtain the nominal wage:

$$W_t = \frac{(1 - \gamma)\theta P_{jt}Y_{jt}}{H_{jt}} = \frac{(1 - \gamma)\theta \int P_{jt}Y_{jt}}{\int H_{jt}} = \frac{(1 - \gamma)\theta P_t Y_t}{H_{Yt}} \tag{22}$$

Let us now perform the same calculations for the firms indexed by i, which produce the human capital intermediates:

$$W_t H_{it} = (1 - \gamma)\theta Q_{it}X_{it} \tag{23}$$

$$R_t K_{it} = \gamma\theta Q_{it}X_{it} \tag{24}$$

$$R_t = \frac{\gamma\theta Q_{it}X_{it}}{K_{it}} = \frac{\gamma\theta \int Q_{it}X_{it}}{\int K_{it}} = \frac{\gamma\theta Q_t X_t}{K_{Xt}} \tag{25}$$

$$W_t = \frac{(1 - \gamma)\theta Q_{it}X_{it}}{H_{it}} = \frac{(1 - \gamma)\theta \int Q_{it}X_{it}}{\int H_{it}} = \frac{(1 - \gamma)\theta Q_t X_t}{H_{Xt}} \tag{26}$$

Putting together (21) and (25), (22) and (26), we obtain the following expressions for the return on capital R_t and the wage W_t:

$$R_t = \frac{\gamma\theta P_t Y_t}{K_{Yt}} = \frac{\gamma\theta Q_t X_t}{K_{Xt}} = \frac{\gamma\theta(P_t Y_t + Q_t X_t)}{K_t} \tag{27}$$

$$W_t = \frac{(1-\gamma)\theta P_t Y_t}{H_{Yt}} = \frac{(1-\gamma)\theta Q_t X_t}{H_{Xt}} = \frac{(1-\gamma)\theta(P_t Y_t + Q_t X_t)}{H_t} \tag{28}$$

We see from formulas (27) and (28) that other things being equal, imperfect competition (i.e., a low value of θ) will reduce the returns on both factors. We will see below that these lower returns lead to reduced rates of factor accumulation.

8.4.3   Households

The program of a household (we omit any index since everything is symmetrical) is simply to maximize its expected utility (7) subject to the sequence of its budget constraints (8):

$$\max \sum_t \beta^t \left[\log C_t + \omega \log \left(\frac{M_t}{P_t} \right) \right] \quad \text{s.t.}$$

$$C_t + \frac{M_t}{P_t} + K_{t+1} + \frac{Q_t}{P_t} H_{t+1} = \frac{R_t K_t}{P_t} + \frac{W_t H_t}{P_t} + \frac{\mu_t M_{t-1}}{P_t} + \frac{\Pi_t}{P_t}$$

The first-order conditions for this program are

$$\frac{1}{C_t} = \beta E_t \left(\frac{R_{t+1}}{P_{t+1} C_{t+1}} \right) \tag{29}$$

$$\frac{Q_t}{P_t C_t} = \beta E_t \left(\frac{W_{t+1}}{P_{t+1} C_{t+1}} \right) \tag{30}$$

$$\frac{1}{P_t C_t} = \frac{\omega}{M_t} + \beta E_t \left(\frac{\mu_{t+1}}{P_{t+1} C_{t+1}} \right) \tag{31}$$

8.4.4   Dynamic Equilibrium

Equation (31) yields, since $\mu_{t+1} = M_{t+1}/M_t$,

$$\frac{M_t}{P_t C_t} = \omega + \beta E_t \left(\frac{M_{t+1}}{P_{t+1} C_{t+1}} \right) \tag{32}$$

which solves as

$$\frac{M_t}{P_t C_t} = \frac{\omega}{1 - \beta} \tag{33}$$

Now we combine (29) and (30) with the expressions for R_t and W_t found in (27) and (28), and use (5), (6) to find

$$\frac{I_t}{C_t} = \beta \gamma \theta E_t \left(\frac{P_{t+1} Y_{t+1} + Q_{t+1} X_{t+1}}{P_{t+1} C_{t+1}} \right) \tag{34}$$

$$\frac{Q_t X_t}{P_t C_t} = (1 - \gamma) \beta \theta E_t \left(\frac{P_{t+1} Y_{t+1} + Q_{t+1} X_{t+1}}{P_{t+1} C_{t+1}} \right) \tag{35}$$

Summing these two relations, we obtain

$$\frac{P_t I_t + Q_t X_t}{P_t C_t} = \beta \theta E_t \left(\frac{P_{t+1} Y_{t+1} + Q_{t+1} X_{t+1}}{P_{t+1} C_{t+1}} \right) \tag{36}$$

which, using $Y_t = C_t + I_t$, solves as

$$\frac{P_t I_t + Q_t X_t}{P_t C_t} = \frac{\beta \theta}{1 - \beta \theta} \tag{37}$$

What formula (37) tells us is that the total value of investment (physical and human capital) is equal to $\beta\theta$ times the value of total income:

$$P_t I_t + Q_t X_t = \beta \theta (P_t Y_t + Q_t X_t) \tag{38}$$

The reduced rates of return associated with a low θ seen in equations (27) and (28) induce therefore a lower overall rate of factor accumulation. Let us now insert (37) back into (34). We obtain

$$\frac{I_t}{C_t} = \frac{\beta\gamma\theta}{1 - \beta\theta} \tag{39}$$

Combining (39) with $Y_t = C_t + I_t$, we obtain (11) and (12). From (37) and (39) we compute the ratio

$$\frac{Q_t X_t}{P_t Y_t} = \frac{(1 - \gamma)\beta\theta}{1 - \beta\theta + \beta\gamma\theta} \tag{40}$$

From (27) and (28) we obtain

$$\frac{K_{Yt}}{K_t} = \frac{H_{Yt}}{H_t} = \frac{P_t Y_t}{P_t Y_t + Q_t X_t} \tag{41}$$

$$\frac{K_{Xt}}{K_t} = \frac{H_{Xt}}{H_t} = \frac{Q_t X_t}{P_t Y_t + Q_t X_t} \tag{42}$$

Inserting (40) into (41) and (42), we obtain formulas (9) and (10).

8.5   Dynamics and the Growth Rate

We can now, with the help of formulas (9) to (12), study the dynamics of the model. Insert first (9) and (10) into the production functions (1) to (4) to obtain the current productions of physical goods and human capital:

$$Y_t = Z_t K_{Yt}^{\gamma} H_{Yt}^{1-\gamma} = [1 - \beta\theta(1 - \gamma)] Z_t K_t^{\gamma} H_t^{1-\gamma} \tag{43}$$

$$X_t = A_t K_{Xt}^{\gamma} H_{Xt}^{1-\gamma} = [\beta\theta(1 - \gamma)] A_t K_t^{\gamma} H_t^{1-\gamma} \tag{44}$$

We next proceed to logarithms:[2]

$$y_t = z_t + \gamma k_t + (1 - \gamma)h_t + \log[1 - \beta\theta(1 - \gamma)] \tag{45}$$

$$x_t = a_t + \gamma k_t + (1 - \gamma)h_t + \log[\beta\theta(1 - \gamma)] \tag{46}$$

---

2 Lowercase letters represent the logarithms of the variables denoted by the corresponding uppercase letters.

Using equation (12) and the equality $h_{t+1} = x_t$, we obtain the level of accumulated factors in the next period:

$$k_{t+1} = z_t + \gamma k_t + (1 - \gamma)h_t + \log(\beta\gamma\theta) \qquad (47)$$

$$h_{t+1} = a_t + \gamma k_t + (1 - \gamma)h_t + \log[\beta\theta(1 - \gamma)] \qquad (48)$$

from which we deduce the rates of growth of each factor:

$$k_{t+1} - k_t = z_t - (1 - \gamma)(k_t - h_t) + \log(\beta\gamma\theta) \qquad (49)$$

$$h_{t+1} - h_t = a_t + \gamma(k_t - h_t) + \log[\beta\theta(1 - \gamma)] \qquad (50)$$

These rates of growth are of course stochastic, and they depend also on the initial ratio of factors in the economy. The "endogenous growth" aspect shows up particularly well if we consider the "composite factor" $\gamma k_t + (1 - \gamma)h_t$. We find indeed that

$$\gamma k_{t+1} + (1 - \gamma)h_{t+1} = \gamma k_t + (1 - \gamma)h_t + \gamma z_t + (1 - \gamma)a_t$$
$$+ \gamma \log(\beta\gamma\theta) + (1 - \gamma) \log[\beta\theta(1 - \gamma)] \qquad (51)$$

From formula (51), if z_t and a_t are constant, physical and human capital will grow at the same rate given by (in logarithms)

$$g = \gamma z + (1 - \gamma)a + \log \beta\theta + \gamma \log \gamma + (1 - \gamma) \log(1 - \gamma) \qquad (52)$$

We see, in particular, that the higher is θ (i.e., the more competitive the economy), the higher is the rate of growth.

8.6 Conclusions

We studied in this chapter an endogenous growth model with imperfect competition in order to see how the competitiveness of the economy affects the rate of growth. The rates of technical progress A_t and Z_t were taken as exogenous. We found that the less competitive the economy, the lower is the rate of growth.

The basic intuitions for that result were seen along the proof of proposition 1: other things equal, imperfect competition (i.e., a low θ) cuts into the remuneration of the two accumulated factors, physical and human capital, as formulas (27) and (28) show. As a consequence households are less willing to accumulate these factors (e.g., see formula 38, which shows that the "aggregate propensity to invest" is proportional to θ). In a model of endogenous growth this naturally results in a lower rate of growth.

8.7   References

This chapter extends to an imperfectly competitive framework the basic competitive endogenous growth model with two accumulated factors found, for example, in Lucas (1988).

We took here technical progress as given. The effects of the competitiveness of the economy on this rate of technical progress itself is a much more unsettled issue, as the reader could find out by comparing, for example, the different answers in Aghion and Howitt (1998), Grossman and Helpman (1991), Romer (1990), or Young (1998).

Appendix 8.1: Different Production Functions

We generalize here the model of this chapter by differentiating the production functions for physical goods and human capital.[3] The production function for intermediate physical goods is, as before,

$$Y_{jt} = Z_t K_{jt}^{\gamma} H_{jt}^{1-\gamma} \qquad (53)$$

but the production function for human capital intermediates is now

$$X_{it} = A_t K_{it}^{\varphi} H_{it}^{1-\varphi} \qquad (54)$$

We do not need to give here an explicit derivation of the equilibrium and dynamics of this model, since it essentially parallels that in the main text of this chapter. So we give only the corresponding results. First, the results of

---

3 We could also consider different degrees of substitutability between physical and human capital intermediates, or we could add some utility for leisure, but then the formulas would become too cumbersome.

proposition 1 are replaced by the following ones:

Proposition 2 *Equilibrium quantities are determined by the relations*

$$\frac{K_{jt}}{K_t} = \frac{\gamma(1 - \beta\theta + \beta\varphi\theta)}{\gamma + \beta\theta(\varphi - \gamma)} \tag{55}$$

$$\frac{K_{it}}{K_t} = \frac{\varphi(1 - \gamma)\beta\theta}{\gamma + \beta\theta(\varphi - \gamma)} \tag{56}$$

$$\frac{H_{jt}}{H_t} = 1 - \beta\theta + \beta\varphi\theta \tag{57}$$

$$\frac{H_{it}}{H_t} = (1 - \varphi)\beta\theta \tag{58}$$

$$K_{t+1} = I_t = \beta\theta\frac{\gamma + \beta\theta(\varphi - \gamma)}{1 - \beta\theta + \beta\theta\varphi}Y_t \tag{59}$$

Using these formulas, we can compute the rates of growth for each of the accumulated factors:

$$k_{t+1} - k_t = z_t - (1 - \gamma)(k_t - h_t) + \log\beta\theta$$
$$+ \gamma\log\gamma + (1 - \gamma)\log[\gamma + \beta\theta(\varphi - \gamma)] \tag{60}$$

$$h_{t+1} - h_t = a_t + \varphi(k_t - h_t) + \log\beta\theta$$
$$+ (1 - \varphi)\log(1 - \varphi) + \varphi\log\frac{(1 - \gamma)\varphi}{\gamma + \beta\theta(\varphi - \gamma)} \tag{61}$$

Again, endogenous growth shows up best if we consider the evolution of the composite factor $\varphi k_t + (1 - \gamma)h_t$:

$$\varphi k_{t+1} + (1 - \gamma)h_{t+1} = \varphi k_t + (1 - \gamma)h_t + \varphi z_t + (1 - \gamma)a_t$$
$$+ (1 - \gamma + \varphi)\log\beta\theta + \gamma\varphi\log\gamma + \varphi(1 - \gamma)\log\varphi$$
$$+ \varphi(1 - \gamma)\log(1 - \gamma) + (1 - \gamma)(1 - \varphi)\log(1 - \varphi) \tag{62}$$

If z_t and a_t are constant, respectively z and a, physical and human capital will grow at the same rate given by (in logarithms)

$$
g = \log \beta \theta + \frac{\varphi z + (1 - \gamma)a}{1 - \gamma + \varphi}
$$
$$
+ \frac{\gamma \varphi \log \gamma + (1 - \gamma)(1 - \varphi) \log(1 - \varphi) + \varphi(1 - \gamma) \log[(1 - \gamma)\varphi]}{1 + \varphi - \gamma} \tag{63}
$$

which is an expression that generalizes formula (52).

Part V

Nominal Rigidities and Fluctuations

9

Wage Rigidities and Employment Fluctuations

9.1 Introduction

The dynamic general equilibrium models we considered so far had only "real" rigidities due to imperfect competition. As a result the dynamic evolutions were essentially influenced by real productivity shocks, and monetary shocks had essentially no impact. In the three chapters of this part we will incorporate nominal rigidities, and as a consequence we will see that demand shocks can also have an important impact on the dynamics of employment and output.

There are several reasons why one may want to construct models where demand shocks matter. The first is that several empirical studies have shown that demand shocks, and in particular, monetary shocks, have substantial and long-lasting effects on employment and output.[1] Second, within the literature on real business cycles, a number of authors have recently convincingly demonstrated that the consideration of price, and especially wage rigidities, in economies subject to real and monetary shocks enables them to substantially improve the capacity of these business cycle models to match a number of stylized facts in actual economies. These contributions are generally made in "calibrated" models. We will, as in the previous chapters, follow here a complementary line of research and consider a model with explicit solutions that make obvious the economic mechanisms at work.

---

1 See notably the recent studies of Christiano, Eichenbaum, and Evans (1999, 2001) and the references therein.

Of course, there are many ways to introduce nominal rigidities. A particularly popular approach is to assume some degree of presetting of prices or wages. In this chapter we will follow this line, and consider wage contracts in the tradition initiated by Gray (1976), whereby wage contracts are signed at the beginning of each period without knowing the shocks of that period, but of course on the basis of rational expectations. More complex staggered contracts will be considered in the next chapter.

We will initially consider a one-sector economy as in McCallum (1989), and extend it in two directions: We will first introduce money into the model, while maintaining the market-clearing assumption for all markets. We will observe that this model has properties very similar to those of traditional RBC models, as we already saw in chapter 6 for an imperfectly competitive framework.

We will next study the same monetary model under the assumption of predetermined wages, and we will see that this presetting of wages makes a big difference in the results. In particular, monetary shocks now have an effect on employment and production.

We will finally apply the results to a few stylized facts on prices, real wages, and inflation, and show that the introduction of preset wages alleviates some empirical problems of standard Walrasian business cycles models, such as the too high procyclicality of real wages or the too high countercyclicality of prices. Our analytical solutions will make fully transparent the mechanisms by which these improvements take place.

In most of the chapter we make the traditional assumption that the preset wage is equal to the expected value of the Walrasian wage. In section 9.6 we extend the model to a multisectoral framework where wages are set by maximizing trade unions. It turns out that up to constant terms, all the results previously obtained still hold.

9.2   The Model

The economy studied is a monetary economy with two markets in each period t: goods for money at the price P_t and labor for money at the wage W_t. There are two types of representative agents: firms and households. Firms have a Cobb-Douglas technology:

$$Y_t = Z_t K_t^{\gamma} N_t^{1-\gamma} \tag{1}$$

where K_t is capital, N_t labor input, and Z_t a stochastic technological shock.

Capital fully depreciates in one period so that

$$K_{t+1} = I_t \tag{2}$$

where I_t is investment in period t.[2]

In period t the representative household works N_t, consumes C_t, and ends the period with a quantity of money M_t. It maximizes the expected value of discounted future utilities with the following utility:

$$U = E_0 \sum_{t=0}^{\infty} \beta^t \left[\log C_t + \omega \log \frac{M_t}{P_t} - V(N_t) \right] \tag{3}$$

where V is a convex function. At the beginning of period t there is a stochastic multiplicative monetary shock denoted as μ_t. Money holdings M_{t-1} carried from the previous period are multiplied by μ_t, so that the household starts period t with a quantity of money $\mu_t M_{t-1}$. His budget constraint for period t is thus

$$C_t + \frac{M_t}{P_t} + I_t = \frac{W_t}{P_t} N_t + \kappa_t I_{t-1} + \frac{\mu_t M_{t-1}}{P_t} \tag{4}$$

where κ_t is the real return in period t on capital invested in $t - 1$.

9.3 The Walrasian Regime

We will first study a benchmark case where the two markets clear in each period, as in the traditional real business cycle theory, and see how the economy reacts to the shocks on technology and money.

9.3.1 Solving the Model

In each period firms demand labor competitively. The real wage is equal to the marginal productivity of labor:

$$\frac{W_t}{P_t} = \frac{\partial Y_t}{\partial N_t} = (1 - \gamma) \frac{Y_t}{N_t} \tag{5}$$

2 The case of incomplete depreciation with a loglinearized accumulation of capital equation is treated in the appendix at the end of the chapter.

Also the real return on capital is simply the marginal productivity of capital:

$$\kappa_t = \frac{\partial Y_t}{\partial K_t} = \gamma \frac{Y_t}{K_t} \tag{6}$$

The representative households maximize the expected value of their discounted utility (3), subject to the sequence of budget constraints (4). Call $\beta^t \lambda_t$ the marginal utility of real wealth in period t (i.e., the Lagrange multiplier associated with the corresponding budget constraint 4). Then the usual first-order conditions for the consumer's program yield

$$\frac{1}{C_t} = \lambda_t \tag{7}$$

$$V'(N_t) = \lambda_t \frac{W_t}{P_t} \tag{8}$$

$$\lambda_t = \beta E_t(\lambda_{t+1} \kappa_{t+1}) \tag{9}$$

$$\lambda_t = \frac{\omega P_t}{M_t} + \beta E_t \left(\lambda_{t+1} \frac{\mu_{t+1} P_t}{P_{t+1}} \right) \tag{10}$$

Combining (7), (9), the condition $Y_t = C_t + I_t$, and the definition of κ_t in (6), we obtain

$$\frac{I_t}{C_t} = \beta\gamma + \beta\gamma E_t \left(\frac{I_{t+1}}{C_{t+1}} \right) \tag{11}$$

This solves as

$$\frac{I_t}{C_t} = \frac{\beta\gamma}{1 - \beta\gamma} \tag{12}$$

so that

$$C_t = (1 - \beta\gamma)Y_t \tag{13}$$

$$I_t = K_{t+1} = \beta\gamma Y_t \tag{14}$$

The equilibrium condition for money is that the quantity of money demanded by the household, M_t, be equal to the initial money holdings $\mu_t M_{t-1}$:

$$M_t = \mu_t M_{t-1} \tag{15}$$

Now condition (10), using (7) and (15), is rewritten as

$$\frac{M_t}{P_t C_t} = \omega + \beta E_t \left(\frac{M_{t+1}}{P_{t+1} C_{t+1}} \right) \tag{16}$$

This solves as

$$\frac{M_t}{P_t C_t} = \frac{\omega}{1 - \beta} \tag{17}$$

Combining (13) and (17), we obtain the level of real money balances:

$$\frac{M_t}{P_t} = \frac{\omega(1 - \beta\gamma)}{1 - \beta} Y_t = \varrho Y_t \tag{18}$$

Finally, combining condition (8) with the expression of the real wage (5) and the value of consumption (13), we find that N_t is constant and equal to N, where N is given by

$$N V'(N) = \frac{1 - \gamma}{1 - \beta\gamma} \tag{19}$$

As an example we consider the specification

$$V(N_t) = \frac{\xi N_t^\nu}{\nu} \tag{20}$$

Then formula (19) yields a Walrasian quantity of labor equal to

$$N = \left[\frac{1 - \gamma}{\xi (1 - \beta\gamma)} \right]^{1/\nu} \tag{21}$$

9.3.2   Walrasian Dynamics

In order to compare it later with the dynamics under preset wages, we now briefly describe the dynamic evolution of this Walrasian economy. Let us start with the "real" variables, whose evolution is summarized by the following equations:

$$N_t = N \tag{22}$$

$$Y_t = Z_t K_t^{\gamma} N_t^{1-\gamma} \tag{23}$$

$$\frac{W_t}{P_t} = (1 - \gamma) \frac{Y_t}{N_t} \tag{24}$$

$$K_{t+1} = \beta \gamma Y_t \tag{25}$$

Immediately we note that although the economy is perpetually subjected to monetary shocks, fluctuations in real variables are driven by real shocks *only*. In fact the dynamics of the real variables are exactly the same as in the model without money. We see that the introduction of money per se does not give necessarily a role for monetary shocks.[3]

Combining equations (23) and (25), we obtain the expression for output in terms of current and past technology shocks, in logarithms:[4]

$$y_t = n + \frac{z_t}{1 - \gamma L} + \frac{\gamma \log \beta \gamma}{1 - \gamma} \tag{26}$$

where L is the "lag operator," defined by

$$L^j(X_t) = X_{t-j} \tag{27}$$

We see that the propagation mechanism is exactly the same as in the "pure" real models, going through the accumulation of capital. We can also compute

---

3 As we already mentioned, the total lack of effect of monetary shocks is due to our specific money creation process and utility for money, and is thus not a robust feature. But dynamic models with money usually yield relatively small effects for these shocks under market clearing.

4 As before, lowercase letters denote the logarithm of the corresponding uppercase variables.

the nominal wage and price:

$$w_t = m_t + \log(1 - \gamma) - \log \varrho - n \tag{28}$$

$$p_t = m_t - \frac{z_t}{1 - \gamma L} - \log \varrho - n - \frac{\gamma \log \beta \gamma}{1 - \gamma} \tag{29}$$

where ϱ has been defined in equation (18). At this point, although we will not embark on any actual calibrations, we may note a few correlations that have puzzled researchers working in the real business cycles area.

The first problem is that real wages are too procyclical in this model. To illustrate, we combine equations (22) and (24):

$$\frac{W_t}{P_t} = \frac{(1 - \gamma) Y_t}{N} \tag{30}$$

Note that the coefficient of correlation between W_t/P_t and Y_t is equal to one. Although this correlation is a little weaker in calibrated models where N_t varies, it is usually much higher than what is observed in reality.

The second problem concerns prices. A comparison of equations (26) and (29) shows that prices in this model are always countercyclical, whatever the relative size of technological and monetary shocks (we assume that they are independent). Although it is not believed anymore, as during the Keynesian era, that prices are always procyclical, it is nevertheless admitted that there are periods when prices have been countercyclical but also some periods when they have been procyclical.[5] Clearly, this Walrasian model cannot reproduce this variety of experiences in the cyclical behavior of prices.

The third problem concerns the correlation between inflation and output (an issue related to the Phillips curve literature). Whereas this correlation is most generally viewed as positive, the Walrasian model above delivers a negative correlation for most sensible specifications of the productivity shocks.

We will now consider wage contracts, and see that this can help alleviate the problems above.

9.4 Wage Contracts

Suppose that instead of being determined by Walrasian market clearing, the level of wages is predetermined at the beginning of each period, and that at

5 See, for example, Cooley and Ohanian (1991) and Smith (1992).

this contract wage the household supplies all labor demanded by the firm (such contracts were introduced by Gray 1976).

As for the level at which the contract wage is fixed, let us assume that parties to the contract aim at clearing the market ex ante (in logarithmic terms). To that effect the contract wage is set equal to the expected value of the Walrasian wage, which, by formula (28), yields

$$w_t = E_{t-1}w_t^* = E_{t-1}m_t + \log(1-\gamma) - \log\varrho - n \tag{31}$$

where $E_{t-1}m_t$ denotes the expectation of m_t formed at the beginning of period t, before the shocks occurred.

9.4.1 Solving the Model

Since the goods market clears and the firm's demand for labor is always satisfied, equations (5) and (6) concerning the firm still hold. As for the household, it maximizes the utility function (3) subject to the budget constraints (4), but this time taking N_t as *given* (and determined by firms's demands) instead of choosing it. As it turns out, except for the fact that N_t is not chosen by the household, and thus equations (8) and (19) are not valid anymore, the rest of the resolution of the model goes through unchanged, and in particular, equations (14) and (18) still hold. Rewriting equations (1), (5), (14), and (18) in logarithmic form, we obtain the dynamic system

$$y_t = z_t + \gamma k_t + (1-\gamma)n_t \tag{32}$$

$$w_t - p_t = y_t - n_t + \log(1-\gamma) \tag{33}$$

$$m_t = p_t + y_t + \log\varrho \tag{34}$$

$$k_{t+1} = y_t + \log\beta\gamma \tag{35}$$

9.4.2 Dynamics

Combining equations (31) to (34), we first obtain the level of employment in period t:

$$n_t = n + m_t - E_{t-1}m_t \tag{36}$$

For what follows it will actually be convenient to define the monetary innovation at time t:

$$\varepsilon_{mt} = m_t - E_{t-1}m_t \tag{37}$$

So employment is given by

$$n_t = n + \varepsilon_{mt} \tag{38}$$

Now, combining (32) and (38), we obtain the expression for output:

$$y_t = (1-\gamma)n + \gamma k_t + z_t + (1-\gamma)\varepsilon_{mt} \tag{39}$$

Contrary to what happened in the Walrasian model, unexpected money shocks now have an impact on the levels of employment and output. The mechanism is simple. Consider, for example, a positive money shock. This results in a greater demand for goods and labor. Since here wages are blocked in the short run, this demand increase will naturally translate into an increase in employment, and therefore output.

Further combining equations (35) and (39) and lagging appropriately, we obtain

$$y_t = n + \frac{z_t + (1-\gamma)\varepsilon_{mt}}{1 - \gamma L} + \frac{\gamma \log \beta\gamma}{1-\gamma} \tag{40}$$

where we see that unexpected money shocks get propagated in time via the same mechanism as technology shocks, namely through capital accumulation. We should note, however, an important difference between the effects of monetary and technology shocks. Here a more persistent technology shock z_t will lead to more persistent output, since the shock z_t itself appears in formula (40) giving output. This is not the case for monetary shocks, since it is only the innovation in money ε_{mt}, and not the monetary shock m_t itself, which appears in formula (40). We will see in the next chapter that this feature changes with more complex wage contracts.

Now the real wage and price are deduced from y_t through the simple formulas

$$w_t - p_t = y_t - n - \varepsilon_{mt} + \log(1-\gamma) \tag{41}$$

$$p_t = m_t - y_t - \log \varrho \tag{42}$$

9.5   The Cyclical Behavior of Real Wages, Prices, and Inflation

We will use the preceding results to throw some light on the cyclical properties of a few variables in response to technological and monetary shocks.

9.5.1   Real Wages

We begin with real wages, for which we saw that the Walrasian model yields a much too high positive correlation with output. To make these correlations clearer, let us rewrite output and real wages in the following form (suppressing all irrelevant constant terms):

$$y_t = (1 - \gamma)\varepsilon_{mt} + \frac{\gamma(1 - \gamma)\varepsilon_{mt-1}}{1 - \gamma L} + \frac{z_t}{1 - \gamma L} \qquad (43)$$

$$w_t - p_t = -\gamma\varepsilon_{mt} + \frac{\gamma(1 - \gamma)\varepsilon_{mt-1}}{1 - \gamma L} + \frac{z_t}{1 - \gamma L} \qquad (44)$$

We see that although all supply shocks and *lagged* money shocks induce a positive correlation between real wage and output, *contemporary* money shocks induce inversely a negative correlation between real wage and output. Our model thus allows to mix this last feature, which is characteristic of traditional Keynesian models, with the more standard results of real business cycles models.

In order to have a simple example of potential correlations, let us consider the (unrealistic) case where z_t is trend-stationary with the following characteristics[6]

$$z_t = a_z t + \varepsilon_{zt} \qquad (45)$$

The ε_{zt} and ε_{m_t} are uncorrelated white noises, with

$$\text{var}(\varepsilon_{zt}) = \sigma_z^2, \quad \text{var}(\varepsilon_{mt}) = \sigma_m^2 \qquad (46)$$

---

6 Correlations are easy to compute for more complex processes, but the formulas can become somewhat messy.

In that case we obtain the following correlation:

$$\text{corr}(w_t - p_t, y_t) = \frac{\sigma_z^2 - \gamma(1-\gamma)^2\sigma_m^2}{\left[\sigma_z^2 + (1-\gamma)^2\sigma_m^2\right]^{1/2}\left[\sigma_z^2 + 2\gamma^2(1-\gamma)\sigma_m^2\right]^{1/2}} \quad (47)$$

Formula (47) shows that the correlation between real wages and output is still one if there are *only* supply shocks. But this correlation diminishes as soon as monetary shocks are present, and can even become negative. The relatively low actual correlations can thus be reproduced by adequate combinations of technological and monetary shocks.

9.5.2 Prices

Let us now move to the expression of the price level, which can be rewritten as

$$p_t = E_{t-1}m_t + \gamma\varepsilon_{mt} - \frac{\gamma(1-\gamma)\varepsilon_{mt-1}}{1-\gamma L} - \frac{z_t}{1-\gamma L} \quad (48)$$

Comparing this expression with that of output (43), we see that although all supply shocks and *lagged* money shocks induce a negative correlation between output and prices, *contemporary* money shocks induce inversely a positive correlation between prices and output. Again, we have a synthesis of traditional Keynesian features with those of standard real business cycles models.

To have an example of potential correlations, let us take again the example of equations (45) and (46), assuming further that m_t is also trend-stationary:

$$m_t = a_m t + \varepsilon_{m_t} \quad (49)$$

As a result we obtain the correlation[7]

$$\text{corr}(p_t, y_t) = \frac{\gamma(1-\gamma)^2\sigma_m^2 - \sigma_z^2}{\left[\sigma_z^2 + (1-\gamma)^2\sigma_m^2\right]^{1/2}\left[\sigma_z^2 + 2\gamma^2(1-\gamma)\sigma_m^2\right]^{1/2}} \quad (50)$$

7 We may note that the two correlation coefficients between real wages and output, on the one hand, and prices and output, on the other hand, are exactly opposite. This is due to the particular process for money (49), which makes the wage w_t fully deterministic (see equation 31). This particular relation would not hold for a more general money process.

Formula (50) shows that we can obtain procyclical prices if demand shocks are prevalent, and countercyclical prices if technology shocks are prevalent. The different behavior of prices over different historical subperiods may thus simply be due to the nature of shocks faced by the economies during these periods.

9.5.3 The Inflation-Output Correlation

We will finally study another well-known relation in macroeconomics, that between inflation and output, which are usually thought to be positively correlated, at least in the Keynesian tradition. We can compute this correlation for various processes for monetary and technological shocks.

For example, if we assume the two trend-stationary processes above (equations 45 and 49), we find that

$$\text{corr}(\Delta p_t, y_t) = \frac{(1-\gamma)^{1/2}\left[\gamma(1-\gamma)^2\sigma_m^2 - \sigma_z^2\right]}{\left[\sigma_z^2 + (1-\gamma)^2\sigma_m^2\right]^{1/2}\left[2\gamma^2(3-\gamma)^2\sigma_m^2 + 2\sigma_z^2\right]^{1/2}} \quad (51)$$

Formula (51), and similar ones for different processes of money or technology, shows us that the positive inflation-output correlation is closely related to the presence of monetary shocks, and that the sign of this correlation can actually be reversed if there are sufficiently strong technological shocks.

9.6 Endogenizing Wage Formation

So far we assumed that in each period wages are preset at the expected value of the Walrasian wage (in logarithms). We will now show how a highly similar wage formation scheme can be derived rigorously as the result of maximizing behavior by rational trade unions.

9.6.1 The Model

As before, we assume a Cobb-Douglas technology

$$Y_t = Z_t K_t^\gamma N_t^{1-\gamma} \quad (52)$$

where the labor index N_t is actually an aggregate of a continuum of labor types, indexed by $i \in [0, 1]$:

$$N_t = \left(\int_0^1 N_{it}^\theta \, di \right)^{1/\theta} \tag{53}$$

Each type is represented by a trade union, and these trade unions compete through their wages W_{it}. All wages are set at the beginning of the period, before shocks are known.

The representative household's utility is, as above,

$$U = E_0 \sum_{t=0}^{\infty} \beta^t \left[\log C_t + \omega \log \frac{M_t}{P_t} - V(N_t) \right] \tag{54}$$

9.6.2 Wage Contracts: The Demand for Labor

At any time firms are confronted with a multiplicity of wage contracts, since wages W_{it} may differ depending on index i. For a given aggregate labor index N_t, they will minimize costs. That is to say, they will solve the following program:

$$\min \int_0^1 W_{it} N_{it} \, di \quad \text{s.t.}$$

$$\left(\int_0^1 N_{it}^\theta \, di \right)^{1/\theta} = N_t \tag{55}$$

The solution is

$$N_{it} = N_t \left(\frac{W_{it}}{W_t} \right)^{-1/(1-\theta)} \tag{56}$$

$$W_t = \left(\int_0^1 W_{it}^{-\theta/(1-\theta)} \, di \right)^{-(1-\theta)/\theta} \tag{57}$$

9.6.3 Optimal Wage Contracts

We now derive the wage level that will be chosen by a rational trade union. From this point on we will assume the particular disutility of labor

$$V(N_t) = \frac{\xi N_t^\nu}{\nu} \tag{58}$$

Wage contracts are characterized by the following proposition:

Proposition 1   *The wages W_{it} chosen by the various trade-unions are given by*

$$W_{it} = W_t \qquad \forall i \tag{59}$$

$$W_t = \left[\frac{\xi(1-\beta\gamma)}{\theta(1-\gamma)}\right]^{1/\nu} \frac{(1-\beta)(1-\gamma)}{\omega(1-\beta\gamma)} \left[E_{t-1}M_t^\nu\right]^{1/\nu} \tag{60}$$

Proof   Consider a household working in a firm i. The household has to choose at the beginning of period t its wage W_{it}. This household will maximize the expected value, using information up to period $t-1$, of its discounted utility:

$$\sum_{s\geq t} \beta^{s-t} \left[\log C_{is} + \omega\log\frac{M_{is}}{P_s} - \frac{\xi N_{is}^\nu}{\nu}\right] \tag{61}$$

subject to the budget constraints in each period

$$C_{is} + \frac{M_{is}}{P_s} + I_{is} = \frac{W_{is}}{P_s}N_{is} + \kappa_s I_{is-1} + \frac{\mu_s M_{is-1}}{P_s} \tag{62}$$

and to the equation giving the demand for labor (56),

$$N_{is} = N_s \left(\frac{W_{is}}{W_s}\right)^{-1/(1-\theta)} \tag{63}$$

Inspection of this maximization problem shows that all households face exactly the same circumstances, independently of their index i. So at equilibrium we have

$$W_{it} = W_t \qquad \forall i \tag{64}$$

which is equation (59). As a consequence all consumers will have the same income, and therefore the same consumption, money holdings, investments, and employment levels:

$$C_{is} = C_s, \quad M_{is} = M_s, \quad I_{is} = I_s, \quad N_{is} = N_s, \qquad \forall i \tag{65}$$

Households indexed by i maximize (61) subject to (62) and (63). Let us insert the value of N_{is} (equation 63) into (61) and (62). Taking into account (65), the corresponding Lagrangean is the expected value in $t-1$ of (we omit the terms that are not used in the following derivation)

$$\sum_{s\geq t} \beta^{s-t} \left\{ \log C_s - \frac{\xi}{\nu} \left[N_s \left(\frac{W_{is}}{W_s} \right)^{-1/(1-\theta)} \right]^{\nu} \right\}$$

$$+ \sum_{s\geq t} \beta^{s-t} \lambda_{is} \left[\frac{W_s N_s}{P_s} \left(\frac{W_{is}}{W_s} \right)^{-\theta/(1-\theta)} - C_s \right] \qquad (66)$$

Maximization in C_s yields

$$\lambda_{is} = \frac{1}{C_s} \qquad (67)$$

Now, when choosing the wage W_{it}, the household will maximize the sum of the terms that actually include W_{it}. Moreover it will do so on the basis of information up to period $t-1$, since the wage is preset before period t shocks are known. As a consequence the relevant maximand is

$$E_{t-1} \left\{ \frac{W_t N_t}{P_t C_t} \left(\frac{W_{it}}{W_t} \right)^{1-1/(1-\theta)} - \frac{\xi}{\nu} N_t^{\nu} \left(\frac{W_{it}}{W_t} \right)^{-\nu/(1-\theta)} \right\} \qquad (68)$$

Both W_{it} and W_t are known when deciding individual wages, so we can take them out of expectations. Moreover from equations (5), (13), and (17), which are still valid here,

$$W_t N_t = (1-\gamma) P_t Y_t = \frac{1-\gamma}{1-\beta\gamma} P_t C_t = \frac{(1-\beta)(1-\gamma)}{\omega(1-\beta\gamma)} M_t \qquad (69)$$

So the term in W_{it} (equation 68) becomes

$$\frac{1-\gamma}{1-\beta\gamma} \left(\frac{W_{it}}{W_t} \right)^{-\theta/(1-\theta)} - \frac{\xi}{\nu} \left[\frac{(1-\beta)(1-\gamma)}{\omega(1-\beta\gamma)} \right]^{\nu} \left(\frac{W_{it}}{W_t} \right)^{-\nu/(1-\theta)} E_{t-1} \left(\frac{M_t}{W_t} \right)^{\nu} \qquad (70)$$

Differentiating with respect to W_{it}, we find the first-order condition:

$$\frac{(1-\gamma)\theta}{1-\beta\gamma} \left(\frac{W_{it}}{W_t} \right)^{(\nu-\theta)/(1-\theta)} = \xi \left[\frac{(1-\beta)(1-\gamma)}{\omega(1-\beta\gamma)} \right]^{\nu} E_{t-1} \left(\frac{M_t}{W_t} \right)^{\nu} \qquad (71)$$

As we saw above (equation 64), in equilibrium $W_{it} = W_t$ for all i. So (71) simplifies as

$$W_t^\nu = \frac{\xi(1 - \beta\gamma)}{\theta(1 - \gamma)} \left[\frac{(1 - \beta)(1 - \gamma)}{\omega(1 - \beta\gamma)} \right]^\nu E_{t-1} M_t^\nu \tag{72}$$

from which we immediately obtain equation (60).   ∎

9.6.4 Relation with the Gray Contracts

We may have a more intuitive interpretation of equation (60) giving the value of the preset wage, as well as a simple relation with the Gray contracts used until section 9.5, if we first compute the value of the Walrasian wage W_t^*. Combining equations (5), (18), and (21), we find that

$$W_t^* = \frac{(1 - \beta)(1 - \gamma)}{\omega(1 - \beta\gamma)} \left[\frac{\xi(1 - \beta\gamma)}{1 - \gamma} \right]^{1/\nu} M_t \tag{73}$$

Now, using (73), equation (60) simplifies as

$$W_t^\nu = \frac{1}{\theta} E_{t-1}(W_t^*)^\nu \tag{74}$$

where it appears that the preset wage at the power ν is equal to the expected value of its Walrasian counterpart, multiplied by the "monopolistic markup" $1/\theta$. For example, if M_t is a lognormal variable whose innovation ε_{mt} has variance σ_m^2, then

$$w_t = E_{t-1}w_t^* - \frac{\log\theta}{\nu} + \frac{\nu\sigma_m^2}{2} \tag{75}$$

So we see that up to a constant term, the wage resulting from explicit maximization looks exactly like the wage given by the "Gray contract."

9.7 Conclusions

We constructed in this chapter a fully computable model of a business cycle with optimizing agents, adding money and nonclearing markets to the traditional real business cycles framework. A few observations can be made.

First, in the Walrasian version of this model, the real variables do not respond to monetary shocks. The presence of money per se does not necessarily create a role for monetary shocks.

Second, the combination of money *and* nonclearing markets does change things substantially. In particular, nonforecasted money shocks have an impact on employment and production, and the effect on production is transmitted through time via the accumulation of capital. These effects give a balanced view between usual real business cycles results and traditional Keynesian ones. In particular, monetary shocks induce countercyclical real wages and procyclical prices, whereas technological shocks induce procyclical real wages and countercyclical prices. This synthetic blend of "classical" and "Keynesian" outcomes is obtained via fully computable solutions to a rigorous intertemporal optimization problem under stochastic shocks.

Now we have seen that although employment and output do react to monetary shocks, these effects are not persistent. If indeed the depreciation rate is small, the appendix to this chapter shows that the effects of money shocks will be essentially concentrated in the first period, whereas empirical studies indicate fairly persistent effects. We will see in the next chapter that such persistence can actually be obtained with more sophisticated wage contracts.

9.8   References

This chapter is based on Bénassy (1995a). Another model with wage rigidities and closed-form solutions is found in Cho, Cooley, and Phaneuf (1997). A pioneering dynamic general equilibrium model with preset prices is Svensson (1986).

A detailed empirical analysis of the effects of monetary shocks is found notably in Christiano, Eichenbaum, and Evans (1999, 2001).

Initial real business cycles models assuming full market clearing were developed by Kydland and Prescott (1982) and Long and Plosser (1983). King and Plosser (1984) and Cooley and Hansen (1989) introduced money in market-clearing models, while nonclearing markets in real economies were introduced by Danthine and Donaldson (1990, 1991, 1992). Money and nonclearing markets were then successfully integrated by a number of researchers (Cho 1993; Cho and Cooley 1995; Hairault and Portier 1993), who showed that the introduction of price, and especially wage rigidities, in monetary economies subject to real and monetary shocks brought several important correlations much closer to those observed in actual economies.

Appendix 9.1: Incomplete Depreciation

We investigate here the case of incomplete capital depreciation. To obtain a closed form solution, we will use a loglinearized approximation of the capital accumulation equation, as in Hercowitz and Sampson (1991):

$$K_{t+1} = AK_t^{1-\delta}I_t^{\delta}, \qquad 0 < \delta \le 1 \tag{76}$$

where δ is the rate of depreciation. The case studied in the main text corresponds to $\delta = 1$ and $A = 1$. We will see how this modifies the analysis. We still call κ_t the real return on capital K_t. The household's budget constraint is

$$C_t + \frac{M_t}{P_t} + I_t = \frac{W_t}{P_t}N_t + \kappa_t K_t + \frac{\mu_t M_{t-1}}{P_t} \tag{77}$$

The household maximizes the expected value of its utility:

$$E_0 \sum_t \beta^t \left[\log C_t + \omega \log \frac{M_t}{P_t} - V(L_t) \right] \tag{78}$$

subject to its budget constraints (77) and the capital accumulation equations (76). The Lagrangean for this program is the expected value of

$$\sum_t \beta^t \left[\log C_t + \omega \log \frac{M_t}{P_t} - V(L_t) \right] + \sum_t \beta^t \zeta_t \left(AK_t^{1-\delta}I_t^{\delta} - K_{t+1} \right)$$

$$+ \sum_t \beta^t \lambda_t \left[\frac{W_t}{P_t}N_t + \kappa_t K_t + \frac{\mu_t M_{t-1}}{P_t} - C_t - I_t - \frac{M_t}{P_t} \right] \tag{79}$$

The first-order conditions for consumption, investment and capital yield

$$\lambda_t = \frac{1}{C_t} \tag{80}$$

$$\lambda_t = \delta A \zeta_t K_t^{1-\delta} I_t^{\delta-1} \tag{81}$$

$$\zeta_t = \beta E_t \left[\lambda_{t+1}\kappa_{t+1} + (1-\delta)AK_{t+1}^{-\delta}I_{t+1}^{\delta}\zeta_{t+1} \right] \tag{82}$$

After inserting the value $\kappa_t = \alpha Y_t / K_t$ into (82) and combining with (76), (80), and (81), we obtain

$$
\begin{aligned}
\frac{I_t}{C_t} &= \beta\gamma\delta E_t \left(\frac{Y_{t+1}}{C_{t+1}} \right) + \beta(1-\delta)E_t \left(\frac{I_{t+1}}{C_{t+1}} \right) \\
&= \beta\gamma\delta + [\beta\gamma\delta + \beta(1-\delta)]E_t \left(\frac{I_{t+1}}{C_{t+1}} \right)
\end{aligned}
\tag{83}
$$

which solves as

$$
\frac{I_t}{C_t} = \frac{\beta\gamma\delta}{1 - \beta(1 - \delta + \gamma\delta)}
\tag{84}
$$

So

$$
C_t = \frac{1 - \beta(1 - \delta + \gamma\delta)}{1 - \beta + \beta\delta} Y_t
\tag{85}
$$

$$
I_t = \frac{\beta\gamma\delta}{1 - \beta + \beta\delta} Y_t
\tag{86}
$$

Now equation (17) is still valid, and combining it with (85), we obtain

$$
\frac{M_t}{P_t} = \frac{\omega[1 - \beta(1 - \delta + \gamma\delta)]}{(1 - \beta)(1 - \beta + \beta\delta)} Y_t
\tag{87}
$$

Finally, equations (5), (7), (8), and (85) yield a Walrasian quantity of labor N now given by

$$
N V'(N) = \frac{(1 - \gamma)(1 - \beta + \beta\delta)}{1 - \beta + \beta\delta - \beta\gamma\delta}
\tag{88}
$$

Let us now move to the situation with wage contracts and denote as σ the savings rate, so that (86) is rewritten as

$$
I_t = \sigma Y_t, \quad \sigma = \frac{\beta\gamma\delta}{1 - \beta + \beta\delta}
\tag{89}
$$

Combining (89) with equations (1) and (76), we find that output is given by

$$y_t = \frac{[1 - (1 - \delta)L][z_t + (1 - \gamma)n_t]}{1 - (1 - \delta + \gamma\delta)L} + \frac{\gamma\delta\log\sigma + \gamma\log A}{\delta(1 - \gamma)} \tag{90}$$

Moreover employment is still given by

$$n_t = n + \varepsilon_{mt} \tag{91}$$

Combining (90) and (91), we obtain the final expression for output:

$$y_t = n + \frac{[1 - (1 - \delta)L][z_t + (1 - \gamma)\varepsilon_{mt}]}{1 - (1 - \delta + \gamma\delta)L} + \frac{\gamma\delta\log\sigma + \gamma\log A}{\delta(1 - \gamma)} \tag{92}$$

which generalizes and replaces equation (40) in the main text.

10

Staggered Contracts and Persistence

10.1 Introduction

In the previous chapter the introduction of nominal wage rigidities into a rigorous stochastic intertemporal model enabled us to explain a number of stylized facts that traditional models failed to reproduce. At this stage our model is nevertheless still vulnerable to a well-known critique of standard real business cycles models, that is, their almost total inability to generate an internal propagation mechanism in the business cycle. For example, Cogley and Nason (1995), among others, showed that most of the dynamics in the standard RBC model is that contained in the dynamics of the productivity shocks themselves. It is, of course, troublesome to have everything one tries to explain deriving directly from an exogenously given stochastic process.

Moreover, when money is introduced in such models, the effects of monetary shocks are weak and display little persistence for reasonable values of the parameters. On the contrary, empirical studies show that the response of output to monetary shocks is quite persistent, and even displays a "hump-shaped" response (Christiano, Eichenbaum, and Evans 1999, 2001).

So the purpose of this chapter is to construct a structural dynamic model with wage contracts deriving from rigorous microfoundations. We will introduce wage stickiness into dynamic general equilibrium models in a way that is analytically tractable, and that enables us to reproduce the persistence of output and employment response to monetary shocks.

The first question we ask is naturally: Which contracts do we use? Several forms of wage contracts have been developed since the early 1970's, notably associated with the names of Gray (1976), Fischer (1977), Taylor (1979, 1980), and Calvo (1983). The contracts introduced by Calvo (1983) are particularly interesting for our purposes because with a single parameter one can describe economies ranging from full wage flexibility to full rigidity. To be a little more precise, this parameter, say ϕ, is the probability that a wage contract survives unchanged from one period to the next. Every new contract is set on the basis of the information of the current period. So, for $\phi = 0$, wages are fully flexible, and for $\phi = 1$ they are totally rigid.

A particularity of Calvo contracts is that, following Taylor (1979, 1980), the value of the wage set in a particular contract remains constant throughout the duration of the contract. Although this particularity appeared initially beneficial, because it seemed to create more persistence than alternative formulations, one may consider it today a less desirable feature for at least two reasons. The first is a simple empirical one: in reality multiperiod contracts typically stipulate different wages for different periods. The second one is normative: in an inflationary environment, since one has to pick a unique wage for periods with highly different price levels, such contracts can potentially create enormous inefficiencies.

Therefore what we will do is to construct a new contract that, while retaining the central elegant feature of Calvo contracts, allows the value of the negotiated wages to depend on time. This will solve the two problems above. We will see that these contracts give persistence in output, so that this attractive feature of the Calvo contracts is preserved. Another important feature is that the value of a wage contract is derived from the behavior of utility-maximizing trade unions, and not postulated, as in most of this literature.

10.2   The Model

10.2.1   Markets and Agents

The economy studied is a monetary economy with markets for goods at price P_t and markets for labor at (average) wage W_t. The goods market is competitive, while the labor markets function under a system of imperfectly competitive labor contracts, as will be explained below. The agents are representative firms, households, and the government.

The representative firm has a Cobb-Douglas technology:

$$Y_t = Z_t K_t^{\gamma} N_t^{1-\gamma} \tag{1}$$

where K_t is capital, N_t is the aggregate quantity of labor used in production, and Z_t is a stochastic technology skock. Capital fully depreciates in one period so that

$$K_{t+1} = I_t \tag{2}$$

where I_t is investment in period t.[1] The labor index N_t is an aggregate of a continuum of labor types,[2] indexed by $i \in [0, 1]$:

$$\log N_t = \int_0^1 \log N_{it} \, di \tag{3}$$

The essential difference between these types, as we will see below, is that usually they will have signed different wage contracts at different times. Now each index N_{it} is itself the aggregate of another infinity of labor types indexed by k:[3]

$$N_{it} = \left(\int_0^1 N_{ikt}^\theta \, dk \right)^{1/\theta} \tag{4}$$

All individuals with the same index i face exactly the same situation in terms of wage contracts, whatever their subindex k. We may think of the index i as representing sectors, while the index k represents firms within these sectors. We thus assume that all firms within a sector, although they compete through prices and wages, negotiate wages at exactly the same time. These negotiations need not be synchronized across sectors.

The representative household (we omit the indexes i or k at this stage) works N_t, consumes C_t, and ends the period with a quantity of money M_t. It maximizes the expected value of its discounted utilities with the following intertemporal

---

1 The case of incomplete depreciation is treated in appendix 10.1.

2 Throughout this chapter we will aggregate across labor types because it simplifies the exposition. The alternative (and perhaps more intuitive) aggregation across output types is sketched in appendix 10.2. The results are, up to an unimportant constant, essentially the same.

3 To be fully rigorous, we should use a notation like k_i, but this would make notation more cumbersome and with little gain in understanding. Note also that the double subdivision of workers, which may seem to complicate matters at this stage, is actually the key to a simple solution, as will be seen below.

utility:

$$U = E_0 \sum_t \beta^t \left[\log C_t + \omega \log \frac{M_t}{P_t} - V(N_t) \right] \qquad (5)$$

At the beginning of period t there is a stochastic multiplicative monetary shock whereby money holdings carried from the previous period M_{t-1} are multiplied by the same factor μ_t for all agents. The representative household's budget constraint in period t is thus

$$C_t + \frac{M_t}{P_t} + I_t = \frac{W_t}{P_t} N_t + \kappa_t I_{t-1} + \frac{\mu_t M_{t-1}}{P_t} \qquad (6)$$

where κ_t is the real return in t on capital invested in $t - 1$.

10.2.2 Wage Contracts

Let us now describe the wage contracts. As in Calvo (1983), in each period there is a random draw for all contracts, after which any particular contract will continue unchanged with probability ϕ, or be terminated with probability $1 - \phi$. In this last case the corresponding contract wage is renegotiated on the basis of all information currently available.

We denote by W_t the average wage, and by X_{ts} the wage contract signed in period t to be in effect in period $s \geq t$ (as we will find out below, all workers who sign a new contract in t for period s choose the same wage level, so we do not need to index X_{ts} by i or k). The assumption in Calvo (1983) is that X_{ts} is independent of s for all $s \geq t$. On the contrary, we will assume that these can be different for all periods.

10.3   The Walrasian Regime

We will first, as a benchmark for what follows, describe the Walrasian equilibrium of this economy. The economy is actually the same as that of the previous chapter, and it has the same Walrasian equilibrium. So we need only to recall the main formulas. The real wage is equal to the marginal productivity of labor:

$$\frac{W_t}{P_t} = \frac{\partial Y_t}{\partial N_t} = (1 - \gamma) \frac{Y_t}{N_t} \qquad (7)$$

Consumption, investment, and real money balances are given by

$$C_t = (1 - \beta\gamma)Y_t \tag{8}$$

$$K_{t+1} = I_t = \beta\gamma Y_t \tag{9}$$

$$\frac{M_t}{P_t C_t} = \frac{\omega}{1 - \beta} \tag{10}$$

Walrasian employment is constant and equal to N, which is solution of

$$NV'(N) = \frac{1 - \gamma}{1 - \beta\gamma} \tag{11}$$

and the Walrasian wage W_t^* is equal to

$$W_t^* = \frac{(1 - \gamma)(1 - \beta)}{(1 - \beta\gamma)\omega N} M_t \tag{12}$$

If $V(N_t) = \xi N_t^\nu / \nu$, which we will use below, formula (11) yields

$$N = \left[\frac{1 - \gamma}{\xi(1 - \beta\gamma)} \right]^{1/\nu} \tag{13}$$

10.4 Wage Contracts

We will now study our model under staggered wage contracts. We assume that the households, perhaps through trade unions, decide on the level of wages, and supply the amount of labor demanded by firms at these wages. We will compute the demand for labor addressed to households, then derive the optimal contract wages, and finally characterize the evolution of the average wage.

10.4.1 The Demand for Labor

In any period t the firms are confronted with a multiplicity of wage contracts, which were signed at different points in time. So, for a given aggregate labor index N_t, the firms will minimize costs. This cost minimization can be broken into two steps. First, firms will solve the following program:

$$\min \int_0^1 W_{it} N_{it} \, di \quad \text{s.t.}$$

$$\int_0^1 \log N_{it} \, di = \log N_t$$

whose solution is

$$N_{it} = \frac{W_t N_t}{W_{it}} \tag{14}$$

$$\log W_t = \int_0^1 \log W_{it} \, di \tag{15}$$

For a given index N_{it}, the firms will similarly choose the N_{ikt} that minimize cost, meaning they will solve

$$\min \int_0^1 W_{ikt} N_{ikt} \, dk \quad \text{s.t.}$$

$$\left(\int_0^1 N_{ikt}^\theta \, dk \right)^{1/\theta} = N_{it}$$

whose solution is

$$N_{ikt} = N_{it} \left(\frac{W_{ikt}}{W_{it}} \right)^{-1/(1-\theta)} \tag{16}$$

$$W_{it} = \left(\int_0^1 W_{ikt}^{-\theta/(1-\theta)} \, dk \right)^{-(1-\theta)/\theta} \tag{17}$$

Putting together equations (14) and (16), we obtain the final expression of the demand for labor in firm (i, k):

$$N_{ikt} = \frac{W_t N_t}{W_{it}} \left(\frac{W_{ikt}}{W_{it}} \right)^{-1/(1-\theta)} \tag{18}$$

An important thing to remember for what follows is that, in view of equation (14), all households, whatever their contract and their wage, will have exactly the same wage income:

$$W_{it} N_{it} = W_t N_t \qquad \forall i \tag{19}$$

10.4.2 Optimal Wage Contracts

We will derive the optimal wage contracts assuming from now on the particular disutility of labor:

$$V(N_t) = \frac{\xi N_t^\nu}{\nu} \tag{20}$$

Wage contracts are characterized by the following proposition:

Proposition 1 *The wage contract X_{ts} signed at time t for period s is given by*

$$X_{ts} = \left[\frac{\xi(1 - \beta\gamma)}{\theta(1 - \gamma)} \right]^{1/\nu} \frac{(1 - \gamma)(1 - \beta)}{\omega(1 - \beta\gamma)} \left[E_t \ M_s^\nu \right]^{1/\nu} \tag{21}$$

Proof Since we do not know yet that all households will sign the same contracts, we denote by X_{ikts} the contract signed at time t, to be in effect in period s, by household (i, k). To determine X_{ikts}, household (i, k) maximizes its discounted expected utility. We consider here only the terms corresponding to the contracts signed in t and still in effect at some time $s \geq t$. Since contracts have a probability ϕ to survive each period, the contract signed in t has a probability ϕ^{s-t} to be still in effect in period s, and the household will thus maximize the expected value of the following discounted utility:

$$E_t \sum_{s \geq t} \beta^{s-t} \phi^{s-t} \left[\log C_{iks} + \omega \log \frac{M_{iks}}{P_s} - \frac{\xi N_{iks}^\nu}{\nu} \right] \tag{22}$$

subject to the budget constraints in each period,

$$C_{iks} + \frac{M_{iks}}{P_s} + I_{iks} = \frac{W_{iks}}{P_s} N_{iks} + \kappa_s I_{iks-1} + \frac{\mu_s M_{iks-1}}{P_s} \tag{23}$$

The quantity of labor N_{iks} in these two formulas is given by equation (18) characterizing the demand for labor:

$$N_{iks} = \frac{W_s N_s}{W_{is}} \left(\frac{W_{iks}}{W_{is}} \right)^{-1/(1-\theta)} \tag{24}$$

Since we consider only wage contracts signed in t, and still in effect in period s, then $W_{iks} = X_{ikts}$. W_{is} is equal to the average of these contracts across households indexed by i, that is, in view of formula (17):

$$W_{is} = \left(\int_0^1 X_{ikts}^{-\theta/(1-\theta)} \, dk \right)^{-(1-\theta)/\theta} = X_{its} \tag{25}$$

Consequently formula (24) is rewritten as

$$N_{iks} = \frac{W_s N_s}{X_{its}} \left(\frac{X_{ikts}}{X_{its}} \right)^{-1/(1-\theta)} \tag{26}$$

Household (i, k) will thus maximize expected utility (22) subject to the budget constraints (23) and the equation giving the demand for labor (26). Inspecting this maximization problem, we see that all households sharing the same index i face exactly the same circumstances. So in equilibrium we will have

$$X_{ikts} = X_{its} \qquad \forall k \tag{27}$$

Moreover, in view of equation (19), all consumers have the same income, and therefore the same consumption, money holdings, and investments (but they will differ, of course, in their wages and employment levels):

$$C_{iks} = C_s, \quad I_{iks} = I_s, \quad M_{iks} = M_s, \qquad \forall i, k \tag{28}$$

Households indexed by (i, k) thus maximize (22) subject to (23) and (26). Let us insert the value of N_{iks} (equation 26) into (22) and (23). Taking into account (28), the corresponding Lagrangean is the expected value of (we omit the terms that will not be used)

$$\sum_{s \geq t} \beta^{s-t} \phi^{s-t} \left\{ \log C_s - \frac{\xi}{\nu} \left[\frac{W_s N_s}{X_{its}} \left(\frac{X_{ikts}}{X_{its}} \right)^{-1/(1-\theta)} \right]^{\nu} \right\}$$

$$+ \sum_{s \geq t} \beta^{s-t} \phi^{s-t} \lambda_{iks} \left[\frac{W_s N_s}{P_s} \left(\frac{X_{ikts}}{X_{its}} \right)^{-\theta/(1-\theta)} - C_s \right] \tag{29}$$

Maximization in C_s yields

$$\lambda_{iks} = \frac{1}{C_s} \tag{30}$$

So, when choosing in period t the various contract wages X_{ikts} $s \geq t$, the household maximizes the expected value in t of the maximand (29). The part concerning the contract wage X_{ikts} is, suppressing unimportant constants,

$$E_t \left\{ \frac{W_s N_s}{P_s C_s} \left(\frac{X_{ikts}}{X_{its}} \right)^{-\theta/(1-\theta)} - \frac{\xi}{\nu} \left(\frac{W_s N_s}{X_{its}} \right)^{\nu} \left(\frac{X_{ikts}}{X_{its}} \right)^{-\nu/(1-\theta)} \right\} \tag{31}$$

Equations (7), (8), and (10) are still valid. Consequently

$$W_s N_s = (1 - \gamma) P_s Y_s = \frac{1 - \gamma}{1 - \beta \gamma} P_s C_s = \frac{(1 - \gamma)(1 - \beta)}{\omega(1 - \beta \gamma)} M_s \tag{32}$$

and the term in X_{ikts} (equation 31) becomes

$$\frac{1 - \gamma}{1 - \beta \gamma} \left(\frac{X_{ikts}}{X_{its}} \right)^{-\theta/(1-\theta)} - \frac{\xi}{\nu} \left[\frac{(1 - \gamma)(1 - \beta)}{\omega(1 - \beta \gamma) X_{its}} \right]^{\nu} \left(\frac{X_{ikts}}{X_{its}} \right)^{-\nu/(1-\theta)} E_t \left(M_s^{\nu} \right) \tag{33}$$

Maximizing with respect to X_{ikts}, we obtain the first-order condition

$$\frac{\theta(1 - \gamma)}{1 - \beta \gamma} \left(\frac{X_{ikts}}{X_{its}} \right)^{(\nu-\theta)/(1-\theta)} = \xi \left[\frac{(1 - \gamma)(1 - \beta)}{\omega(1 - \beta \gamma) X_{its}} \right]^{\nu} E_t \left(M_s^{\nu} \right) \tag{34}$$

Now we know from (27) that in equilibrium, $X_{ikts} = X_{its}$ for all k. So we first simplify (34) as

$$\frac{\theta(1 - \gamma)}{1 - \beta \gamma} = \xi \left[\frac{(1 - \gamma)(1 - \beta)}{\omega(1 - \beta \gamma) X_{its}} \right]^{\nu} E_t \left(M_s^{\nu} \right) \tag{35}$$

We see that the solution in X_{its} is the same for all agents i, and we denote it as X_{ts}. We then rewrite (35) as

$$\frac{\theta(1 - \gamma)}{1 - \beta \gamma} X_{ts}^{\nu} = \xi \left[\frac{(1 - \gamma)(1 - \beta)}{\omega(1 - \beta \gamma)} \right]^{\nu} E_t M_s^{\nu} \tag{36}$$

from which we immediately obtain equation (21). ∎

We may note that in using equations (12) and (13) which give the value of the Walrasian wage W_s^*, we can rewrite equation (21) in a simpler and more intuitive form:

$$X_{ts}^\nu = \frac{1}{\theta} E_t (W_s^*)^\nu \qquad (37)$$

So X_{ts}^ν is equal to the expected value in period t of $(W_s^*)^\nu$, multiplied by the "monopolistic markup" $1/\theta$. The contract wage is thus very directly related to a particular expected value of the Walrasian wage W_s^*.

10.4.3   The Average Wage

We will derive the average wage index W_t as a function of all contracts signed in the past, X_{st}, $s \le t$. We first recall the general formula (15) giving W_t:

$$\log W_t = \int_0^1 \log W_{it}\, di \qquad (38)$$

Because of the law of large numbers, and in view of the survival rate ϕ, a proportion $1 - \phi$ of the wage contracts comes from period t, a proportion $\phi(1 - \phi)$ from period $t - 1, \dots$, a proportion $\phi^{t-s}(1 - \phi)$ from period $s \le t$, and so on. As a result formula (38) is rewritten as

$$\log W_t = (1 - \phi) \sum_{s=-\infty}^{t} \phi^{t-s} \log X_{st} \qquad (39)$$

10.5   Macroeconomic Dynamics

10.5.1   Employment Dynamics

We will now compute the wage and employment dynamics for the following standard monetary process:

$$m_t - m_{t-1} = \frac{u_t}{1 - \rho L} \qquad (40)$$

where u_t is a white noise with mean zero and variance σ^2. We can characterize the resulting employment process through the following proposition:

Proposition 2 *Under the monetary process (40) employment dynamics is given by*

$$n_t = n + \frac{\phi u_t}{(1 - \phi L)(1 - \phi \rho L)} + \Phi \tag{41}$$

$$\Phi = \frac{\log \theta}{\nu} - \frac{(1 + \phi \rho) \phi \nu \sigma^2}{2(1 - \phi \rho)(1 - \phi \rho^2)(1 - \phi)} \tag{42}$$

Proof Appendix 10.3. ∎

We see that market power decreases average employment, and so does uncertainty. Formula (41) also tells us that, unlike in the previous chapter, the response to a monetary shock can be quite persistent. We can get a first idea of the time profile of this response by computing the impulse response functions of employment and output to a monetary shock. The important parameters are, of course, ϕ and ρ. A value for ρ usually found in the literature is $\rho = 0.5$. As for ϕ, let us first compute the average duration of wage contracts: a contract has a probability $(1 - \phi)\phi^j$ to be in effect j periods after the initial date, so the average duration is

$$(1 - \phi) \sum_{j=0}^{\infty} j \phi^j = \frac{\phi}{1 - \phi} \tag{43}$$

The average duration of wage contracts is usually considered to be between one and two years. So two impulse responses are plotted in figures 10.1 and 10.2. Both use the value $\rho = 0.5$. Figure 10.1 takes $\phi = 8/9$ (which corresponds to a two-year, or 8 quarters, duration of contracts), while figure 10.2 takes $\phi = 4/5$ (which corresponds to a one-year duration of contracts).

We see that both response functions show persistence, and even display a hump that is more marked for the two-year contract case than for the one-year contract case. The response of output is easy to derive. From formulas (1) and (9) we obtain

$$y_t = \frac{(1 - \gamma)n_t}{1 - \gamma L} + \frac{z_t}{1 - \gamma L} + \frac{\gamma \log \beta \gamma}{1 - \gamma} \tag{44}$$

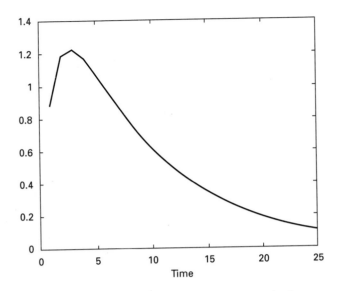

Figure 10.1   Employment IRF to a monetary shock

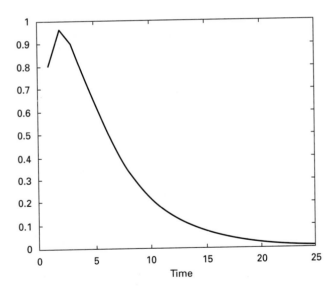

Figure 10.2   Employment IRF to a monetary shock

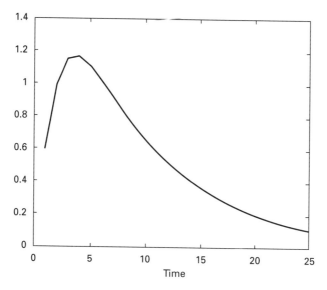

Figure 10.3 Output IRF to a monetary shock

Combining (44) with the expression for n_t (formula 41), we find

$$y_t = n + \Phi + \frac{(1 - \gamma)\phi u_t}{(1 - \gamma L)(1 - \phi L)(1 - \phi \rho L)} + \frac{z_t}{1 - \gamma L} + \frac{\gamma \log \beta \gamma}{1 - \gamma} \quad (45)$$

where the value of Φ is given in formula (42). The response of output to a monetary shock is displayed in figure 10.3 for the two-year contract case.[4]

10.5.2 The Hump

Formula (41) suggests, and figures 10.1 and 10.2 confirm, that the response of employment to a money shock may be first increasing, and then decreasing, giving thus rise to the "hump" that apparently characterizes the actual response of the economy to money shocks. We will make this more precise through the following proposition, which tells us under which conditions a

---

4 The expression of output response in the more general case of incomplete depreciation is computed in appendix 10.1.

hump will occur, as well as its timing:

Proposition 3 *Under the monetary process (40) there will be a hump in the response of employment to money if*

$$\phi > \frac{1}{1+\rho} \tag{46}$$

In that case the time at which the hump occurs is the integer $\hat{j}$ given by

$$\hat{j} < \frac{1}{\log \rho} \log \left(\frac{1-\phi}{1-\phi\rho} \right) < \hat{j} + 1 \tag{47}$$

Proof We saw above that up to a constant,

$$n_t = \frac{\phi u_t}{(1-\phi L)(1-\phi\rho L)} = \frac{\phi u_t}{1-\rho} \left[\frac{1}{1-\phi L} - \frac{\rho}{1-\phi\rho L} \right] \tag{48}$$

The term of order j is a multiple of

$$\phi^j - \rho(\phi\rho)^j \tag{49}$$

The hump will thus occur for the integer value j such that

$$\phi^{j-1} - \rho(\phi\rho)^{j-1} < \phi^j - \rho(\phi\rho)^j > \phi^{j+1} - \rho(\phi\rho)^{j+1} \tag{50}$$

These two inequalities are rewritten as

$$\rho^{j+1} < \frac{1-\phi}{1-\phi\rho} < \rho^j \tag{51}$$

Going to logarithms, (51) yields

$$j < \frac{1}{\log \rho} \log \left(\frac{1-\phi}{1-\phi\rho} \right) < j + 1 \tag{52}$$

which is equation (47). Now, for this to correspond to an actual hump, the value of j so obtained must be greater than one:

$$\frac{1}{\log \rho} \log \left(\frac{1 - \phi}{1 - \phi \rho} \right) > 1 \tag{53}$$

which yields equation (46). ∎

10.5.3 The Autocorrelations of Employment Variations

Another stylized fact that traditional models often fail to reproduce is the positive autocorrelations of output and employment variations, at least at short lags. We see, via the following proposition, that the model of this chapter enables us to reproduce this feature.

Proposition 4 *Denote by* $\Delta n_t = n_t - n_{t-1}$ *the variations in employment. Then these employment variations are autocorrelated in time according to the formula*

$$\text{cov}(\Delta n_t, \Delta n_{t-j}) = \left[\frac{a^2 \phi^j}{1 - \phi^2} + \frac{b^2 \zeta^j}{1 - \zeta^2} + \frac{ab(\phi^j + \zeta^j)}{1 - \phi \zeta} \right] \sigma_u^2 \tag{54}$$

where

$$\zeta = \phi \rho, \quad a = -\frac{1 - \phi}{1 - \rho}, \quad b = \frac{1 - \zeta}{1 - \rho} \tag{55}$$

Proof Appendix 10.3. ∎

Using formula (54), we can actually compute explicitly autocorrelations at various lags. The autocorrelation at lag one is relatively simple:

$$\text{corr}(\Delta n_t, \Delta n_{t-1}) = \frac{\phi + \phi \rho + \phi^2 \rho - 1}{2} \tag{56}$$

This autocorrelation is clearly positive for large enough ϕ and ρ. For greater lags, formulas become very rapidly clumsy, but the computer easily generates the autocorrelations profiles. Figure 10.4 depicts the autocorrelations of employment variations at various lags, for the same parameter values as in figure 10.1. We see that at low values of the lags, these autocorrelations are indeed positive.

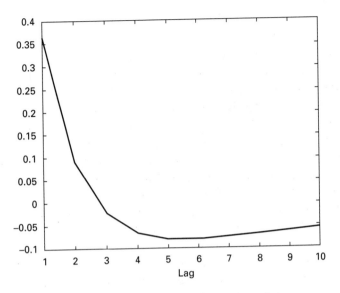

Figure 10.4   Employment variations autocorrelations

10.6   Conclusions

In this chapter we developed a new form of staggered wage contracts, close in spirit to those due to Calvo (1983). We explicitly modeled maximizing trade unions, and integrated these contracts into a rigorous business cycle model. We were able to obtain closed-form solutions throughout, for both the optimal wage contracts and the resulting macroeconomic dynamics. We found that we could generate a strong propagation mechanism and, in particular, produce a hump-shaped response of employment and output to monetary shocks, or positive autocorrelations of employment and output variations at short lags. These are features that have been observed in the data, and that traditional RBC models often have difficulties to reproduce.

From our closed-form solutions it appears also that the parameter ϕ describing the "survival rate" of contracts, which is the basis of Calvo's and our contract, is a central parameter in explaining the capacities of the model to create an endogenous propagation mechanism. In particular, most differences in the literature on this subject seem to boil down to different values in the (implicit or explicit) value of this parameter.

10.7 References

This chapter is based on Bénassy (2000), which develops the new contract used in this chapter. An earlier exploration of the same issues using Taylor contracts (which implicitly correspond to a value of ϕ equal to two thirds) is found in Ascari (2000). A comparison of price and wage contracts from the point of view of persistence is carried out in Andersen (1998).

A detailed empirical analysis of the effects of money shocks is carried out in Christiano, Eichenbaum, and Evans (1999, 2001). They show notably that the output response is persistent and hump-shaped. The latter paper also shows that wage staggering performs better than price staggering in explaining the data. Cogley and Nason (1995) examine notably whether various modifications of the standard RBC model can help to obtain a persistent and hump-shaped response of output and positive autocorrelations of output variations at short lags.

Calibrated dynamic general equilibrium models with various forms of staggered price or wage contracts are found in Chari, Kehoe, and McGrattan (2000), Collard and Ertz (2000), Jeannc (1998), and Yun (1996). These authors arrive at fairly different conclusions, but the model of this chapter allows one to easily interpret these differences.

Appendix 10.1: Incomplete Depreciation

We investigate here the case of incomplete capital depreciation. In order to obtain a closed-form solution, we use, as in appendix 9.1, a loglinearized approximation of the capital accumulation equation:

$$K_{t+1} = A K_t^{1-\delta} I_t^{\delta} \tag{57}$$

As it turns out, many important elements of the solution are the same. In particular, the Walrasian equilibria are identical. Moreover, in the case of wage contracts, which we will study here, the investment equation is the same:

$$I_t = \sigma Y_t, \quad \sigma = \frac{\beta \gamma \delta}{1 - \beta + \beta \delta} \tag{58}$$

Combining (58) with equations (1) and (57), we find that output is given by

$$y_t = \frac{[1 - (1 - \delta)L][z_t + (1 - \gamma)n_t]}{1 - (1 - \delta + \gamma \delta)L} + \frac{\gamma \delta \log \sigma + \gamma \log A}{\delta(1 - \gamma)} \tag{59}$$

which replaces equation (44) in the main text. We can insert into (59) the value of n_t found in (41), which turns out to be also valid here. This yields the final expression for output:

$$y_t = n + \Phi + \frac{[1 - (1 - \delta)L](1 - \gamma)\phi u_t}{[1 - (1 - \delta + \gamma\delta)L](1 - \phi L)(1 - \phi\rho L)}$$

$$+ \frac{[1 - (1 - \delta)L]z_t}{1 - (1 - \delta + \gamma\delta)L} + \frac{\gamma\delta\log\sigma + \gamma\log A}{\delta(1 - \gamma)} \qquad (60)$$

which generalizes equation (45) in the main text.

Appendix 10.2: Aggregation across Output Types

We briefly indicate here how the analysis of chapter 10 has to be modified when the aggregation across sectors and firms takes place on output types, instead of taking place on labor types as in the main body of the chapter.

There are thus, as in chapter 10, sectors indexed by i, themselves composed of firms indexed by k. The output index Y_t is an aggregate of a continuum of output types, indexed by $i \in [0, 1]$:

$$\log Y_t = \int_0^1 \log Y_{it}\, di \qquad (61)$$

The sectoral index Y_{it} is itself the aggregate of another infinity of output types indexed by k:

$$Y_{it} = \left(\int_0^1 Y_{ikt}^\theta\, dk \right)^{1/\theta} \qquad (62)$$

Again, all firms with the same index i face exactly the same situation in terms of wage contracts, and notably negotiate at the same time. Firms have the same Cobb-Douglas technology:

$$Y_{ikt} = Z_t K_{ikt}^\gamma N_{ikt}^{1-\gamma}, \qquad (63)$$

where K_{ikt} is capital, N_{ikt} is the quantity of labor used in production, and Z_t is a common stochastic technology shock.

The representative household is exactly the same, so we omit its description. The Walrasian equilibrium is characterized by the same equations (7) to (13).

In particular, the Walrasian wage is

$$W_t^* = \frac{(1-\beta)(1-\gamma)}{(1-\beta\gamma)\omega} \left[\frac{\xi(1-\beta\gamma)}{1-\gamma} \right]^{1/\nu} M_t \tag{64}$$

The Demand for Labor

Labor demand will here directly derive from the demand for goods. Using the same method as in the main text, we find that the sectoral and firm demands are

$$Y_{it} = \frac{P_t Y_t}{P_{it}} \tag{65}$$

$$Y_{ikt} = Y_{it} \left(\frac{P_{ikt}}{P_{it}} \right)^{-1/(1-\theta)} \tag{66}$$

where the price indexes P_t and P_{it} are given by:

$$\log P_t = \int_0^1 \log P_{it} \, di \tag{67}$$

$$P_{it} = \left(\int_0^1 P_{ikt}^{-\theta/(1-\theta)} \, dk \right)^{-(1-\theta)/\theta} \tag{68}$$

Combining (65) and (66), we find the following expression for the demand for goods addressed to firm k in sector i:

$$Y_{ikt} = \frac{P_t Y_t}{P_{it}} \left(\frac{P_{ikt}}{P_{it}} \right)^{-1/(1-\theta)} \tag{69}$$

Firm (i, k) competitively maximizes profits $P_{ikt} Y_{ikt} - W_{ikt} N_{ikt} - R_t K_{ikt}$, taking P_{ikt}, W_{ikt}, and R_t as exogenous, where R_t is the nominal return on capital. This yields the usual first-order conditions:

$$W_{ikt} N_{ikt} = (1-\gamma) P_{ikt} Y_{ikt} \tag{70}$$

$$R_t K_{ikt} = \gamma P_{ikt} Y_{ikt} \tag{71}$$

Combining these two equations with the production function (63) and the equation of demand for goods (69), we obtain the final expression for the demand for labor in firm (i, k):

$$N_{ikt} = \Omega_{it} W_{ikt}^{-(1-\gamma\theta)/(1-\theta)} \tag{72}$$

$$\Omega_{it} = \left[\gamma^{\gamma\theta}(1-\gamma)^{1-\gamma\theta} R_t^{-\gamma\theta}(P_t Y_t)^{1-\theta} P_{it}^{\theta} Z_t^{\theta}\right]^{1/(1-\theta)} \tag{73}$$

Wage Contracts

We continue to assume the particular disutility of labor:

$$V(N_t) = \frac{\xi N_t^{\nu}}{\nu} \tag{74}$$

Using the same method as in proposition 1, we find that the optimal wage contracts are given by the following formula, which replaces formula (21) in the text:

$$X_{ts} = \frac{(1-\beta)(1-\gamma)}{(1-\beta\gamma)\omega} \left[\frac{\xi(1-\gamma\theta)(1-\beta\gamma)}{\theta(1-\gamma)^2}\right]^{1/\nu} [E_t M_s^{\nu}]^{1/\nu} \tag{75}$$

We can actually give a more intuitive presentation of formula (75). Using (64), it can indeed be rewritten as

$$X_{ts}^{\nu} = \frac{1-\gamma\theta}{\theta(1-\gamma)} E_t [W_s^*]^{\nu} \tag{76}$$

This formula is easy to interpret. Call ε the absolute value of the elasticity of the demand for labor. From formula (72), $\varepsilon = (1-\gamma\theta)/(1-\theta)$. The associated markup factor is therefore, according to the usual formula in monopolistic competition,

$$\frac{\varepsilon - 1}{\varepsilon} = \frac{1-\gamma\theta}{\theta(1-\gamma)} \tag{77}$$

We thus see that X_{ts}^{ν} is equal to the expected value in t of $[W_s^*]^{\nu}$ multiplied by the monopolistic markup.

Now using the same methods as in appendix 10.3, we find that employment is given by the formulas

$$n_t = n + \frac{\phi u_t}{(1 - \phi L)(1 - \phi \rho L)} + \Phi \tag{78}$$

$$\Phi = \frac{1}{\nu} \log \left[\frac{\theta(1 - \gamma)}{1 - \gamma \theta} \right] - \frac{(1 + \phi \rho) \phi \nu \sigma^2}{2(1 - \phi \rho)(1 - \phi \rho^2)(1 - \phi)} \tag{79}$$

We see that, except for the first part of the constant Φ, things are exactly the same as in the main body of the chapter, and we will thus not repeat the corresponding analysis.

Appendix 10.3: Proofs of Propositions 2 and 4

Proof of Proposition 2

We first want to compute the value of the aggregate wage, as given by equation (39):

$$w_t = \log W_t = (1 - \phi) \sum_{s=-\infty}^{t} \phi^{t-s} \log X_{st} \tag{80}$$

Using formula (21) giving the value of newly negotiated wages, this yields

$$w_t = \frac{1}{\nu} \log \left[\frac{\xi(1 - \beta \gamma)}{\theta(1 - \gamma)} \right] + \log \left[\frac{(1 - \gamma)(1 - \beta)}{\omega(1 - \beta \gamma)} \right]$$
$$+ (1 - \phi) \sum_{s=-\infty}^{t} \phi^{t-s} \frac{\log \left[E_s \, M_t^\nu \right]}{\nu} \tag{81}$$

Let us make the change of variable $j = t - s$. The formula above becomes

$$w_t = \frac{1}{\nu} \log \left[\frac{\xi(1 - \beta \gamma)}{\theta(1 - \gamma)} \right] + \log \left[\frac{(1 - \gamma)(1 - \beta)}{\omega(1 - \beta \gamma)} \right]$$
$$+ (1 - \phi) \sum_{j=0}^{\infty} \phi^j \log \left[E_{t-j} \, M_t^\nu \right]^{1/\nu} \tag{82}$$

Since the monetary variables are lognormal, we use the standard formula:

$$\log\left[E_{t-j}\left(M_t^\nu\right)\right]^{1/\nu} = E_{t-j}(m_t) + \nu\frac{\text{var}_{t-j}(m_t)}{2} \tag{83}$$

with

$$m_t = m_{t-j} + \frac{u_{t-j+1}}{1-\rho L} + \cdots + \frac{u_t}{1-\rho L} \tag{84}$$

Let us compute in turn the mean and variance:

$$E_{t-j}m_t = m_{t-j} + \frac{\rho u_{t-j}}{1-\rho L} + \cdots + \frac{\rho^j u_{t-j}}{1-\rho L} = m_{t-j} + \frac{\rho(1-\rho^j)u_{t-j}}{(1-\rho)(1-\rho L)} \tag{85}$$

$$m_t - E_{t-j}m_t = (1 + \cdots + \rho^{j-1})u_{t-j+1} + (1 + \cdots + \rho^{j-2})u_{t-j+2} + \cdots + u_t$$
$$= \frac{1-\rho^j}{1-\rho}u_{t-j+1} + \frac{1-\rho^{j-1}}{1-\rho}u_{t-j+2} + \cdots + u_t \tag{86}$$

$$\text{var}_{t-j}(m_t) = \sigma^2\left[\left(\frac{1-\rho^j}{1-\rho}\right)^2 + \left(\frac{1-\rho^{j-1}}{1-\rho}\right)^2 + \cdots + 1\right]$$
$$= \frac{\sigma^2}{(1-\rho)^2}\left[j - \frac{2\rho(1-\rho^j)}{1-\rho} + \frac{\rho^2(1-\rho^{2j})}{1-\rho^2}\right] \tag{87}$$

Combining (83), (85), and (87), we obtain

$$\log\left[E_{t-j}\left(M_t^\nu\right)\right]^{1/\nu} = m_{t-j} + \frac{\rho(1-\rho^j)u_{t-j}}{(1-\rho)(1-\rho L)}$$
$$+ \frac{\nu\sigma^2}{2(1-\rho)^2}\left[j - \frac{2\rho(1-\rho^j)}{1-\rho} + \frac{\rho^2(1-\rho^{2j})}{1-\rho^2}\right] \tag{88}$$

Inserting (88) into (82), we find that the wage is equal to

$$w_t = (1 - \phi) \sum_{j=0}^{\infty} \phi^j \left[m_{t-j} + \frac{\rho(1 - \rho^j)u_{t-j}}{(1 - \rho)(1 - \rho L)} \right]$$

$$+ (1 - \phi) \sum_{j=0}^{\infty} \phi^j \frac{v\sigma^2}{2(1 - \rho)^2} \left[j - \frac{2\rho(1 - \rho^j)}{1 - \rho} + \frac{\rho^2(1 - \rho^{2j})}{1 - \rho^2} \right]$$

$$+ \frac{1}{v} \log \left[\frac{\xi(1 - \beta\gamma)}{\theta(1 - \gamma)} \right] + \log \left[\frac{(1 - \gamma)(1 - \beta)}{\omega(1 - \beta\gamma)} \right] \tag{89}$$

We compute separately the first and second terms:

$$(1 - \phi) \sum_{j=0}^{\infty} \phi^j \left[m_{t-j} + \frac{\rho(1 - \rho^j)u_{t-j}}{(1 - \rho)(1 - \rho L)} \right] = m_t - \frac{\phi u_t}{(1 - \phi L)(1 - \phi\rho L)} \tag{90}$$

$$(1 - \phi) \sum_{j=0}^{\infty} \phi^j \frac{v\sigma^2}{2(1 - \rho)^2} \left[j - \frac{2\rho(1 - \rho^j)}{1 - \rho} + \frac{\rho^2(1 - \rho^{2j})}{1 - \rho^2} \right]$$

$$= \frac{(1 + \phi\rho)\phi v\sigma^2}{2(1 - \phi\rho)(1 - \phi\rho^2)(1 - \phi)} \tag{91}$$

Finally, after inserting (90) and (91) into (89), we find the wage:

$$w_t = m_t - \frac{\phi u_t}{(1 - \phi L)(1 - \phi\rho L)} + \frac{(1 + \phi\rho)\phi v\sigma^2}{2(1 - \phi\rho)(1 - \phi\rho^2)(1 - \phi)}$$

$$+ \frac{1}{v} \log \frac{\xi(1 - \beta\gamma)}{\theta(1 - \gamma)} + \log \frac{(1 - \gamma)(1 - \beta)}{\omega(1 - \beta\gamma)} \tag{92}$$

To compute employment, we have, from formulas (7), (8), and (10),

$$n_t = m_t - w_t + \log \frac{(1 - \gamma)(1 - \beta)}{\omega(1 - \beta\gamma)} \tag{93}$$

Also from formula (13) we have Walrasian employment:

$$n = \frac{1}{v} \log \frac{1 - \gamma}{\xi(1 - \beta\gamma)} \tag{94}$$

Combining (92), (93), and (94), we obtain the final expression for employment:

$$n_t = n + \frac{\phi u_t}{(1 - \phi L)(1 - \phi\rho L)} + \frac{\log\theta}{v} - \frac{(1 + \phi\rho)\phi v\sigma^2}{2(1 - \phi)(1 - \phi\rho)(1 - \phi\rho^2)} \tag{95}$$

■

Proof of Proposition 4

We saw above (formula 41) that employment is given, up to a constant, by

$$n_t = \frac{\phi u_t}{(1 - \phi L)(1 - \phi\rho L)} \tag{96}$$

Consequently employment variations Δn_t are given by

$$\Delta n_t = \frac{\phi(1 - L)u_t}{(1 - \phi L)(1 - \phi\rho L)} = \frac{1 - \phi\rho}{1 - \rho}\frac{u_t}{1 - \phi\rho L} - \frac{1 - \phi}{1 - \rho}\frac{u_t}{1 - \phi L} \tag{97}$$

which is of the form

$$\Delta n_t = \left[\frac{a}{1 - \phi L} + \frac{b}{1 - \zeta L}\right]u_t \tag{98}$$

with

$$\zeta = \phi\rho, \quad a = -\frac{1 - \phi}{1 - \rho}, \quad b = \frac{1 - \zeta}{1 - \rho} \tag{99}$$

So

$$\Delta n_t = a\sum_{i=0}^{\infty}\phi^i u_{t-i} + b\sum_{i=0}^{\infty}\zeta^i u_{t-i} \tag{100}$$

and hence

$$\Delta n_{t-j} = a\sum_{i=0}^{\infty}\phi^i u_{t-j-i} + b\sum_{i=0}^{\infty}\zeta^i u_{t-j-i} \tag{101}$$

To compute the covariance between Δn_t and Δn_{t-j}, we rewrite Δn_t, omitting all shocks with a lag below j, since these will be uncorrelated with Δn_{t-j}:

$$\Delta n_t = a \sum_{k=j} \phi^k u_{t-k} + b \sum_{k=j} \zeta^k u_{t-k} \tag{102}$$

Take $k = i + j$:

$$\Delta n_t = a\phi^j \sum_{i=0}^{\infty} \phi^i u_{t-j-i} + b\zeta^j \sum_{i=0}^{\infty} \zeta^i u_{t-j-i} \tag{103}$$

Putting together formulas (101) and (103), we obtain

$$\text{cov}(\Delta n_t, \Delta n_{t-j}) = \frac{a^2 \phi^j}{1 - \phi^2} + \frac{b^2 \zeta^j}{1 - \zeta^2} + \frac{ab(\phi^j + \zeta^j)}{1 - \phi\zeta} \tag{104}$$

∎

11

Market Power, Voluntary Exchange, and Unemployment Fluctuations

11.1 Introduction

In the two preceding chapters we made the assumption, traditional in macro-economic models of Keynesian inspiration, that whenever there is a discrepancy between demand and supply, demand is always satisfied and suppliers adjust their supplies. Although this assumption has a long tradition, it is clearly a simplification, as it violates the hypothesis of voluntary exchange that we encountered, in particular, in chapters 1 to 3.

The reader may thus legitimately inquire how results will be modified if this simplification is abandoned. What we will do in this chapter is to construct a model where wages are set in advance by trade unions maximizing the expected utility of the workers they represent in a framework of monopolistic competition between firms, and where the assumption of voluntary exchange is satisfied.

As we will see, this modification automatically introduces a nonlinearity in employment determination. As it turns out, several authors have found such nonlinearities in macroeconomic series, and notably in the employment series. Thus the model of this chapter gives us a very natural formalization of these nonlinearities, which themselves have interesting consequences. For example, we will find that a higher variance of shocks induces a higher average level of unemployment.

11.2   The Model

We consider an overlapping generations model. All households have the same utility function, which is, for the household born at time t:

$$U_t = \alpha \log C_t + (1 - \alpha) \log C'_{t+1} \tag{1}$$

where C_t is consumption when young and C'_{t+1} consumption when old. Consumption goods are produced by competitive firms using intermediate goods indexed by $j \in [0, 1]$, with production function:

$$Y_t = \left(\int_0^1 Y_{jt}^\theta \, dj \right)^{1/\theta} \tag{2}$$

The intermediate goods $j \in [0, 1]$ are produced by monopolistically competitive firms with production functions:

$$Y_{jt} = Z_t N_{jt}^\nu \tag{3}$$

where Z_t is a technology shock common to all firms j.

   To simplify some of the calculations, it is convenient to separate again households, as in chapter 5, between workers and capitalists. The profits of the intermediate firms are distributed to the young capitalists. Young workers supply a fixed quantity of labor, and they are allocated uniformly between the intermediate goods sectors, so that the labor supply in each sector j is fixed and equal to N_0.

11.3   Equilibrium with Flexible Wages

As a benchmark we first solve the model for the case where wages are set at the same time the other markets are held, meaning when the values of the shocks are known. Presetting and nominal rigidity will be studied in the next section.

11.3.1   Households and Aggregate Demand

Let us denote by M_t the quantity of money in the economy. This money is entirely in the hands of the old households who spend all of it so that

$$C'_t = \frac{M_t}{P_t} \tag{4}$$

In view of the utility function (1), the young households, whether workers or capitalists, spend a fraction α of their income. Since their total real income is equal to Y_t, we have

$$C_t = \alpha Y_t \tag{5}$$

Now, since the goods market always clears, we have $Y_t = C_t + C'_t$, which, together with (4) and (5), yields

$$Y_t = \frac{M_t}{(1 - \alpha) P_t} \tag{6}$$

11.3.2   Final Goods Firms

The competitive final goods firms maximize their profits:

$$P_t \left(\int_0^1 Y_{jt}^\theta \, dj \right)^{1/\theta} - \int_0^1 P_{jt} Y_{jt} \, dj \tag{7}$$

This gives the following demand for intermediate j:

$$Y_{jt} = Y_t \left(\frac{P_{jt}}{P_t} \right)^{-1/(1-\theta)} \tag{8}$$

where the aggregate price index P_t is given by the usual CES formula:

$$P_t = \left(\int_0^1 P_{jt}^{-\theta/(1-\theta)} \, dj \right)^{-(1-\theta)/\theta} \tag{9}$$

11.3.3   Intermediate Goods Firms

The intermediate firm j maximizes profits subject to the production function (3) and the demand function (8). It solves the following program:

$$\max P_{jt} Y_{jt} - W_{jt} N_{jt} \quad \text{s.t.}$$

$$Y_{jt} = Z_t N_{jt}^\nu$$

$$Y_{jt} \le Y_t \left(\frac{P_{jt}}{P_t} \right)^{-1/(1-\theta)}$$

The solution yields, in particular, firm j's demand for labor:

$$N_{jt} = \left(\frac{\theta v P_t Z_t^\theta Y_t^{1-\theta}}{W_{jt}} \right)^{1/(1-\theta v)}$$

(10)

11.3.4 Trade Unions

In view of utility function (1) the utility of a worker in firm j is equal, up to a constant, to $\log(W_{jt} N_{jt} / P_t)$. So, in setting the wage W_{jt}, the trade union in firm j maximizes the value of this utility, subject to the demand for labor (10) and a maximal labor supply N_0. It solves the program

$$\max \log \left(\frac{W_{jt} N_{jt}}{P_t} \right) \quad \text{s.t.}$$

$$N_{jt} \leq \left(\frac{\theta v P_t Z_t^\theta Y_t^{1-\theta}}{W_{jt}} \right)^{1/(1-\theta v)}$$

$$N_{jt} \leq N_0$$

Since, in view of equation (10), $W_{jt} N_{jt} / P_t$ is increasing in N_{jt}, and since there is no disutility of employment below N_0, the trade union will always choose a value of the wage W_{jt} such that $N_{jt} = N_0$, that is, in view of equation (10),

$$W_{jt} = \theta v P_t Z_t^\theta Y_t^{1-\theta} N_0^{\theta v - 1}$$

(11)

We note that this value does not depend on j, so all trade unions will set the same wage, denoted as W_t.

11.3.5 Macroeconomic Equilibrium

The macroeconomic equilibrium will thus be described by

$$N_{jt} = N_0 \quad \forall j$$

(12)

$$Y_t = Z_t N_0^v$$

(13)

Combining equations (6), (11), (12), and (13), we obtain simple expressions for the nominal and real wage:

$$W_t = \frac{\theta \nu M_t}{(1-\alpha)N_0} \tag{14}$$

$$\frac{W_t}{P_t} = \theta \nu Z_t N_0^{\nu-1} \tag{15}$$

11.4   Preset Wages

We assume that wages are set by trade unions at the beginning of each period, and this without knowing the value of the shocks. In order to characterize the resulting dynamic equilibrium, let us denote by $\Phi(m_t)$ the cumulative density function for money at time t. The equilibrium is described by the following proposition:

Proposition 1   *The wage and employment strategies of trade unions in the various sectors j are given by*

$$w_{jt} = w_t, \quad n_{jt} = n_t, \qquad \forall j \tag{16}$$

$$w_t = \overline{\omega}_t - n_0 + \log \theta \nu - \log(1-\alpha) \tag{17}$$

$$n_t = n_0 + \min(0, m_t - \overline{\omega}_t) \tag{18}$$

where $\overline{\omega}_t$, a threshold value for the money shock, is defined by

$$\Phi(\overline{\omega}_t) = 1 - \theta \nu \tag{19}$$

Proof   Part of the analysis carried for the case of flexible wages remains valid here, and in particular, the demand for labor in firm j is that given by (10). Of course, because wages are preset, this demand may exceed the supply N_0. So the actual transaction will be

$$N_{jt} = \min\left[N_0, \left(\frac{\theta \nu P_t Z_t^\theta Y_t^{1-\theta}}{W_{jt}} \right)^{1/(1-\theta\nu)} \right] \tag{20}$$

Now let us define an aggregate index of labor:[1]

$$N_t = \left(\int_0^1 N_{jt}^{\theta v} \right)^{1/\theta v} \tag{21}$$

It is easy to compute by combining (2), (3), and (21):

$$Y_t = Z_t N_t^v \tag{22}$$

Putting together (6) and (22), we obtain

$$P_t Z_t^\theta Y_t^{1-\theta} = \frac{M_t N_t^{-\theta v}}{1 - \alpha} \tag{23}$$

and formula (20) becomes

$$N_{jt} = \min \left\{ N_0, \left[\frac{\theta v M_t N_t^{-\theta v}}{(1 - \alpha) W_{jt}} \right]^{1/(1-\theta v)} \right\} \tag{24}$$

Let us denote by $\Psi(M_t)$ the solution in N_t to the system of equations (21) and (24), or in logarithmic terms,

$$n_t = \psi(m_t) \tag{25}$$

In logarithms, equation (2) becomes

$$(1 - \theta v)n_{jt} = \min[(1 - \theta v)n_0, m_t - \theta v \psi(m_t) - w_{jt} + \log \theta v - \log(1 - \alpha)] \tag{26}$$

We denote by $\overline{\omega}_{jt}$ the threshold value of m_t at which the demand for labor in firm j is exactly equal to n_0. From formula (26) we immediately obtain

$$(1 - \theta v)n_0 = \overline{\omega}_{jt} - \theta v \psi(\overline{\omega}_{jt}) - w_{jt} + \log \theta v - \log(1 - \alpha) \tag{27}$$

Next we compute the union's objective $E(w_{jt} + n_{jt} - p_t)$ in the two regimes. We take $\overline{\omega}_{jt}$ as our working variable, because, as we will see below, the condition giving the optimal $\overline{\omega}_{jt}$ is particularly simple.

---

1 At this stage N_t is only a convenient intermediate variable for calculations. In symmetric equilibrium it will be, of course, equal to employment.

From equation (27) we compute the value of the wage in sector j:

$$w_{jt} = \overline{\omega}_{jt} - \theta v \psi(\overline{\omega}_{jt}) + \log \theta v - \log(1 - \alpha) - (1 - \theta v)n_0 \qquad (28)$$

Combining (6), (22), and (25), we obtain the value of the aggregate price:

$$p_t = m_t - v\psi(m_t) - z_t - \log(1 - \alpha) \qquad (29)$$

The two possible values of n_{jt} are given in equation (26), which becomes, after taking into account the value of w_{jt} in (28),

$$n_{jt} = n_0 + \min \left[0, \frac{m_t - \theta v \psi(m_t) - \overline{\omega}_{jt} + \theta v \psi(\overline{\omega}_{jt})}{1 - \theta v}\right] \qquad (30)$$

Combining (28), (29), and (30), we find that the value of the trade union's maximand $E(w_{jt} + n_{jt} - p_t)$ is, denoting by $\phi(m_t)$ the density function of the logarithm of money,

$$
\begin{aligned}
&E(w_{jt} + n_{jt} - p_t) \\
&= Ez_t + \int_{\overline{\omega}_{jt}}^{\infty} [\overline{\omega}_{jt} - \theta v \psi(\overline{\omega}_{jt})]\phi(m_t)\, dm_t \\
&\quad + \int_{-\infty}^{\overline{\omega}_{jt}} \left[\frac{m_t - \theta v \psi(m_t) - \theta v \overline{\omega}_{jt} + \theta^2 v^2 \psi(\overline{\omega}_{jt})}{1 - \theta v}\right] \phi(m_t)\, dm_t \\
&\quad + \int_{-\infty}^{+\infty} \left[v\psi(m_t) - m_t + \log \theta v + \theta v n_0\right] \phi(m_t)\, dm_t
\end{aligned}
\qquad (31)
$$

We can differentiate this with respect to $\overline{\omega}_{jt}$, and we obtain the first-order condition:

$$[1 - \theta v \psi'(\overline{\omega}_{jt})]\left[\int_{\overline{\omega}_{jt}}^{\infty} \phi(m_t)\, dm_t - \frac{\theta v}{1 - \theta v} \int_{-\infty}^{\overline{\omega}_{jt}} \phi(m_t)\, dm_t\right] = 0 \qquad (32)$$

It is easy to check, using formulas (21) and (24), that the derivative of ψ is between zero and one[2] so that the first bracket can be ignored. Hence equation (32)

2 Actually ψ has a discontinuous derivative at some points, so at these points the statement applies to the left and right derivatives.

can be rewritten as

$$(1 - \theta v)[1 - \Phi(\overline{\omega}_{jt})] - \theta v \Phi(\overline{\omega}_{jt}) = 0 \tag{33}$$

where, we recall, Φ is the cumulative distribution of m_t. This yields immediately the condition giving the optimal $\overline{\omega}_{jt}$:

$$\Phi(\overline{\omega}_{jt}) = 1 - \theta v \tag{34}$$

We see that all sectors will choose the same $\overline{\omega}_{jt}$, which we denote $\overline{\omega}_t$. This yields equation (19). Second, recall from the definition of $\overline{\omega}_{jt}$ that $\psi(\overline{\omega}_{jt}) = n_0$, so equation (28) with a uniform $\overline{\omega}_t$ gives equation (17). Finally, from equation (24) with a uniform wage, we obtain

$$n_t = \min[n_0, m_t - w_t + \log \theta v - \log(1 - \alpha)] \tag{35}$$

which, combined with (17), yields (18).   ∎

We see that the wage policy of the trade unions is particularly simple: trade unions choose a value of the wage such that the probability of being in the unemployment regime is $1 - \theta v$. This probability is also the probability that the demand for labor is served. That is to say, the less competitive the labor market (i.e., the lower the θ), the higher is the probability that demand is served on the market considered. In appendix 11.1 we further study this issue for a market with a storable good.

11.5 Macroeconomic Equilibrium

We want to study the macroeconomic equilibrium with a particular distribution of money shocks. Let us assume that m_t is uniformly distributed on the interval $[-\sigma, \sigma]^3$ so that the density $\phi(m_t) = 1/2\sigma$ on this interval. Employment is given by

$$n_{jt} - n_0 = \min(0, m_t - \varpi_t) \tag{36}$$

3 A nonzero mean for m_t yields exactly the same final results. Note that the variance of money for this uniform distribution is $\sigma^2/3$.

A good approximate indicator of unemployment is

$$E(n_0 - n_t) = \int_{-\infty}^{\overline{\omega}_t} (\overline{\omega}_t - m_t)\phi(m_t)\, dm_t \tag{37}$$

It is easy to compute for the uniform distribution above that $\overline{\omega}_t = (1 - 2\theta v)\sigma$, so

$$E(n_0 - n_t) = \int_{-\sigma}^{\overline{\omega}_t} (\overline{\omega}_t - m_t)\frac{1}{2\sigma}\, dm_t = \frac{1}{2\sigma}\left[\overline{\omega}_t m_t - \frac{m_t^2}{2}\right]_{-\sigma}^{\overline{\omega}_t} \tag{38}$$

$$E(n_0 - n_t) = (1 - \theta v)^2 \sigma \tag{39}$$

We see that the indicator of average unemployment increases with the dispersion of money shocks. We can do a similar computation for the absolute level of employment:

$$N_t = N_0 \min[1, \exp(m_t - \overline{\omega}_t)] \tag{40}$$

The expected value of the unemployment rate $(N_0 - N_t)/N_0$ is

$$E\left(\frac{N_0 - N_t}{N_0}\right) = \int_{-\sigma}^{\overline{\omega}_t} [1 - \exp(m_t - \overline{\omega}_t)]\frac{1}{2\sigma}\, dm_t$$

$$= 1 - \theta v + \frac{\exp[-2(1-\theta v)\sigma] - 1}{2\sigma} \tag{41}$$

We can further compute how expected unemployment varies with the dispersion of monetary shocks. Let us call $\chi = 2(1 - \theta v)\sigma$. Then

$$\frac{\partial}{\partial \sigma}E\left(\frac{N_0 - N_t}{N_0}\right) = \frac{1 - e^{-\chi} - \chi e^{-\chi}}{2\sigma^2} > 0 \tag{42}$$

Hence both (39) and (42) show that the average rate of unemployment increases with the variance of money shocks.

11.6 Conclusions

We developed in this chapter a simple dynamic model where trade unions rationally set wages under the assumption of voluntary exchange. We saw that in such a case price (or wage) setters will rationally choose a price such that contrary to the usual assumption, the agents on the other side are rationed with some positive probability. This probability depends notably on the market power of the price setting agents. The appendix also shows that storability plays an important role.

Another immediate consequence of introducing voluntary exchange is to introduce asymmetries and nonlinearities. Since such nonlinearities have been observed in the data by a number of authors, this seems to be a particularly natural and realistic way to obtain them.

11.7   References

This chapter is based on Bénassy (1995b). An early dynamic stochastic model with voluntary exchange and imperfectly competitive price setting is Svensson (1986).

The relation between shocks' variability and the mean levels of employment and output is stressed in Portier and Puch (2000). The nonlinearity of various macroeconomic series, and notably, as is the case here, of employment and output series, has been documented by several authors, including Neftci (1984), Rothman (1991), Acemoglu and Scott (1994), Altug, Ashley, and Patterson (1999), and Koop and Potter (1999).

The inventory problem in the appendix has been treated by, among many others, Mills (1962), Zabel (1972), and Bénassy (1982).

Appendix 11.1: Storability and the Probability of Rationing

We show here in a purely microeconomic model why the probability of rationing the consumers is much smaller in the market for a storable good than for a nonstorable good like labor, and therefore why the "traditional" assumption that demand is always served is more likely to be satisfied in that case.

Let us consider a firm that can produce a storable good at a unitary cost c. Let us denote by P_t the price of the good which is set by the firm, by Q_t the production, by D_t the demand, and by I_t the inventory that the firm holds at the beginning of the period. We assume that the firm must decide its production before the demand is known, hence the utility of having inventories. Sales are the minimum of demand and supply, where supply includes both current production and the inventories already available:

$$S_t = \min(Q_t + I_t, D_t) \tag{43}$$

Now inventories deteriorate at the rate $1 - \varphi$. So the next period inventories are given by

$$I_{t+1} = \varphi(Q_t + I_t - S_t) \tag{44}$$

We assume that the demand function is stochastic, with a multiplicative random term:

$$D_t = \xi_t g(P_t) \tag{45}$$

where the ξ_t are iid stochastic variables with a probability density $\phi(\xi_t)$ and a cumulative density function $\Phi(\xi_t)$. The firm maximizes discounted profits:

$$\max E_0 \left\{ \sum_{t=0}^{\infty} \beta^t (P_t S_t - cQ_t) \right\} \tag{46}$$

Resolution

We will solve the problem using the traditional methods of dynamic programming. For that we construct a valuation function for inventories, denoted $V(I)$. To find the recursive equation characterizing $V(I)$, we note that the firm can be in one of two regimes: excess supply where transactions are equal to demand $\xi_t g(P_t)$, or excess demand where transactions are equal to supply $Q_t + I_t$. The transition occurs for a value of the stochastic shock ξ_t such that the two are equal:

$$\xi_t = \frac{Q_t + I_t}{g(P_t)} \tag{47}$$

As a consequence $V(I)$ is characterized by the following recursive equation (we omit the time index since the problem is stationary):

$$V(I) = \max \left\{ \int_0^{(Q+I)/g(P)} [P\xi g(P) + \beta V(\varphi[Q + I - \xi g(P)])]\phi(\xi)\,d\xi \right.$$
$$\left. + \int_{(Q+I)/g(P)}^{\infty} [P(Q + I) + \beta V(0)]\phi(\xi)\,d\xi - cQ \right\} \tag{48}$$

Assuming an interior solution in P and Q, which means that I is small enough for current production to be positive, we obtain the optimal price-production strategy by equating to zero the partial derivatives of the right-hand side of (48) with respect to P and Q. This yields the two equations:

$$\int_0^{(Q+I)/g(P)} [g(P) + Pg'(P) - \beta\varphi g'(P)V'(\varphi[Q + I - \xi g(P)])]\xi\phi(\xi)\,d\xi$$

$$+ \int_{(Q+I)/g(P)}^{\infty} (Q + I)\phi(\xi)\,d\xi = 0 \tag{49}$$

$$\int_0^{(Q+I)/g(P)} \beta\gamma V'(\varphi[Q + I - \xi g(P)])\phi(\xi)\,d\xi + \int_{(Q+I)/g(P)}^{\infty} P\phi(\xi)\,d\xi - c = 0$$

$$\tag{50}$$

We note immediately that these two equations are actually equations in $Q + I$ and P. This means that for I smaller than a threshold value $\hat{I}$ (which we will assume henceforth), the optimal price is independent of I while the optimal production is given by

$$Q = \hat{I} - I \tag{51}$$

Inserting this optimal strategy into equation (48), we find that $V'(I) = c$ for all $I \leq \hat{I}$. We then introduce this value into equations (49) and (50) and obtain the following two equations, which determine the optimal P and $\hat{I}$:

$$\int_0^{\hat{I}/g(P)} [g(P) + Pg'(P) - \beta\varphi cg'(P)]\xi\phi(\xi)\,d\xi + \int_{\hat{I}/g(P)}^{\infty} \hat{I}\phi(\xi)\,d\xi = 0 \tag{52}$$

$$\int_0^{\hat{I}/g(P)} \beta\varphi c\phi(\xi)\,d\xi + \int_{\hat{I}/g(P)}^{\infty} P\phi(\xi)\,d\xi - c = 0 \tag{53}$$

Equation (53) can be rewritten more simply, using the cumulative density function Φ:

$$\Phi\left[\frac{\hat{I}}{g(P)}\right] = \frac{P - c}{P - \beta\varphi c} \tag{54}$$

The probability that demanders be rationed is thus

$$1 - \Phi\left[\frac{\hat{I}}{g(P)}\right] = 1 - \frac{P - c}{P - \beta\varphi c} = \frac{(1 - \beta\varphi)c}{P - \beta\varphi c} \tag{55}$$

Of course, this is not the end of the story, since P is an endogenous variable. To obtain an effective bound on the probability of rationing, let us assume, as in the text of the chapter, an isoelastic demand curve:

$$g(P) = P^{-1/(1-\theta)} \tag{56}$$

Under this parameterization, equation (52) is rewritten as

$$\int_0^{\hat{\xi}} (\beta\varphi c - \theta P)\xi\phi(\xi)\,d\xi + \int_{\hat{\xi}}^{\infty} (1-\theta)P\hat{\xi}\phi(\xi)\,d\xi = 0 \tag{57}$$

where $\hat{\xi} = \hat{I}/g(P)$. Since $\xi \leq \hat{\xi}$ in the interval $[0, \hat{\xi}]$, equation (57) then implies that

$$\int_0^{\hat{\xi}} (\beta\varphi c - \theta P)\phi(\xi)\,d\xi + \int_{\hat{\xi}}^{\infty} (1-\theta)P\phi(\xi)\,d\xi \leq 0 \tag{58}$$

This can be rewritten in terms of the probability Φ as

$$(\beta\varphi c - \theta P)\Phi + (1-\theta)P(1-\Phi) \leq 0 \tag{59}$$

Combining (54) and (59), we obtain

$$P \geq \frac{c}{\theta} \tag{60}$$

The price is thus higher than c/θ, the "traditional" value. After inserting (60) into (54), we finally have

$$\Phi \geq \frac{1-\theta}{1-\beta\varphi\theta} \tag{61}$$

and the probability $1 - \Phi$ of being rationed is therefore bounded above:

$$1 - \Phi \leq \frac{\theta(1-\beta\varphi)}{1-\beta\varphi\theta} \tag{62}$$

We see that patience (a high β) and storability (a high φ) lead to a very low probability of rationing. This makes the usual assumption that demand is not rationed a reasonable approximation for such goods.

Part VI

Economic Policy

12

Nominal Rigidities and Policy Activism

12.1 Introduction

A much debated topic in macroeconomic theory is whether nominal rigidities provide a rational foundation to activist policies and, if yes, which policies.

Until the early 1970s it was generally admitted, following Keynesian intuition, that wage (or price) rigidities provide a strong case for activist countercyclical demand policies. Under such rigidities unforecasted negative demand shocks create underemployment of resources, and it was thought that government could successfully fight such underemployment by adequate demand stimulation (and conversely for positive shocks).

This consensus exploded at the start of the 1970s with the advent of rational expectations. Two lines of criticism arose that were particularly destructive to the Keynesian view.

The first was due to Lucas's (1972) seminal work. His critique stemmed from the fact that most models displaying policy effectiveness were not "structural," meaning not based on rigorous microfoundations. As was indeed the case, the results of some "nonstructural" models came from certain ad hoc assumptions introduced into the equations of the model. So, clearly, effectiveness had to be investigated in the framework of a model with explicitly optimizing agents.

The second critique was put forward by Sargent and Wallace (1975, 1976). They show that effectiveness of policy in most traditional Keynesian models is essentially due to an "informational advantage" implicitly conferred to the government in such models. More precisely, the government is allowed to react to some "recent" shocks while the private sector is locked into "old" wage or price contracts.[1] Now, if the government is not allowed to use more information about shocks than the private sector, then government policies become "ineffective." This line of attack was particularly damaging, notably as most Keynesian models, even those constructed with rational expectations after Sargent-Wallace, were totally vulnerable to this critique (Fischer 1977 is a well-known example). Moreover the informational advantage critique was truly compelling since one could consider a duty of a government having more information than the private sector to release any such superior information to private agents, and to intervene only if the result was not sufficient.

The purpose of this chapter is to reexamine this issue in a rigorous maximizing model with preset wages. In this model the economy is subject to both demand and supply shocks, and the government is "less informed" than the private sector, in the sense seen above. More precisely, we will assume that (1) the government takes its policy actions on the basis of information that is never superior to that of the private sector, and (2) the private sector sets wages *after* the government has decided on policy for the same period. That is to say, the government cannot "surprise" the private sector while the latter is locked into fixed wage agreements.

Despite these restrictions we will demonstrate that the optimal policy is nevertheless an activist one. We will notably obtain the remarkable result that although the economy is hit in each period by stochastic demand and supply shocks *after* wages have been preset, our optimal policy will nevertheless succeed in keeping the economy on a full employment track.

12.2   The Model

To make the argument clear, we begin with a very simple model where the government uses a single policy instrument, fiscal policy. We will assume that wages are preset at the expected Walrasian value, which is the traditional assumption. It will be shown in the next two chapters that the results are robust to generalizations. Notably in chapter 13 we will introduce wages set by maximizing trade unions, and in chapter 14 we will introduce the joint determination of monetary and fiscal policies, together with additional shocks and the presetting of prices. We now turn to the description of the model.

1 We give a very simple formalization of the Sargent-Wallace argument in appendix 12.1.

12.2.1 An OLG Model

We choose to use a monetary overlapping generations model (Samuelson 1958) with production. The OLG structure is particularly well suited for this analysis because we will consider in this chapter a simple fiscal policy, operating through lump-sum transfers. If we had chosen an infinitely lived agent model, Ricardian equivalence would hold, making the study of such fiscal policy problematic.

12.2.2 The Agents

The economy includes representative firms and households, and the government.

Households of generation t live for two periods. They work N_t and consume C_t in period t, consume C'_{t+1} in period $t + 1$. Their savings are in the form of money, which is the sole asset in the economy.[2] Households maximize the expected value of their utility U_t, with

$$U_t = \alpha_t \log C_t + \log C'_{t+1} - (1 + \alpha_t)N_t \tag{1}$$

where the α_t's are positive stochastic variables whose variations represent demand shocks, since, as we will see below, the propensity to consume in period t is equal to $\alpha_t/(1 + \alpha_t)$. The coefficient $1 + \alpha_t$ in the disutility of labor was chosen so as to yield a constant Walrasian labor supply in the absence of government intervention (see section 12.3). This way variations in α_t have the characteristics of a pure demand shock.

The representative firm in period t has a production function

$$Y_t = Z_t N_t \tag{2}$$

where Y_t is output, N_t is labor input, and Z_t is a technology shock common to all firms. Firms belong to the young households, to which they distribute their profits, if any. To make the exposition simpler, we will assume that the two shocks, α_t and Z_t, are stochastic iid variables.

---

2 Since there is a unique financial asset, what we call money, and denote as Ω_t, must be understood, as usual in OLG models, as the net sum of financial assets. Although we will keep the convenient denomination of "money" for short, that economic interpretation should be kept in mind throughout. All this will appear more clearly in chapters 14 and 15, where money and interest-bearing assets are separated.

Government has one policy instrument: it can increase or decrease the money stock by taxing the old household.[3] We will constrain government taxes to be conditional only on variables already known to the private sector.

12.2.3   The Timing of Events

Because the issue raised by Sargent and Wallace about the respective informations of the public and private sector is central to the debate, the timing of actions and information is important. So we need to spell things out precisely.

The old households enter period t holding a quantity of money Ω_{t-1} carried from the previous period. In a first step the government taxes them by an amount T_t in *nominal* terms,[4] so these old households are now endowed with a quantity of money Ω_t:

$$\Omega_t = \Omega_{t-1} - T_t \tag{3}$$

Government policy in period t can only react to past developments. To reflect this fact, we will assume that the government's policy variable T_t is a function of observable macroeconomic variables up to period $t - 1$ only, which the private sector already knows.

In a second step the wage is set by the private sector at its expected market-clearing value, without knowing the values of period t shocks α_t and Z_t. Finally the shocks become public knowledge and transactions are carried out.

We may note that as indicated in the introduction, the government does not have the opportunity to use policy to "surprise" the private sector while it is locked into binding nominal contracts, since the contracts are signed *after* the government has taxed households. Also the tax in period t is based on information up to $t - 1$, so the government is no more informed than the private agents.

12.3   Walrasian Equilibrium

To contrast the results with the preset wage case, we will study first the Walrasian equilibria of this economy.

---

3 Taxing only the old households simplifies the notation throughout. Appendix 12.2 shows that the results carry over when both young and old are taxed.

4 So in this and the next three chapters the notation T will represent taxes in nominal terms, whereas it was real taxes in chapters 2 and 4.

Call P_t and W_t the price and nominal wage. The real wage is equal to the marginal productivity of labor:

$$\frac{W_t}{P_t} = Z_t \tag{4}$$

The old consumers have a quantity of money Ω_t, which they spend entirely. So their consumption C'_t is simply

$$C'_t = \frac{\Omega_t}{P_t} \tag{5}$$

Next we write the maximization program of the young household born in t. It receives profits $\Pi_t = P_t Y_t - W_t N_t$ while young, and will pay a tax T_{t+1} to the government when old. It saves a quantity of money S_t. So its program is

$$\max \; E_t[\alpha_t \log C_t + \log C'_{t+1} - (1 + \alpha_t)N_t] \quad \text{s.t.}$$

$$P_t C_t + S_t = W_t N_t + \Pi_t$$

$$P_{t+1} C'_{t+1} = S_t - T_{t+1}$$

Note that since T_{t+1} is a function of variables up to period t, it is known to the household when deciding on quantities supplied and demanded. The first-order conditions for this program yield:

$$P_t C_t = \frac{\alpha_t}{1 + \alpha_t}(W_t N_t + \Pi_t - T_{t+1}) = \frac{\alpha_t}{1 + \alpha_t}(P_t Y_t - T_{t+1}) \tag{6}$$

$$N_t^s = \frac{W_t - \Pi_t + T_{t+1}}{W_t} \tag{7}$$

Equation (6) is the usual consumption function, while equation (7) gives the Walrasian supply of labor. The equilibrium condition on the goods market is

$$C_t + C'_t = Y_t = Z_t N_t \tag{8}$$

Equations (4) to (8) determine all equilibrium values, which depend on Ω_t and $\Omega_{t+1} = \Omega_t - T_{t+1}$. They are easily computed as

$$C_t = \frac{\alpha_t Z_t}{1 + \alpha_t}, \quad C_t' = \frac{Z_t \Omega_t}{(1 + \alpha_t)\Omega_{t+1}} \tag{9}$$

$$N_t = \frac{1}{1 + \alpha_t}\left(\alpha_t + \frac{\Omega_t}{\Omega_{t+1}}\right) \tag{10}$$

$$W_t^* = (1 + \alpha_t)\Omega_{t+1}, \quad P_t^* = \frac{(1 + \alpha_t)\Omega_{t+1}}{Z_t} \tag{11}$$

We see that equation (10) confirms what we indicated in section 12.2, that if there are no taxes, namely if $\Omega_{t+1} = \Omega_t$, then the Walrasian quantity of labor is constant and equal to one.

12.4   Optimality

12.4.1   The Criterion

To assess the optimality properties of various government policies, both in the Walrasian and the non Walrasian case, we need a criterion. Clearly with an infinity of generations the Pareto optimality criterion is not sufficiently demanding. So we will use the criterion proposed by Samuelson for the overlapping generations model (Samuelson 1967, 1968; Abel 1987) and assume that in period t the government maximizes the following discounted sum of expected utilities V_t:

$$V_t = E_t \sum_{s=t-1}^{\infty} \beta^{s-t} U_s \tag{12}$$

Note that the sum starts at $s = t - 1$ because the household born in $t - 1$ is still alive in t. The limit case $\beta = 1$ corresponds to maximizing the representative household's expected utility. The parameter β will play here the same role as that played by the households' discount rate in models with infinitely lived consumers.

Rearranging the terms in the infinite sum (12), we find that up to a constant, the criterion V_t can be rewritten under the more convenient form:

$$V_t = E_t \sum_{s=t}^{\infty} \beta^{s-t} \Delta_s \tag{13}$$

$$\Delta_t = \alpha_t \log C_t + \frac{\log C_t'}{\beta} - (1 + \alpha_t)N_t \tag{14}$$

12.4.2 Optimal Policy in the Walrasian Case

Let us begin our investigation of optimal policies with the Walrasian case. To find the best policy, we simply insert the equilibrium values found in (9) and (10) into the criterion defined by (13) and (14). The term Δ_t corresponding to period t is equal to

$$\Delta_t = \alpha_t \log \left[\frac{\alpha_t Z_t}{1 + \alpha_t} \right] + \frac{1}{\beta} \log \left[\frac{Z_t \Omega_t}{(1 + \alpha_t)\Omega_{t+1}} \right] - \left(\alpha_t + \frac{\Omega_t}{\Omega_{t+1}} \right) \tag{15}$$

Maximizing this with respect to Ω_{t+1}/Ω_t, we immediately find the optimal policy under the Walrasian regime:

$$\frac{\Omega_{t+1}}{\Omega_t} = \beta \tag{16}$$

Looking at the optimal policy (16), we may note two things. The first is that this optimal policy is one of the well-known "Friedman rules" derived from Friedman's (1969) famous "optimal quantity of money" article: let a monetary aggregate grow at a rate equal to the discount rate β. Second the optimal policy is a typical nonactivist one, since the policy defined by (16) does not depend on any event, past or present. We will now see that the introduction of preset wages changes things drastically.

12.5 Preset Wages

Let us suppose that firms and workers sign wage contracts at the beginning of period t, based on information available then (which does *not* include the values of α_t and Z_t), and that at this wage households supply the quantity of labor demanded by firms. We will assume, in order not to add any further distorsion, that the preset wage is equal to the expected value of the Walrasian wage,[5]

---

5 In chapter 13 we study the case where wages are set by maximizing trade unions endowed with some market power.

namely according to formula (11):

$$W_t = E_{t-1} W_t^* = E_{t-1}[(1 + \alpha_t)\Omega_{t+1}] \tag{17}$$

12.5.1 Computing the Equilibrium

In this case equilibrium equations (4) to (8) still hold, with the exception of equation (7) which indicates that the household is on its labor supply curve. Equation (7) is replaced by equation (17). Combining these equations, we find that the preset wage equilibrium is characterized by the following values for employment and consumptions:

$$N_t = \frac{\alpha_t \Omega_{t+1} + \Omega_t}{W_t} \tag{18}$$

$$C_t = \frac{\alpha_t \Omega_{t+1} Z_t}{W_t} \tag{19}$$

$$C_t' = \frac{\Omega_t Z_t}{W_t} \tag{20}$$

12.5.2 The Suboptimality of Nonactivist Policies

To show the suboptimality of nonactivist policies, we now study what happens if the government follows policy (16), which was optimal under Walrasian market clearing. In view of (16) and (17), the preset wage W_t is equal to

$$W_t = \beta(1 + \alpha_a)\Omega_t \tag{21}$$

where

$$\alpha_a = E(\alpha_t) \tag{22}$$

the subscript a meaning "average." Equations (18), (19), and (20) yield the following values:

$$N_t = \frac{1 + \beta \alpha_t}{\beta(1 + \alpha_a)} \tag{23}$$

$$C_t = \frac{\alpha_t Z_t}{1 + \alpha_a} \tag{24}$$

$$C_t' = \frac{Z_t}{\beta(1 + \alpha_a)} \tag{25}$$

It is easy to check that the allocation defined by (23) to (25) is not even a Pareto optimum. Looking now at the labor market, we see, combining (7), (16), (21), and (23), that the discrepancy between the demand and supply of labor is equal to

$$N_t - N_t^s = \frac{\alpha_t - \alpha_a}{1 + \alpha_a} \tag{26}$$

The economy will display either unemployment (when $\alpha_t < \alpha_a$) or over-employment (when $\alpha_t > \alpha_a$), both creating inefficiencies. We now show that an activist policy enables to do much better.

12.6 The Optimality of Activist Policies

12.6.1 The Optimal Policy

Finding an optimal policy consists in finding a strategy where (1) T_t, or Ω_t, are functions only of variables up to period $t - 1$, and (2) the resulting equilibrium values maximize the utility function V_t in (12) to (14) for this class of policies.

To find the optimal policy in a simple manner, we insert into the criterion (14) the "fixwage equilibrium" values of C_t, C_t', and N_t found above (equations 18 to 20). In period t the government will thus maximize the expected value of the following quantity:

$$\alpha_t \log\left(\frac{\alpha_t \Omega_{t+1} Z_t}{W_t}\right) + \frac{1}{\beta} \log\left(\frac{\Omega_t Z_t}{W_t}\right) - (1 + \alpha_t)\left(\frac{\alpha_t \Omega_{t+1}}{W_t} + \frac{\Omega_t}{W_t}\right) \tag{27}$$

subject to (17). In this maximization Ω_t is inherited from the previous period, Ω_{t+1} can be chosen conditional on the value of all shocks up to period t included, while W_t is predetermined according to equation (17). As it turns out, constraint (17) is actually not binding at the optimum, and consequently we obtain exactly the same solution maximizing the expected value of (27) with respect to Ω_{t+1} and W_t. Because the whole problem is homogeneous of degree zero in Ω_{t+1}, W_t, and Ω_t, we will actually maximize with respect to the ratios Ω_{t+1}/W_t and W_t/Ω_t. Let us first maximize (27) in Ω_{t+1}/W_t. This yields

$$\Omega_{t+1} = \frac{W_t}{1+\alpha_t} \tag{28}$$

We immediately note that by combining (11) and (28), we obtain

$$W_t^* = (1+\alpha_t)\Omega_{t+1} = W_t \tag{29}$$

Under policy rule (28), the Walrasian wage in period t is *independent* of period t shocks, α_t and Z_t, and thus fully predetermined. As a result the contract wage W_t, which is equal to the expected value of W_t^*, is always at its market-clearing value, and therefore under policy (28) the economy will always be at full employment!

Now inserting the value of Ω_{t+1}/W_t so obtained into the expression of the expected value of Δ_t, we obtain, up to a constant term,

$$\frac{1}{\beta}\log\left(\frac{\Omega_t}{W_t}\right) - \frac{(1+\alpha_a)\Omega_t}{W_t} \tag{30}$$

Maximization of this term in W_t/Ω_t yields

$$W_t = \beta(1+\alpha_a)\Omega_t \tag{31}$$

Combining (28) and (31) finally gives the formula for the optimal monetary policy:

$$\frac{\Omega_{t+1}}{\Omega_t} = \frac{\beta(1+\alpha_a)}{1+\alpha_t} \tag{32}$$

We see that rule (32) combines in a nutshell both some Friedmanian and Keynesian insights. Indeed we can observe that if there were no demand shocks, namely if α_t was constant, equation (32) would yield $\Omega_{t+1} = \beta\Omega_t$, the traditional Friedmanian rule (16), which we found to be optimal in the Walrasian case. However, we should also see that as soon as demand shocks are present, the optimal policy calls for the government to respond countercyclically to these shocks, since a negative demand shock today (low α_t) will trigger low or negative taxes tomorrow (low T_{t+1} and therefore high Ω_{t+1}), and conversely for a positive demand shock. The optimal policy is thus an activist one.

12.6.2 An Intuitive Explanation

The fact that a government with no more information than the private sector can nevertheless succeed in stabilizing the economy, despite wages being set in advance without knowledge of the shocks, may be somewhat surprising. So we will give here a simple intuition behind this remarkable result. Let us rewrite the household's consumption function (6):

$$P_t C_t = \frac{\alpha_t}{1 + \alpha_t}(P_t Y_t - T_{t+1}) \qquad (33)$$

Suppose that after the wage has been set, a negative demand shock (a low α_t) hits the economy. If the government has no systematic policy, this shock will clearly lead, in view of consumption function (33), to a *decrease* in the demand for goods and labor, and therefore to an underemployment of labor. Now, if the government is known to lead the countercyclical policy (32), then the private sector will know in advance that the future taxes T_{t+1} will be low, and from the formula above this will, on the contrary, tend to *increase* the demand for goods and labor. When policy is calibrated to be (32), these two conflicting effects cancel out, and the economy remains at full employment. Of course, the zero unemployment result is due to our particular specifications, but the optimality of an activist policy is a robust result, as appendix 12.3 shows.

12.6.3 Implementation

Policy (32) is expressed as a function of the shocks α_t. But these shocks, which are shocks to the households' utility functions, are a priori not directly observable by the government. So we will now check whether such policy can actually be implemented, namely whether the value of α_t can be recouped from the observable macroeconomic series. We will see that this is feasible.

Let us indeed insert the value of the optimal policy (32) into the values of the wage and employment in a preset wage equilibrium (equations 17 and 18). We obtain

$$W_t = \beta(1 + \alpha_a)\Omega_t \qquad (34)$$

$$N_t = \frac{\beta(1 + \alpha_a)}{1 + \alpha_t}\frac{\alpha_t \Omega_t}{W_t} + \frac{\Omega_t}{W_t} \qquad (35)$$

Combining these equations, we find the value of employment as a function of the current shock:

$$N_t = \frac{\alpha_t}{1 + \alpha_t} + \frac{1}{\beta(1 + \alpha_a)} \tag{36}$$

The shock α_t can therefore be deduced from the value of employment,

$$\frac{1}{1 + \alpha_t} = 1 - N_t + \frac{1}{\beta(1 + \alpha_a)} \tag{37}$$

and the policy function (32) can be rewritten directly as a function of observable employment:

$$\frac{\Omega_{t+1}}{\Omega_t} = 1 + \beta(1 + \alpha_a) - \beta(1 + \alpha_a)N_t \tag{38}$$

Under this form it is clear that the optimal policy can be implemented, since the policy rule is now directly function of observable macroeconomic variables.

12.7 Conclusions

We constructed in this chapter a model of an economy with preset wages where agents maximize under rational expectations, and showed that it was optimal for a "less informed" government to lead nevertheless an activist countercyclical fiscal policy. With our specification of the model the government can even maintain the economy at all times on a full-employment trajectory.

An issue that has been often raised against traditional activist policies is that they might impart an inflationary bias to the economy. This is clearly not at all the case with the optimal policy we just found, since all nominal values will increase on average at the rate β, thus following a nonincreasing trend. The traditional opposition between employment stabilization and price stability therefore does not hold here.

12.8 References

This chapter is based on Bénassy (1997b, 2001).

The "ineffectiveness" argument according to which a government no more informed than the private sector would be powerless against employment fluctuations was developed by Sargent and Wallace (1975, 1976).

Subsequently the important idea that a "less informed government" can nevertheless have stabilizing powers was developed in insightful articles by Turnovsky (1980), Weiss (1980), King (1982, 1983), and Andersen (1986). All of these papers embed a sophisticated treatment of rational expectations into an otherwise fairly traditional framework, with a priori given demand-supply functions and government objectives. So the question of whether these results would carry over in a model with explicit maximization has remained open.

The "Friedman rule", which originates in Friedman (1969), was subsequently derived by numerous authors working with infinitely lived representative agents, for example, Dornbusch and Frenkel (1973), Grandmont and Younès (1973), Brock (1975), and many others since. The same rule was derived in an OLG framework by Abel (1987).

There are also some contributions showing that activist policies can be useful in a Walrasian framework without nominal rigidities (e.g., Bulow and Polemarchakis 1983). We deliberately chose a model where this is not the case in order to focus on the central role of nominal rigidities.

Appendix 12.1: The Sargent-Wallace Argument

We give here a particularly simple version of Sargent and Wallace's argument against activist policies when the government is no more informed than the private sector. Although this argument would hold in more complex models, the basic idea remains the same. So for expositional simplicity, we consider a highly streamlined version.

The Model

Let us consider an economy with the simple production function (everything is expressed in logarithms):

$$y_t = n_t \tag{39}$$

The supply of labor is fixed,

$$n_t^s = n_0 \tag{40}$$

and we have a simple loglinear demand,

$$y_t = m_t + v_t - p_t \tag{41}$$

where v_t is a velocity shock. This model solves particularly easily. The price is equal to the wage,

$$p_t = w_t \tag{42}$$

and the demand for labor is thus

$$n_t = m_t + v_t - w_t \tag{43}$$

Equating this demand for labor to the fixed labor supply immediately yields the Walrasian wage:

$$w_t^* = m_t + v_t - n_0 \tag{44}$$

Now, as in the main body of the chapter, we assume that the actual wage is preset at the expected value of the Walrasian wage:

$$w_t = E_{t-1}(w_t^*) = E_{t-1}(m_t) + E_{t-1}(v_t) - n_0 \tag{45}$$

Combining (43) and (45), we immediately obtain the employment level:

$$n_t = n_0 + (m_t - E_{t-1}m_t) + (v_t - E_{t-1}v_t) \tag{46}$$

Let us assume that the government's objective is to stabilize employment (the policies we will derive actually also stabilize inflation). We want to investigate two distinct possibilities, depending on which information the government is allowed to use.

Traditional Keynesian Analysis

In traditional Keynesian analysis, say of the IS-LM type, it is implicitly assumed that the government can use all information up to and with period t included. Then one optimal policy is of the type:

$$m_t = \mu - v_t \tag{47}$$

In this case employment is

$$n_t = n_0 \tag{48}$$

We see that government can completely stabilize employment. But clearly here the government has an enormous informational advantage over the private sector. The private sector is locked into wage contracts based on period $t - 1$ information, whereas the government can react with full knowledge of period t shocks.

The Ineffectiveness Result

Let us suppose, as Sargent-Wallace suggested, that government can only use period $t - 1$ information. Then $m_t - E_{t-1}m_t$ and $v_t - E_{t-1}v_t$ in formula (46) are independant. If the government wants to reduce fluctuations in employment, then the best it can do is to have a fully predictable policy:

$$m_t = E_{t-1}m_t \tag{49}$$

Under condition (49), employment is equal to

$$n_t = n_0 + (v_t - E_{t-1}v_t) \tag{50}$$

No matter which policy it uses, government will therefore be unable to suppress a minimal amount of fluctuations, driven by the innovation in velocity $v_t - E_{t-1}v_t$. This is the famous "ineffectiveness" result.

We may note that although it cannot stabilize employment, the government can, in this very simple model, stabilize inflation by selecting, among policies characterized by (49), a policy of the type

$$m_t = \mu - E_{t-1}v_t \tag{51}$$

Appendix 12.2: Taxing All Households

In order to make the exposition simple, we assumed in the main text of chapter 12 that the government taxes only the old households. Let us see what happens if government taxes both young and old households.

We assume that young and old are equally taxed by an amount T_t in period t. The young household born in t will thus pay T_t today and T_{t+1} tomorrow. As a consequence its maximization program becomes

$$\max \; E_t[\alpha_t \log C_t + \log C'_{t+1} - (1 + \alpha_t)N_t] \quad \text{s.t.}$$

$$P_t C_t + S_t = W_t N_t + \Pi_t - T_t$$

$$P_{t+1} C'_{t+1} = S_t - T_{t+1}$$

The first-order conditions for this program yield

$$P_t C_t = \frac{\alpha_t}{1 + \alpha_t}(P_t Y_t - T_t - T_{t+1}) \tag{52}$$

$$N_t^s = \frac{W_t - \Pi_t + T_t + T_{t+1}}{W_t} \tag{53}$$

We continue to denote as Ω_t the quantity of money held by old households after they have been taxed. In view of this definition, the law of evolution of Ω_t is now

$$\Omega_{t+1} = \Omega_t - T_t - T_{t+1} \tag{54}$$

Combining equations (52), (53), and (54) with equations (4), (5), and (8), which are still valid, we find the following Walrasian equilibrium values:

$$C_t = \frac{\alpha_t Z_t}{1 + \alpha_t}, \quad C'_t = \frac{Z_t \Omega_t}{(1 + \alpha_t)\Omega_{t+1}} \tag{55}$$

$$N_t = \frac{1}{1 + \alpha_t}\left(\alpha_t + \frac{\Omega_t}{\Omega_{t+1}}\right) \tag{56}$$

$$W_t^* = (1 + \alpha_t)\Omega_{t+1} \tag{57}$$

We recognize that these are the same formulas as (9) to (11).

Optimal Policy in the Walrasian Case

To find the best policy in the Walrasian case, we simply insert the equilibrium values found in (55) and (56) into the criterion (13) and (14). The term corresponding to period t is equal to

$$\Delta_t = \alpha_t \log \left(\frac{\alpha_t Z_t}{1 + \alpha_t} \right) + \frac{1}{\beta} \log \left[\frac{Z_t \Omega_t}{(1 + \alpha_t)\Omega_{t+1}} \right] - \left(\alpha_t + \frac{\Omega_t}{\Omega_{t+1}} \right) \quad (58)$$

This is exactly the same maximization as in section 12.4, and therefore we have the same rule:

$$\frac{\Omega_{t+1}}{\Omega_t} = \beta \quad (59)$$

Preset Wage Equilibrium

Now the preset wage is equal to

$$W_t = E_{t-1} W_t^* = E_{t-1}[(1 + \alpha_t)\Omega_{t+1}] \quad (60)$$

The preset wage equilibrium is characterized by the combination of equations (2), (4), (5), (52), (54), and (60). This yields notably

$$N_t = \frac{\alpha_t \Omega_{t+1} + \Omega_t}{W_t} \quad (61)$$

$$C_t = \frac{\alpha_t \Omega_{t+1} Z_t}{W_t} \quad (62)$$

$$C_t' = \frac{\Omega_t Z_t}{W_t} \quad (63)$$

Optimal Activist Policies

In period t the government will maximize the expected value of the following quantity:

$$\alpha_t \log \left(\frac{\alpha_t \Omega_{t+1} Z_t}{W_t} \right) + \frac{1}{\beta} \log \left(\frac{\Omega_t Z_t}{W_t} \right) - (1 + \alpha_t) \left(\frac{\alpha_t \Omega_{t+1}}{W_t} + \frac{\Omega_t}{W_t} \right) \quad (64)$$

Again, this is exactly the same maximization program as in section 12.6, and it therefore yields the same optimal activist rule:

$$\frac{\Omega_{t+1}}{\Omega_t} = \frac{\beta(1+\alpha_a)}{1+\alpha_t} \tag{65}$$

Appendix 12.3: A Robustness Argument

The model in chapter 12 has the particular features that the disutility of labor (equation 1) and the production function (equation 2) are both linear in labor. We now develop a simple argument to show that our result on the optimality of activist policies has nothing to do with these linearities, and continues to hold under nonlinear specifications. For that purpose we will use the more general nonlinear utility and production functions:

$$U_t = \alpha_t \log C_t + \log C'_{t+1} - (1+\alpha_t)N_t^a, \qquad a \geq 1 \tag{66}$$

$$Y_t = Z_t N_t^b, \qquad 0 < b \leq 1 \tag{67}$$

All of the arguments that were developed in the main text could be developed similarly, with the important difference that we do not have an explicit solution to this more general problem. What we know is that in the end there is an optimal policy function of the government that will take the form

$$\frac{\Omega_{t+1}}{\Omega_t} = \Phi(\alpha_t, Z_t, a, b) \tag{68}$$

Since we conducted our investigation in the main text with the values $a = 1$ and $b = 1$, we know further that

$$\Phi(\alpha_t, Z_t, 1, 1) = \frac{\beta(1+\alpha_a)}{1+\alpha_t} \tag{69}$$

Because the problem is continuous, we know that for a and b close to 1, the optimal response function will be close to $\beta(1+\alpha_a)/(1+\alpha_t)$, which means that governmental policy will respond "actively" to demand shocks. This shows that our result on the optimality of activist policies is robust, and does not depend on the linearity of some specifications.

13

Imperfect Competition and Activist Policies

13.1 Introduction

In the preceding chapter we saw that wage rigidities provide a strong rationale for activist policies, even in a "structural" model and even when the informational constraints suggested by Sargent and Wallace (1975) are taken into account. In order to have a simple exposition, the wage rigidity considered was a "traditional" one, as we assumed wages to be preset at their expected market-clearing value. We now investigate the same problem assuming that wages are set by utility-maximizing trade unions. We will see that although more complex, the basic result on the desirability of activist policies very much remains.

13.2 The Model

As in the previous chapter we study a model with overlapping generations. Households have the same utility functions:

$$U_t = \alpha_t \log C_t + \log C_t' - (1 + \alpha_t)N_t \tag{1}$$

Now output is produced by competitive firms from intermediate goods indexed by $j \in [0, 1]$, with a production function

$$Y_t = \left(\int_0^1 Y_{jt}^\theta \, dj \right)^{1/\theta} \tag{2}$$

Intermediate goods are produced by firms indexed by $j \in [0, 1]$, with production functions

$$Y_{jt} = Z_t N_{jt} \tag{3}$$

where Z_t is a technology shock common to all firms. Wages W_{jt} are set in each firm j by a firm-specific trade union.

Finally the government taxes all incomes proportionately at the rate τ_t. This taxation policy (instead of the lump-sum policy of the previous chapter) is assumed so as to have a closed-form solution throughout. Taxes are paid by households when old, but the tax rate is applied to the income they received when young. So the relation between the tax rate of this chapter and the taxes of the previous chapter is

$$T_{t+1} = \tau_{t+1} P_t Y_t = \tau_{t+1}(W_t N_t + \Pi_t) \tag{4}$$

13.3   Some Basic Relations

Since we are studying this model under both flexible and preset wages, we will derive in this section a number of basic relations that are valid in both circumstances.

13.3.1   Macroeconomic Relations

We begin with a few macroeconomic relations that are valid whether wages are flexible or preset:

Proposition 1   *The values of consumptions and output are given by*

$$P_t C_t' = \Omega_t \tag{5}$$

$$P_t C_t = \alpha_t \Omega_{t+1} \tag{6}$$

$$P_t Y_t = \alpha_t \Omega_{t+1} + \Omega_t \tag{7}$$

$$\Omega_{t+1} = \Omega_t - T_{t+1} \tag{8}$$

Proof The old generation has a monetary wealth Ω_t, which they consume entirely, hence (5). Now the program of the young household is

$$\max E_t\{\alpha_t \log C_t + \log C'_{t+1} - (1 + \alpha_t)N_t\} \quad \text{s.t.}$$

$$P_t C_t + S_t = W_t N_t + \Pi_t$$

$$P_{t+1} C'_{t+1} = S_t - \tau_{t+1}(W_t N_t + \Pi_t)$$

For any given value of N_t the solutions in C_t and C'_t are such that

$$P_t C_t = \frac{\alpha_t}{1 + \alpha_t}(1 - \tau_{t+1})(W_t N_t + \Pi_t) \tag{9}$$

$$P_{t+1} C'_{t+1} = \frac{1}{1 + \alpha_t}(1 - \tau_{t+1})(W_t N_t + \Pi_t) \tag{10}$$

Combined with definition (4), equation (9) becomes

$$P_t C_t = \frac{\alpha_t}{1 + \alpha_t}(1 - \tau_{t+1})P_t Y_t = \frac{\alpha_t}{1 + \alpha_t}(P_t Y_t - T_{t+1}) \tag{11}$$

Adding (5) and (11), we obtain

$$P_t Y_t = (1 + \alpha_t)\,\Omega_t - \alpha_t T_{t+1} \tag{12}$$

which, since $\Omega_{t+1} = \Omega_t - T_{t+1}$, yields (7). Inserting this result into (11) yields equation (6). ∎

13.3.2 The Demand for Labor

We now derive the demand for labor in the firms producing intermediate outputs:

Proposition 2 *The demand for labor in sector j is equal to*

$$N_{jt} = \frac{Y_t}{Z_t}\left(\frac{W_{jt}}{W_t}\right)^{-1/(1-\theta)} \tag{13}$$

where

$$W_t = \left(\int_0^1 W_{jt}^{-\theta/(1-\theta)} \, dj \right)^{-(1-\theta)/\theta} \tag{14}$$

Proof Let us start with the firms producing the final output. They competitively maximize their profits, which yields

$$Y_{jt} = Y_t \left(\frac{P_{jt}}{P_t} \right)^{-1/(1-\theta)} \tag{15}$$

$$P_t = \left(\int_0^1 P_{jt}^{-\theta/(1-\theta)} \, dj \right)^{-(1-\theta)/\theta} \tag{16}$$

The intermediate firm j maximizes profits, subject to its demand curve (15), meaning that it solves the program

$$\max P_{jt} Y_{jt} - W_{jt} N_{jt} \quad \text{s.t.}$$

$$Y_{jt} = Z_t N_{jt}$$

$$Y_{jt} = Y_t \left(\frac{P_{jt}}{P_t} \right)^{-1/(1-\theta)}$$

The solution is

$$P_{jt} = \frac{W_{jt}}{\theta Z_t} \tag{17}$$

Combining (14), (16), and (17), we obtain a similar relation between aggregates:

$$P_t = \frac{W_t}{\theta Z_t} \tag{18}$$

We can now derive the demand for labor. For that, we combine (3) and (15):

$$N_{jt} = \frac{Y_{jt}}{Z_t} = \frac{Y_t}{Z_t} \left(\frac{P_{jt}}{P_t} \right)^{-1/(1-\theta)} \tag{19}$$

Combining finally (17), (18), and (19), we obtain formula (13). ∎

13.4 Flexible Prices and Wages

We will investigate as a benchmark, he characteristics of the equilibrium when both prices and wages are flexible.

13.4.1 Wage Setting

We investigate the case where the trade union sets the wage simultaneously with the quantity decisions. In view of equations (9) and (10), we have, up to a constant,

$$E_t(\alpha_t \log C_{jt} + \log C'_{jt+1}) = (1 + \alpha_t) \log(W_{jt} N_{jt} + \Pi_t) \tag{20}$$

so the trade union's utility maximization program is the following:

$$\max(1 + \alpha_t) \log(W_{jt} N_{jt} + \Pi_t) - (1 + \alpha_t) N_{jt} \quad \text{s.t.}$$

$$N_{jt} = \frac{Y_t}{Z_t} \left(\frac{W_{jt}}{W_t} \right)^{-1/(1-\theta)}$$

The first-order condition in W_{jt} is written as

$$\theta W_{jt} = \frac{Y_t W_t}{Z_t} \left(\frac{W_{jt}}{W_t} \right)^{-\theta/(1-\theta)} + \Pi_t \tag{21}$$

The problem is symmetrical, and wages and employment will be the same in all firms:

$$W_{jt} = W_t, \quad N_{jt} = N_t, \quad \forall j \tag{22}$$

Inserting (22) into (21), and using (7), we obtain

$$W_{jt} = W_t = \frac{P_t Y_t}{\theta} = \frac{\Omega_t + \alpha_t \Omega_{t+1}}{\theta} \tag{23}$$

13.4.2 General Equilibrium

Combining (18) and (23), we find the general price level:

$$P_t = \frac{\Omega_t + \alpha_t \Omega_{t+1}}{\theta Z_t} \tag{24}$$

Combining this with (5), (6), and (7), we can compute the values of consumptions and labor:

$$C_t = \frac{\alpha_t \Omega_{t+1}}{P_t} = \theta^2 Z_t \frac{\alpha_t \Omega_{t+1}}{\Omega_t + \alpha_t \Omega_{t+1}} \tag{25}$$

$$C'_t = \frac{\Omega_t}{P_t} = \theta^2 Z_t \frac{\Omega_t}{\Omega_t + \alpha_t \Omega_{t+1}} \tag{26}$$

$$N_t = \theta^2 \tag{27}$$

We note that the parameter θ appears in all these formulas to the square. This is because $1/\theta$ is actually an index of market power on both the goods and labor markets.

13.4.3 Optimal Policy

We can now characterize the optimal policy when both prices and wages are flexible:

Proposition 3 *The optimal policy under flexible prices and wages is given by*

$$\frac{\Omega_{t+1}}{\Omega_t} = \beta \tag{28}$$

Proof The optimal policy is solution of

$$\max E\left\{ \alpha_t \log C_t + \frac{1}{\beta} \log C'_t - (1 + \alpha_t)N_t \right\} \tag{29}$$

where C_t, C'_t, and N_t are given by formulas (25) to (27). This amounts to maximize the expected value of

$$\alpha_t \log\left(\frac{\alpha_t \Omega_{t+1}}{\Omega_t + \alpha_t \Omega_{t+1}} \right) + \frac{1}{\beta} \log\left(\frac{\Omega_t}{\Omega_t + \alpha_t \Omega_{t+1}} \right) - (1 + \alpha_t)\theta^2 \tag{30}$$

The solution is policy (28).   ∎

13.5 Preset Wages

We will assume that wages W_{jt} are set in each firm j at the beginning of each period by utility-maximizing trade unions.

13.5.1 Wage Setting

In this framework of preset prices, the program of the trade union in firm j is to fix W_{jt} *before* knowing the shocks so as to maximize expected utility, which is done by solving the program

$$\max E_{t-1}[(1 + \alpha_t) \log(W_{jt} N_{jt} + \Pi_t) - (1 + \alpha_t) N_t] \quad \text{s.t.}$$

$$N_{jt} = \frac{Y_t}{Z_t} \left(\frac{W_{jt}}{W_t} \right)^{-1/(1-\theta)}$$

Inserting the value of N_{jt} into the maximand and differentiating with respect to W_{jt} we obtain the first-order condition:

$$E_{t-1}\left[\frac{\theta(1 + \alpha_t)Y_t(W_{jt}/W_t)^{-1/(1-\theta)}}{W_{jt}Y_t(W_{jt}/W_t)^{-1/(1-\theta)} + Z_t\Pi_t} \right] = E_{t-1}\left[\frac{(1 + \alpha_t)Y_t}{W_t Z_t} \left(\frac{W_{jt}}{W_t} \right)^{-1/(1-\theta)} \right]$$

$$(31)$$

This is symmetrical in j, and all trade unions will choose the same wage $W_{jt} = W_t$. Equation (31) thus becomes

$$E_{t-1}\left[\frac{\theta(1 + \alpha_t)Y_t}{Z_t(W_t N_t + \Pi_t)} \right] = E_{t-1}\left[\frac{(1 + \alpha_t)Y_t}{W_t Z_t} \right] \qquad (32)$$

which simplifies to

$$\theta^2 (1 + \alpha_a) = E_{t-1}\left[(1 + \alpha_t) N_t \right] \qquad (33)$$

13.5.2 The Preset Wage Equilibrium

We thus have a symmetric equilibrium, defined by equations (5), (6), (7), (18), and (33). Combining the first four, we find the values of consumptions and labor:

$$C_t = \frac{\alpha_t \Omega_{t+1}}{P_t} = \frac{\theta \alpha_t \Omega_{t+1} Z_t}{W_t} \qquad (34)$$

$$C_t' = \frac{\Omega_t}{P_t} = \frac{\theta \Omega_t Z_t}{W_t} \qquad (35)$$

$$N_t = \frac{\theta(\Omega_t + \alpha_t \Omega_{t+1})}{W_t} \qquad (36)$$

Inserting the expression of N_t (36) into equation (33), we obtain the value of the wages:

$$W_{jt} = W_t = E_{t-1}\left[\frac{(1 + \alpha_t)(\Omega_t + \alpha_t \Omega_{t+1})}{\theta(1 + \alpha_a)}\right] \qquad (37)$$

13.6 Optimal Government Policy

We can characterize the optimal government policy through the following proposition:

Proposition 4 *Under preset wages the optimal policy is activist and characterized by*

$$\frac{\Omega_{t+1}}{\Omega_t} = \frac{\beta(1 + \alpha_a)}{1 + \alpha_t} \qquad (38)$$

Proof Optimal government policy is given by the maximization of the following expected utility:

$$E_{t-1}\left[\alpha_t \log\left(\frac{\theta \alpha_t \Omega_{t+1} Z_t}{W_t}\right) + \frac{1}{\beta}\log\left(\frac{\theta \Omega_t Z_t}{W_t}\right)\right]$$
$$- E_{t-1}\left[\frac{\theta(1 + \alpha_t)(\Omega_t + \alpha_t \Omega_{t+1})}{W_t}\right] \qquad (39)$$

subject to the wage equation (37). The Lagrangean of this program is

$$
E_{t-1}\left[\alpha_t \log\left(\frac{\theta\alpha_t\Omega_{t+1}Z_t}{W_t}\right) + \frac{1}{\beta}\log\left(\frac{\theta\Omega_t Z_t}{W_t}\right) - \frac{\theta(1+\alpha_t)(\Omega_t + \alpha_t\Omega_{t+1})}{W_t}\right]
$$
$$
+ \lambda_t\left[W_t - E_{t-1}\frac{(1+\alpha_t)(\Omega_t + \alpha_t\Omega_{t+1})}{\theta(1+\alpha_a)}\right] \tag{40}
$$

Let us first differentiate with respect to Ω_{t+1}. We obtain the following first-order condition:

$$
\frac{\alpha_t}{\Omega_{t+1}} - \frac{\theta\alpha_t(1+\alpha_t)}{W_t} - \frac{\lambda_t(1+\alpha_t)\alpha_t}{(1+\alpha_a)\theta} = 0 \tag{41}
$$

We see that the solution will be of the form

$$
\Omega_{t+1} = \frac{\psi\Omega_t}{1+\alpha_t} \tag{42}
$$

Inserting this into (37), we find that the wage is equal to

$$
W_t = \frac{(1+\alpha_a + \psi\alpha_a)\Omega_t}{\theta(1+\alpha_a)} \tag{43}
$$

Let us now introduce these values (42) and (43) into the maximand (39). We obtain the following maximization program:

$$
\max E_{t-1}\left\{\alpha_t\log\left[\frac{\theta^2(1+\alpha_a)\alpha_t\psi Z_t}{(1+\alpha_t)(1+\alpha_a + \psi\alpha_a)}\right] + \frac{1}{\beta}\log\left[\frac{\theta^2(1+\alpha_a)Z_t}{1+\alpha_a + \psi\alpha_a}\right]\right\}
$$
$$
- \frac{\theta^2(1+\alpha_a)}{1+\alpha_a + \psi\alpha_a}E_{t-1}(1+\alpha_t + \psi\alpha_t) \tag{44}
$$

After we simplify and eliminate irrelevant terms, this maximization problem becomes

$$
\max \alpha_a\log\left(\frac{\psi}{1+\alpha_a + \psi\alpha_a}\right) + \frac{1}{\beta}\log\left(\frac{1}{1+\alpha_a + \psi\alpha_a}\right) - \theta^2(1+\alpha_a)
$$
$$
\tag{45}
$$

Maximizing this with respect to ψ, we obtain

$$\psi = \beta(1 + \alpha_a) \qquad (46)$$

which, combined with (42), gives the optimal policy (38).   ∎

Proposition 4 shows that it is again optimal to use an activist countercyclical policy.

13.7   Conclusions

The previous chapter showed that it is optimal to use countercyclical activist policies in a framework where wages are preset at their expected Walrasian equilibrium value. In this chapter we assumed instead that wages are determined by utility-maximizing trade unions. It turns out that although the algebra is somewhat heavier, exactly the same type of results are obtained.

In the next two chapters we will introduce several generalizations of the model. So to simplify the exposition, we will revert to the simpler preset wages (or prices) framework used in chapter 12.

14

The Optimal Policy Mix

14.1 Introduction

In this chapter we extend the analysis of chapter 12 in a number of important directions. The first is the simultaneous consideration of fiscal and monetary policies, namely what has been called the determination of the optimal "policy mix." Clearly, the results of chapter 12 on the desirability of activist policies would be of limited interest if we found out that the prescriptions were severely modified once monetary policies are introduced into the picture. So here we introduce a "cash in advance" motive for holding money, and study the optimal combination of fiscal and monetary policies. We will see that although the algebra is more complex, the conclusions are basically the same.

The second extension is closely related to the preceding one: since we have a cash in advance constraint, it is quite natural to introduce an additional shock, which will be essentially a shock to the velocity of circulation of money. Since we have already real demand shocks, this will enable us to answer the question of whether activist policies should respond in the same manner to all types of demand shocks.

The third extension concerns the nature of the nominal rigidities. We studied so far nominal wage rigidities, and it is obviously worthwhile to investigate whether and how the results may be modified if the nominal rigidity concerns prices instead of wages.

We will thus study a dynamic economy submitted to technological, monetary, and real demand shocks, and investigate the nature of optimal monetary and fiscal policies. As we already discovered in chapter 12, we will see that although the model is structural and the Sargent-Wallace conditions are met, activist countercyclical fiscal policies will be part of the optimal policy package. More precisely the results are the following:

If prices and wages are Walrasian, then the optimal monetary policy is to have the nominal interest rate set to zero, and the optimal fiscal policy is to have the stock of financial assets grow at the rate β, where β is the discount rate. We thus find the two Friedman rules (Friedman 1969), and these policies are of course nonactivist.

If wages are preset, the optimal monetary policy is still to maintain the nominal interest rate at zero, but the optimal fiscal policy becomes activist and countercyclical, in the sense that the fiscal transfer is negatively related to past demand shocks, as was already found in chapter 12.

If prices are preset, the optimal monetary policy remains the same. Fiscal policy reacts negatively to demand shocks, and now positively to technology shocks.

14.2   The Model

We consider again a monetary overlapping generations economy with production. Money will now be explicitly separated from interest bearing financial assets. The two will coexist because of a cash in advance constraint. The economy includes representative firms, households, and the government.

14.2.1   The Agents

As in chapter 12, households have the utility function

$$U_t = \alpha_t \log C_t + \log C'_{t+1} - (1 + \alpha_t) N_t \tag{1}$$

where α_t is a positive stochastic variable. Households are submitted in each period of their life to a cash in advance constraint. These are written for the household born in period t:

$$m_t \geq \omega_t P_t C_t, \quad m'_{t+1} \geq \omega_{t+1} P_{t+1} C'_{t+1} \tag{2}$$

where ω_t, the inverse of the velocity of money, is a stochastic shock. The total quantity of money is simply $M_t = m_t + m'_t$. We see that at least the young household, who starts life without any financial asset, will need to borrow money in order to satisfy this cash in advance constraint. It can do so at the interest rate i_t set by the government.

The representative firm has a production function

$$Y_t = Z_t N_t \tag{3}$$

As in the previous chapters, we assume that the shocks α_t, ω_t, and Z_t are stochastic iid variables.

14.2.2 Government Policies

Now the government has two policy instruments. Monetary policy consists in setting the nominal interest rate i_t. Fiscal policy consists in levying taxes, denoted T_t in nominal terms, on the old households.

Since money and bonds now coexist, we must further specify what is the counterpart of these taxes. So we will assume that the counterpart of taxes T_t is a monetary creation equal to $-T_t$. Note that this fiscal policy is different from "traditional" fiscal policy where the counterpart of taxes is bond creation or destruction.[1]

We will finally assume that the central bank redistributes all its profits to the young household.[2]

14.2.3 The Timing

Again in each period events occur in three steps:

1. Government sets its two policy variables, the interest rate i_t and the taxes T_t. We will assume that i_t and T_t are functions only of macroeconomic variables up to $t - 1$ included (and therefore *not* of any variable or shock revealed in period t).

2. The wage (or price) is set by the private sector at its expected market-clearing value, without knowing the values of period t shocks α_t, ω_t, and Z_t.

3. The shocks become known to the private sector, and transactions are carried out accordingly.

---

1 Since deficits are automatically "monetized," our fiscal policy is somewhat of a hybrid of standard fiscal policy and monetary policy. We nevertheless call it fiscal policy in order to have a simple terminology.

2 This assumption is made to simplify calculations; it does not change anything substantial. The same model without this assumption is found in Bénassy (1998).

14.3   General Equilibrium Relations

In the discussion that follows we will be computing optimal policies under the three alternative assumptions of Walrasian market clearing, preset wages, and preset prices. In these three cases we will need to know the equilibrium values of a number of macroeconomic variables. These general equilibrium relations are summarized in the following proposition, which we will use in all that follows.

Proposition 1   *In all equilibria that we will consider, the following equilibrium relations hold:*

$$P_t Y_t = \frac{(1+i_t)\Omega_t + \alpha_t \Omega_{t+1}}{1 + \omega_t i_t} \tag{4}$$

$$P_t C_t = \frac{\alpha_t \Omega_{t+1}}{1 + \omega_t i_t} \tag{5}$$

$$P_t C'_t = \frac{(1+i_t)\Omega_t}{1 + \omega_t i_t} \tag{6}$$

$$\Omega_{t+1} = \Omega_t - T_{t+1} \tag{7}$$

If the goods market clears, we further have

$$\frac{W_t}{P_t} = Z_t \tag{8}$$

If the labor market clears, we have

$$W_t = (1 + \alpha_t)\Omega_{t+1} \tag{9}$$

Proof   Let us begin with the problem of the old household in period t. Denote by Ω_t the financial wealth that it has at the beginning of period t, *net of taxes* T_t. If the old household consumes C'_t, it has to keep $\omega_t P_t C'_t$ under the form of money, lends $\Omega_t - \omega_t P_t C'_t$ at the rate i_t, and will pay $(1 - \omega_t) P_t C'_t$ at the end of the period, so that it will be left with a financial wealth equal to

$$(1 + i_t)\Omega_t - (1 + \omega_t i_t) P_t C'_t \tag{10}$$

Of course, the old household wants to have zero wealth at the end of its life, so the second period consumption is given by

$$P_t C_t' = \frac{1 + i_t}{1 + \omega_t i_t} \Omega_t \qquad (11)$$

Since the old household borrows $\omega_t P_t C_t' - \Omega_t$ from the bank, the corresponding central bank profit is equal to $i_t(\omega_t P_t C_t' - \Omega_t)$.

Now let us write the maximization program of the young household born in t. When young, it receives wages $W_t N_t$, profits $\Pi_t = P_t Y_t - W_t N_t$ from the firms, and central bank profits denoted as Φ_t. It will be taxed T_{t+1} by the government when old. If it consumes C_t in the first period of its life, it will end up in the second period with a financial wealth:

$$\Omega_{t+1} = (W_t N_t + \Pi_t + \Phi_t - T_{t+1}) - (1 + \omega_t i_t) P_t C_t \qquad (12)$$

In view of (11), the expected value of $\log C_{t+1}'$ is, up to an unimportant constant, equal to $\log \Omega_{t+1}$, so that the household in the first period of his life solves the following program:

$$\max \alpha_t \log C_t + \log \Omega_{t+1} - (1 + \alpha_t) N_t \quad \text{s.t.}$$

$$\Omega_{t+1} = (W_t N_t + \Pi_t + \Phi_t - T_{t+1}) - (1 + \omega_t i_t) P_t C_t$$

The first-order conditions for this program yield

$$P_t C_t = \frac{\alpha_t}{1 + \alpha_t} \frac{W_t N_t + \Pi_t + \Phi_t - T_{t+1}}{1 + \omega_t i_t} = \frac{\alpha_t}{1 + \alpha_t} \frac{P_t Y_t + \Phi_t - T_{t+1}}{1 + \omega_t i_t} \qquad (13)$$

$$N_t^s = \frac{W_t - \Pi_t - \Phi_t + T_{t+1}}{W_t} \qquad (14)$$

The young consumer borrows $\omega_t P_t C_t$ so that the corresponding bank profit is $\omega_t i_t P_t C_t$. Adding the profits made on the young and old generations, we find that total central bank profits are equal to

$$\Phi_t = i_t(\omega_t P_t C_t + \omega_t P_t C_t' - \Omega_t) \qquad (15)$$

The equilibrium condition on the goods market is

$$C_t + C_t' = Y_t = Z_t N_t \tag{16}$$

Combining equations (11), (12), (13), (15), and (16), which are valid in all circumstances, we obtain equations (4) to (7). Now, if the goods market clears, the real wage W_t/P_t is equal to the marginal productivity of labor Z_t (equation 8). Finally, if the labor market clears, equation (14) is valid. Combining it with relations (4), (5), (6), and (15), we obtain (9).   ∎

14.4   Optimality

14.4.1   The Criterion

We will continue to use the same criterion as in the two previous chapters, which we recall here as

$$V_t = E_t \sum_{s=t}^{\infty} \beta^{s-t} \Delta_s \tag{17}$$

with

$$\Delta_t = \alpha_t \log C_t + \frac{\log C_t'}{\beta} - (1 + \alpha_t) N_t \tag{18}$$

14.4.2   A Characterization of Optimal States

We want first to derive the "first-best" allocation. The resource constraint in each period is

$$C_t + C_t' = Z_t N_t \tag{19}$$

In order to find the optimal allocation, we maximize in each period the quantity Δ_t (formula 18) subject to the resource constraint (19). We obtain immediately that the "first-best" allocation is characterized by

$$C_t = \frac{\alpha_t Z_t}{1 + \alpha_t} \tag{20}$$

$$C_t' = \frac{Z_t}{\beta(1 + \alpha_t)} \tag{21}$$

$$N_t = \frac{1}{1 + \alpha_t}\left(\alpha_t + \frac{1}{\beta}\right) \tag{22}$$

14.5 Walrasian Equilibrium

As in the previous chapters we first investigate optimal policies when prices and wages are Walrasian.

14.5.1 Computing the Equilibrium

In Walrasian equilibrium all equations (4) to (9) hold. Combining them, we find the Walrasian equilibrium values:

$$W_t^* = (1 + \alpha_t)\Omega_{t+1} \tag{23}$$

$$P_t^* = \frac{(1 + \alpha_t)\Omega_{t+1}}{Z_t} \tag{24}$$

$$C_t = \frac{\alpha_t Z_t}{(1 + \alpha_t)(1 + \omega_t i_t)} \tag{25}$$

$$C_t' = \frac{(1 + i_t)\Omega_t Z_t}{(1 + \alpha_t)(1 + \omega_t i_t)\Omega_{t+1}} \tag{26}$$

$$N_t = \frac{(1 + i_t)\Omega_t + \alpha_t \Omega_{t+1}}{(1 + \alpha_t)(1 + \omega_t i_t)\Omega_{t+1}} \tag{27}$$

where W_t^* and P_t^* are the Walrasian wage and price. We see from equation (27) that if government policy is "neutral," i.e., if $i_t = 0$ and $T_{t+1} = 0$ (and thus $\Omega_{t+1} = \Omega_t$), then the Walrasian quantity of labor is constant and equal to one.

14.5.2 Optimal Policies in the Walrasian Case

For later comparison with the results under nominal rigidities, we now compute as a benchmark optimal policies in the Walrasian case. They are characterized by the following proposition:

Proposition 2 *Under Walrasian wages and prices the optimal monetary and fiscal policies are given by*

$$i_t = 0 \tag{28}$$

$$\frac{\Omega_{t+1}}{\Omega_t} = \beta \tag{29}$$

Proof Intuition tells us that under the optimal policies the Walrasian equilibrium will be a first best. We can thus find the optimal policy by equating the first best values of C_t and C'_t (equations 20 and 21) and those obtained at the Walrasian equilibrium (equations 25 and 26). We therefore obtain the two conditions

$$C_t = \frac{\alpha_t Z_t}{(1 + \alpha_t)(1 + \omega_t i_t)} = \frac{\alpha_t Z_t}{1 + \alpha_t} \tag{30}$$

$$C'_t = \frac{(1 + i_t)\Omega_t Z_t}{(1 + \alpha_t)(1 + \omega_t i_t)\Omega_{t+1}} = \frac{Z_t}{\beta(1 + \alpha_t)} \tag{31}$$

Simplifying equations (30) and (31), we obtain the two conditions (28) and (29).
∎

As compared with the results of chapter 12, we see that we have with formulas (28) and (29) two Friedman rules, instead of one as in the two previous chapters: set the nominal interest rate at zero, and have a monetary aggregate grow at a rate equal to the discount factor β. Both do originate in Friedman's (1969) "optimal quantity of money" article. We see here that these rules can be implemented independently by the monetary and fiscal authorities.

Again, the fundamental thing to note, in view of our interest in the "activism versus nonactivism" debate, is that rules (28) and (29) are totally nonactivist, since they do not depend in any way on any event, past or present.

We will now see again that the introduction of preset wages or prices changes things quite drastically.

14.6 Preset Wages

We begin our investigation with preset wages, and assume that the preset wage is equal to the expected value of the Walrasian wage:

$$W_t = E_{t-1} W_t^* \tag{32}$$

where the expression of W_t^* is given in formula (23). So the wage is equal to

$$W_t = E_{t-1}[(1 + \alpha_t)\Omega_{t+1}] \tag{33}$$

14.6.1 The Equilibrium

At the preset wage equilibrium, equations (4) to (8) hold. So the preset wage equilibrium is characterized by the following relations:

$$C_t = \frac{\alpha_t \Omega_{t+1} Z_t}{(1 + \omega_t i_t) W_t} \tag{34}$$

$$C_t' = \frac{(1 + i_t)\Omega_t Z_t}{(1 + \omega_t i_t) W_t} \tag{35}$$

$$N_t = \frac{(1 + i_t)\Omega_t + \alpha_t \Omega_{t+1}}{(1 + \omega_t i_t) W_t} \tag{36}$$

14.6.2 Optimal Policies

We now characterize the optimal fiscal and monetary policies through the following proposition:

Proposition 3 *Under preset wages the optimal monetary and fiscal policies are given by*

$$i_t = 0 \tag{37}$$

$$\frac{\Omega_{t+1}}{\Omega_t} = \frac{\beta(1 + \alpha_a)}{1 + \alpha_t} \tag{38}$$

where

$$\alpha_a = E(\alpha_t) \tag{39}$$

Proof To find the optimal policy in a simple manner, we will use a slightly roundabout method. Essentially we use the fact that the value of C_t' in (35) is independent of the demand shock α_t. We will proceed in two steps. (1) We will compute the best possible situation attainable under the constraint that C_t' is independent of α_t, and (2) we will show that the policy defined by (37) and (38) actually leads to this best situation so that it is indeed the optimal policy.

Let us now carry out step 1. For that we maximize the expected value of the "period t utility" Δ_t:

$$\Delta_t = \alpha_t \log C_t + \frac{1}{\beta} \log C_t' - (1 + \alpha_t) L_t \tag{40}$$

subject to the feasibility constraint $C_t + C_t' = Z_t L_t$ and the condition that C_t' be independent of α_t. Let us first insert the feasibility constraint into (40). The maximand becomes

$$\alpha_t \log C_t + \frac{1}{\beta} \log C_t' - (1 + \alpha_t) \frac{C_t + C_t'}{Z_t} \tag{41}$$

Since there is no constraint on C_t, we immediately find its optimal value:

$$C_t = \frac{\alpha_t Z_t}{1 + \alpha_t} \tag{42}$$

Now taking out constant terms, we have to maximize the expected value of

$$\frac{1}{\beta} \log C_t' - (1 + \alpha_t) \frac{C_t'}{Z_t} \tag{43}$$

under the only constraint that C_t' is independent of α_t. This amounts to maximizing, for every value of the shock Z_t, the expectation of the above with respect to α_t, namely the quantity

$$\frac{1}{\beta} \log C_t' - (1 + \alpha_a) \frac{C_t'}{Z_t} \tag{44}$$

which yields immediately

$$C_t' = \frac{Z_t}{\beta(1 + \alpha_a)} \tag{45}$$

We now move to step 2, and see that policies (37) and (38) allow indeed to reach the allocation defined by (42) and (45). To show this, we equalize the values in (34) and (35) to those we just found (42 and 45):

$$C_t = \frac{\alpha_t \Omega_{t+1} Z_t}{(1 + \omega_t i_t) W_t} = \frac{\alpha_t Z_t}{1 + \alpha_t} \tag{46}$$

$$C_t' = \frac{(1 + i_t)\Omega_t Z_t}{(1 + \omega_t i_t) W_t} = \frac{Z_t}{\beta(1 + \alpha_a)} \tag{47}$$

Taking first equation (46), and comparing it with the value of the Walrasian wage W_t^* (equation 23), we obtain

$$W_t = \frac{(1 + \alpha_t)\Omega_{t+1}}{1 + \omega_t i_t} = \frac{W_t^*}{1 + \omega_t i_t} \tag{48}$$

Given that $W_t = E_{t-1} W_t^*$, the only way to make these consistent is to have $i_t = 0$ (equation 37). Inserting this value $i_t = 0$ into equations (46) and (47) yields

$$\Omega_{t+1} = \frac{W_t}{1 + \alpha_t} \tag{49}$$

$$W_t = \beta(1 + \alpha_a)\Omega_t \tag{50}$$

Combining (49) and (50), we finally obtain the optimal fiscal policy (equation 38). ∎

The optimal monetary-fiscal policy consists of equations (37) and (38). The "open-market" rule is the same as in the Walrasian case ($i_t = 0$), but the optimal fiscal policy (38) is now an activist countercyclical one: a negative demand shock today (low α_t) triggers a monetary expansion tomorrow (low T_{t+1}) and conversely for a positive demand shock.

Let us note that since $i_t = 0$, equation (48) is rewritten as

$$W_t = W_t^* \tag{51}$$

This means that, whatever the value of the shocks, the labor market will be cleared at all times despite the preset wages!

We may note that although we added monetary policy, the results are extremely similar to those of chapter 12 where fiscal policy only was available. This is actually not surprising. First, the monetary velocity shocks ω_t are completely taken care of by the zero nominal interest rate. Second, with $i_t = 0$, money and nonmonetary assets become indistinguishable, and we are thus back to the simpler OLG model studied in chapter 12.

As a result the expression of policy (38) as a function of observable variables will be exactly the same as that found in section 12.6.3, namely

$$\frac{\Omega_{t+1}}{\Omega_t} = 1 + \beta(1 + \alpha_a) - \beta(1 + \alpha_a)N_t \tag{52}$$

14.7 Preset Prices

So far we have concentrated on nominal wage rigidities. In order to be complete, we should also investigate price rigidities. We will here assume that instead of wages, it is the prices that are preset according to the formula

$$P_t = E_{t-1}P_t^* \tag{53}$$

where P_t^* is given in equation (24). So

$$P_t = E_{t-1}\left[\frac{(1 + \alpha_t)\Omega_{t+1}}{Z_t}\right] \tag{54}$$

14.7.1 Computing the Equilibrium

Now equation (8), representing the firms' goods supply behavior, does not hold anymore since the price is preset. The other equilibrium equations (4), (5), (6), (7), and (9) are valid. Combining them, we obtain the values of the preset price equilibrium quantities:

$$C_t = \frac{\alpha_t \Omega_{t+1}}{(1 + \omega_t i_t)P_t} \tag{55}$$

$$C'_t = \frac{(1 + i_t)\Omega_t}{(1 + \omega_t i_t)P_t} \tag{56}$$

$$N_t = \frac{(1 + i_t)\Omega_t + \alpha_t \Omega_{t+1}}{(1 + \omega_t i_t)P_t Z_t} \tag{57}$$

14.7.2 Optimal Policies

We characterize the optimal fiscal and monetary policies by the following proposition:

Proposition 4 *Under preset prices the optimal monetary and fiscal policies are given by*

$$i_t = 0 \tag{58}$$

$$\frac{\Omega_{t+1}}{\Omega_t} = \frac{\beta(1 + \alpha_a)Z_t}{(1 + \alpha_t)Z_a} \tag{59}$$

where

$$\alpha_a = E(\alpha_t) \qquad \frac{1}{Z_a} = E\left(\frac{1}{Z_t}\right) \tag{60}$$

Proof Following the method of section 14.6, we note that the value of C'_t in (56) is independent of both the demand shock α_t and productivity shock Z_t. We thus maximize again the expected value of Δ_t:

$$\Delta_t = \alpha_t \log C_t + \frac{1}{\beta} \log C'_t - (1 + \alpha_t)N_t \tag{61}$$

subject this time to the feasibility constraint $C_t + C'_t = Z_t N_t$ and the condition that C'_t be independent of both α_t and Z_t. We obtain

$$C_t = \frac{\alpha_t Z_t}{1 + \alpha_t}, \quad C'_t = \frac{Z_a}{\beta(1 + \alpha_a)} \tag{62}$$

Now, if a set of policies allows to reach these values, it will be the optimal one. We thus equalize the values in (55) and (56) to those we just found (62):

$$C_t = \frac{\alpha_t \Omega_{t+1}}{(1 + \omega_t i_t) P_t} = \frac{\alpha_t Z_t}{1 + \alpha_t} \tag{63}$$

$$C'_t = \frac{(1 + i_t)\Omega_t}{(1 + \omega_t i_t) P_t} = \frac{Z_a}{\beta(1 + \alpha_a)} \tag{64}$$

Using first equation (63), and comparing it with the value of the Walrasian wage P_t^* (equation 24), we obtain

$$P_t = \frac{(1 + \alpha_t)\Omega_{t+1}}{(1 + \omega_t i_t) Z_t} = \frac{P_t^*}{1 + \omega_t i_t} \tag{65}$$

Since $P_t = E_{t-1} P_t^*$, the only way to make these consistent is to have $i_t = 0$ (equation 58). Inserting $i_t = 0$ into equations (63) and (64) results in

$$\Omega_{t+1} = \frac{P_t Z_t}{1 + \alpha_t} \tag{66}$$

$$P_t = \frac{\beta(1 + \alpha_a)\Omega_t}{Z_a} \tag{67}$$

Finally, combining (66) and (67), we arrive at the optimal fiscal policy (equation 59). ∎

The "open market" rule is again the same as in the Walrasian situation ($i_t = 0$). Optimal fiscal policy (59), as in the preset wages case, reacts counter-cyclically to demand shocks α_t. Moreover it reacts now positively to produc-tivity shocks Z_t. This might look like an element of "procyclical" policy, but actually it is not if we look at things from the point of view of the labor mar-ket: under rigid prices, a positive productivity shock creates a *negative* shock on labor market demand. It is thus natural in such a case to want to engineer a demand expansion so as to bring labor market balance, and this policy is countercyclical from the point of view of the labor market.

Our policy has further the same remarkable feature as in the preset wage case. Indeed, with $i_t = 0$, equation (65) becomes

$$P_t = P_t^* \tag{68}$$

So, although the price is preset before the shocks are revealed, the goods market is always cleared under our optimal policy. Note, however, comparing (62) and (21), that this optimal policy does not allow us to reach the first-best optimum (the same was true under preset wages). Nominal rigidities still result in some residual efficiency cost, however attenuated this cost is by our optimal policy.

14.7.3 Implementation

Again, we can express policy (59) in terms of observable variables. The technology shock Z_t is observable, since it is equal to Y_t/N_t. As for the demand shock, combining (3), (54), (57), (58), and (59) we obtain

$$\frac{1}{1+\alpha_t} = 1 - \frac{\beta(1+\alpha_a)Y_t - Z_a}{\beta(1+\alpha_a)Z_t} \tag{69}$$

Inserting this into (59), we obtain the optimal fiscal policy rule:

$$\frac{\Omega_{t+1}}{\Omega_t} = 1 + \beta(1+\alpha_a)\frac{Z_t}{Z_a} - \beta(1+\alpha_a)\frac{Y_t}{Z_a} \tag{70}$$

14.8 Conclusions

We constructed in this chapter a simple but rigorous model of a dynamic economy submitted to three types of shocks (technological, monetary, and real demand shocks), and studied the optimal combination of fiscal and monetary policies under the three regimes of market clearing, preset wages, and preset prices.

An important question that motivated this investigation was whether wage or price rigidities make a valid case for policy activism. The answer is, again, clearly yes. We found the optimal policies to be activist in both cases of preset wages or prices. Our results are not subject to the usual critiques since (1) the model is microfounded and (2) it satisfies the informational restrictions (adequately) prescribed by Sargent and Wallace (1975). We should also note that this optimality of activism was not an a priori obvious property of the model, since in the Walrasian version it is optimal to follow the two (nonactivist) Friedman rules.

We should now qualify our results a bit more, since not any combination of shocks and rigidities is conducive to policy activism.

First, we note that there is a clear-cut difference between the prescriptions for fiscal and monetary policy: the optimal monetary policy is always to maintain the nominal interest rate at zero so that this part of the policy remains nonactivist. On the other hand optimal fiscal policy will respond in a countercyclical manner to real demand shocks α_t, whether wages or prices are rigid.

Second, it was often the case in models of Keynesian inspiration that government should respond countercyclically to all demand shocks. Here we must clearly differentiate between the two types of demand shocks: money velocity shocks ω_t and real demand shocks α_t. As it turns out, only the existence of real demand shocks α_t makes it necessary to run an activist fiscal policy. As for the velocity shocks ω_t, a zero nominal interest rate is sufficient to take care of such shocks in all cases (rigid wages or prices).

Finally we should note that the optimal reaction to a particular shock depends very much on the underlying rigidity. We saw, for example, that in this model, fiscal policy should not react to technology shocks if wages are rigid but should react positively if prices are rigid.

So, while activist policies are superior in treating nominal rigidities, it is clear that detailed knowledge of the economy's rigidities and shocks is necessary before embarking on such policies.

14.9 References

This chapter is based on Bénassy (1998). Similar issues had been studied by Ireland (1996), with actually somewhat different conclusions, because he focused on a subset of the shocks.

The cash in advance formulation originates in Clower (1967). Friedman rules for OLG models are found in Abel (1987) and in Crettez, Michel, and Wigniolle (1999).

15

Monetary Rules and Fiscal Policy

15.1 Introduction

In the last three chapters we studied optimal government policies. We considered either fiscal policy alone (chapters 12 and 13) or the combination of monetary and fiscal policies (chapter 14), paying particular attention to the issues raised many years ago by Sargent and Wallace (1975). However, in recent years another lively line of study has concentrated on optimal monetary rules. The objective of these studies is to find the interest rate policy that should be pursued by a monetary authority faced with the task of optimally stabilizing the economy. A common characteristic of many of these studies is that, unlike the former literature on stabilization and our own approach in this text, they often disregard fiscal policy. In view of the importance of fiscal policy in the optimal stabilization packages that we found in the preceding chapters, a natural question is whether this neglect of fiscal policy makes a big difference in monetary policy prescriptions. We will see next that it does.

The usual argument for ignoring fiscal policy is that it takes time to implement, whereas monetary policy can be implemented fairly quickly. We take this objection into account by introducing a difference of timing between monetary and fiscal policy. We assume, as in most of the literature on monetary rules, that monetary policy can react to all current shocks. On the contrary, fiscal policy, as in the previous chapters, can react only to past shocks. So there is a clear informational advantage to monetary policy.

Our results will show, first, that studying monetary policy alone is likely to lead to major distortions in the design of policy. For example, we find below that although monetary policy when taken alone should be activist, it can become nonactivist when combined with optimal fiscal policies in the same model.

Second, we find out that the fiscal-monetary combination allows us to attain much better outcomes. Of course, this should be expected since we are adding one more policy instrument. But we will see that the stabilization properties of the fiscal-monetary mix are much superior to those of the optimal monetary rule alone.

15.2   The Model

15.2.1   Markets and Agents

Let us consider again a monetary overlapping generations model with production. The economy includes representative firms and households, and the government. Households of generation t work N_t and consume C_t in period t, consume C'_{t+1} in period $t+1$. They maximize the expected value of their utility U_t, with

$$U_t = \alpha_t \log C_t + \log C'_{t+1} - (1 + \alpha_t) N_t \qquad (1)$$

where α_t is a positive iid stochastic variable. Households are submitted in each period of their life to a cash in advance constraint:

$$m_t \geq \omega_t P_t C_t, \quad m'_{t+1} \geq P_{t+1} C'_{t+1} \qquad (2)$$

where ω_t, the inverse of the velocity of money, is a stochastic shock. Note that the old household, which is in the last period of its life, has to pay 100 percent cash. The total quantity of money is simply $M_t = m_t + m'_t$.

The representative firm in period t has a production function

$$Y_t = Z_t N_t \qquad (3)$$

where Y_t is output, N_t labor input and Z_t a technology shock common to all firms. We assume that the firms belong to the young households and distribute their profits to these households.

As in the previous chapter, government has two policy instruments: it sets the interest rate i_t (monetary policy) and taxes T_t in money terms from the old households (fiscal policy). We also assume, as before, that the central bank redistributes its profits Φ_t to the young households.

15.2.2 The Comparison

We will compare two different sets of policies under the assumption of preset wages. We denote these as the "optimal monetary rule" and the "optimal policy mix."

In deriving the optimal monetary rule, we follow the recent trend in disregarding fiscal policy. So we assume either that the fiscal tranfers are zero or that they correspond to a constant (and possibly optimized) growth of financial assets. On the other hand, we assume, again following recent literature, that the central bank is allowed to react to the *current* shocks. This clearly gives a strong informational advantage to the central bank.

In deriving the optimal policy mix, we assume that the government can use fiscal policy, in addition to monetary policy, but that fiscal policy can react to past shocks only, and not to any contemporaneous shocks.

15.2.3 The Criterion

To assess the optimality properties of government policies, we will use the same criterion V_t as in the previous chapters:

$$V_t = E_t \sum_{s=t-1}^{\infty} \beta^{s-t} U_s \tag{4}$$

As before, V_t can be rewritten as

$$V_t = E_t \sum_{s=t}^{\infty} \beta^{s-t} \Delta_s \tag{5}$$

with

$$\Delta_t = \alpha_t \log C_t + \frac{\log C_t'}{\beta} - (1 + \alpha_t) N_t \tag{6}$$

15.3 General Equilibrium Relations

In the policy exercises that follow, we need to know the equilibrium values of a number of macroeconomic variables. These general equilibrium relations are summarized in the following proposition.

Proposition 1 *If the goods market clears, the following equilibrium relations hold:*

$$P_t Y_t = \frac{\alpha_t \Omega_{t+1}}{1 + \omega_t i_t} + \Omega_t \tag{7}$$

$$P_t C_t = \frac{\alpha_t \Omega_{t+1}}{1 + \omega_t i_t} \tag{8}$$

$$P_t C_t' = \Omega_t \tag{9}$$

$$\Omega_{t+1} = \Omega_t - T_{t+1} \tag{10}$$

$$\frac{W_t}{P_t} = Z_t \tag{11}$$

If the labor market clears, we further have

$$W_t = (1 + \alpha_t)\Omega_{t+1} \tag{12}$$

Proof Let us begin with the problem of the old household in period t. We denote by Ω_t the financial wealth that it has at the beginning of period t, *net of taxes* T_t. With a 100 percent cash in advance constraint, its consumption is simply given by

$$P_t C_t' = \Omega_t \tag{13}$$

Next we write the maximization program of the young household born in t. When young, it receives wages $W_t N_t$, firms' profits $\Pi_t = P_t Y_t - W_t N_t$, and central bank profits Φ_t. It will be taxed T_{t+1} by the government when old. If it consumes C_t in the first period of its life, it will end up in the second period with a financial wealth:

$$\Omega_{t+1} = (W_t N_t + \Pi_t + \Phi_t - T_{t+1}) - (1 + \omega_t i_t)P_t C_t \tag{14}$$

In view of (13) the expected value of $\log C_{t+1}'$ is, up to a constant, equal to $\log \Omega_{t+1}$. So the household in the first period of its life solves the following program:

$$\max \alpha_t \log C_t + \log \Omega_{t+1} - (1 + \alpha_t) N_t \quad \text{s.t.}$$

$$\Omega_{t+1} = (W_t N_t + \Pi_t + \Phi_t - T_{t+1}) - (1 + \omega_t i_t) P_t C_t$$

The first-order conditions are

$$P_t C_t = \frac{\alpha_t}{1 + \alpha_t} \frac{W_t N_t + \Pi_t + \Phi_t - T_{t+1}}{1 + \omega_t i_t} = \frac{\alpha_t}{1 + \alpha_t} \frac{P_t Y_t + \Phi_t - T_{t+1}}{1 + \omega_t i_t} \quad (15)$$

$$N_t^s = \frac{W_t - \Pi_t - \Phi_t + T_{t+1}}{W_t} \quad (16)$$

The young household borrows $\omega_t P_t C_t$ so that the central bank profit is

$$\Phi_t = i_t \omega_t P_t C_t \quad (17)$$

We also have the equation of goods market balance

$$C_t + C_t' = Y_t = Z_t N_t \quad (18)$$

Combining (13), (14), (15), (17), and (18), which are valid in all circumstances, we obtain equations (7) to (10). Since the goods market clears, the real wage W_t / P_t is equal to the marginal productivity of labor Z_t (equation 11). Now, if the labor market clears, equation (16) is valid. Combining it with relations (7), (8), and (17), we obtain (12). ∎

15.4 Preset Wages Equilibria

We will make here again the traditional assumption that the preset wage is equal to the expected value of the Walrasian wage, namely

$$W_t = E_{t-1} W_t^* \quad (19)$$

The value of W_t^* is given in equation (12), so the preset wage is equal to

$$W_t = E_{t-1} [(1 + \alpha_t) \Omega_{t+1}] \quad (20)$$

At the preset wage equilibrium equations (7) to (11) hold, and the various quantities are given by the relations

$$C_t = \frac{\alpha_t \Omega_{t+1} Z_t}{(1 + \omega_t i_t) W_t} \tag{21}$$

$$C_t' = \frac{\Omega_t Z_t}{W_t} \tag{22}$$

$$N_t = \frac{\alpha_t \Omega_{t+1}}{(1 + \omega_t i_t) W_t} + \frac{\Omega_t}{W_t} \tag{23}$$

15.5   The Optimal Monetary Rule

We now perform the exercise that is usually carried out by students of optimal monetary rules. We compute the best interest rate policy, assuming that it can react to any shock and that, in contrast, the fiscal policy is "passive." This last assumption is formalized by having taxes equal to a constant ratio of nominal assets:

$$\Omega_{t+1} = \Omega_t - T_{t+1} = \gamma \Omega_t \tag{24}$$

Proposition 2   *Under fiscal policy (24) the optimal interest rate rule is*

$$i_t = \max\left[0, \frac{\alpha_t - \alpha_a}{(1 + \alpha_a)\omega_t}\right] \tag{25}$$

where

$$\alpha_a = E\left(\alpha_t\right) \tag{26}$$

Moreover the optimal value of γ is

$$\gamma = \beta \tag{27}$$

Proof   From (20) and (24) we first find the value of the wage:

$$W_t = E_{t-1}\left[(1 + \alpha_t)\Omega_{t+1}\right] = \gamma(1 + \alpha_a)\Omega_t \tag{28}$$

Inserting this into formulas (21), (22), and (23), we find the values of C_t, C'_t, and N_t at the preset wage equilibrium:

$$C_t = \frac{\alpha_t Z_t}{(1 + \omega_t i_t)(1 + \alpha_a)} \tag{29}$$

$$C'_t = \frac{Z_t}{\gamma(1 + \alpha_a)} \tag{30}$$

$$N_t = \frac{\alpha_t}{(1 + \omega_t i_t)(1 + \alpha_a)} + \frac{1}{\gamma(1 + \alpha_a)} \tag{31}$$

Next we insert these values of consumptions and labor into the criterion Δ_t (equation 6). The government has to maximize, with respect to i_t, and for each value of the shocks

$$\Delta_t = \alpha_t \log\left[\frac{\alpha_t Z_t}{(1 + \omega_t i_t)(1 + \alpha_a)}\right] + \frac{1}{\beta} \log\left[\frac{Z_t}{\gamma(1 + \alpha_a)}\right]$$
$$- \frac{1 + \alpha_t}{1 + \alpha_a}\left(\frac{\alpha_t}{1 + \omega_t i_t} + \frac{1}{\gamma}\right) \tag{32}$$

subject to the constraint $i_t \geq 0$. The solution is rule (25). To find the optimal value of γ, we maximize the expected value of Δ_t (equation 32) with respect to γ. This yields (27). ∎

We may first note that this optimal interest rule is highly nonlinear: it dampens demand shocks when they are above average ($\alpha_t > \alpha_a$). But it is totally inactive for deflationary shocks because of the constraint $i_t \geq 0$.

We may further inquire how well the labor market is stabilized through this rule. We have already computed the demand for labor (equation 31). Let us now compute labor supply:

$$N_t^s = \frac{W_t - \Pi_t - \Phi_t + T_{t+1}}{W_t} = \frac{1 + \gamma\alpha_a}{\gamma(1 + \alpha_a)} - \frac{\alpha_t \omega_t i_t}{(1 + \alpha_a)(1 + \omega_t i_t)} \tag{33}$$

Comparing the two, we obtain

$$N_t - N_t^s = \frac{\alpha_t - \alpha_a}{1 + \alpha_a} \tag{34}$$

Clearly, in all cases interest rate policy is powerless to cure employment imbalances. We will now see that the joint consideration of monetary and fiscal policy, even under much more stringent informational constraints for fiscal policy, allows to remedy that problem.

15.6   The Optimal Policy Mix

The optimal policy mix can be characterized by the following proposition:

Proposition 3   *Under preset wages the optimal policy mix is given by*

$$i_t = 0 \tag{35}$$

$$\frac{\Omega_{t+1}}{\Omega_t} = \frac{\beta(1+\alpha_a)}{1+\alpha_t} \tag{36}$$

Proof   To find the optimal policy in a simple manner, we use the same method that we used in propositions 3 and 4 of chapter 14. We first note that the value of C_t' in (22) is independent of the demand shock α_t. So we must first find the best possible situation that can be attained under such a constraint. For that we maximize the expected value of the "period t utility" Δ_t:

$$\Delta_t = \alpha_t \log C_t + \frac{1}{\beta} \log C_t' - (1+\alpha_t)N_t \tag{37}$$

subject to the feasibility constraint $C_t + C_t' = Z_t N_t$ and the condition that C_t' be independent of α_t. We obtain

$$C_t = \frac{\alpha_t Z_t}{1+\alpha_t}, \quad C_t' = \frac{Z_t}{\beta(1+\alpha_a)} \tag{38}$$

Now, if a policy allows the government to attain these values, it is an optimal policy. To find this policy, we equalize the values in (21) and (22) to those we just found (38):

$$C_t = \frac{\alpha_t \Omega_{t+1} Z_t}{(1+\omega_t i_t) W_t} = \frac{\alpha_t Z_t}{1+\alpha_t} \tag{39}$$

$$C_t' = \frac{(1+i_t)\,\Omega_t Z_t}{(1+\omega_t i_t) W_t} = \frac{Z_t}{\beta(1+\alpha_a)} \tag{40}$$

Using first equation (39), and comparing it with the value of the Walrasian wage W_t^* (equation 12), we obtain

$$W_t = \frac{(1+\alpha_t)\Omega_{t+1}}{1+\omega_t i_t} = \frac{W_t^*}{1+\omega_t i_t} \tag{41}$$

Given that $W_t = E_{t-1}W_t^*$, the only way to make these consistent is to have $i_t = 0$ (equation 35). Next, inserting the value $i_t = 0$ into (39) and (40), we obtain

$$\Omega_{t+1} = \frac{W_t}{1+\alpha_t} \tag{42}$$

$$W_t = \beta(1+\alpha_a)\Omega_t \tag{43}$$

Combining (42) and (43), we obtain the optimal fiscal policy (equation 36).

∎

The optimal policy mix consists of equations (35) and (36). We see that it combines a passive monetary policy ($i_t = 0$) to an activist countercyclical fiscal policy. Let us note that since $i_t = 0$, equation (41) is rewritten as

$$W_t = W_t^* \tag{44}$$

Once again, whatever the value of the shocks, the labor market is cleared at all times despite the preset wages!

15.7 A Comparison

Let us compare the optimal policy mix and the optimal monetary rule. The most striking points are presented in table 15.1. In the table we see particularly well the two points outlined in the introduction:

1. The nature of optimal policies changes completely from one experiment to the other. In the optimal policy mix, the monetary policy is "inactive" (although the zero interest rate plays a central role in neutralizing monetary shocks) and the fiscal policy is activist. In the optimal monetary rule, in the contrary, the interest rate policy becomes activist (although in an asymmetrical manner). We see that this "interest rate activism" is entirely due to the neglect of fiscal policy.

Table 15.1

	Optimal Policy Mix	Optimal Monetary Rule
Fiscal policy	$\dfrac{\Omega_{t+1}}{\Omega_t} = \dfrac{\beta(1+\alpha_a)}{1+\alpha_t}$	$\dfrac{\Omega_{t+1}}{\Omega_t} = \beta$
Monetary policy	$i_t = 0$	$i_t = \max\left[0, \dfrac{\alpha_t - \alpha_a}{(1+\alpha_a)\omega_t}\right]$
$N_t - N_t^s$	$N_t - N_t^s = 0$	$N_t - N_t^s = \dfrac{\alpha_t - \alpha_a}{1+\alpha_a}$

2. Neglect of fiscal policy leads to very suboptimal outcomes. Whereas the optimal policy mix completely eliminates imbalances in the labor market, the optimal monetary rule cannot prevent shocks from creating labor market imbalances, so it appears to be very much a second-best exercise.

15.8 Conclusions

We saw in this chapter that focusing on optimal monetary policy and completely ignoring the accompanying fiscal policy can lead to highly distorted and suboptimal recommendations. The usual justification for ignoring fiscal policy is that unlike monetary policy, it can be time-consuming to implement. Although an important objection, it does not quite apply here, since we precisely constrained fiscal policy to react with a lag. So the next step would be to see how the results of this chapter can be adapted if the lag structure is modified. But, in view of the strong results we obtained, it is clear that the idea of a necessary complementarity between fiscal and monetary policies cannot be dismissed so easily.

15.9 References

This chapter is based on Bénassy (1999).

The study of monetary policy rules has gained popularity since the stimulating article by Taylor (1993) was published. Surveys and original contributions are found, among others, in Clarida, Gali, and Gertler (1999), Erceg, Henderson, and Levin (2000), Mc Callum (1999), and Taylor (1999a, b).

Bibliography

Abel, Andrew B. (1987). Optimal monetary growth. *Journal of Monetary Economics* 19: 437–50.

Acemoglu, Daron, and Andrew Scott (1994). Asymmetries in the cyclical behaviour of U.K. labour markets. *Economic Journal* 104: 1303–23.

Aghion, Philippe, and Peter W. Howitt (1992). A model of growth through creative destruction. *Econometrica* 60: 323–51.

Aghion, Philippe, and Peter W. Howitt (1998). *Endogenous Growth Theory*. Cambridge: MIT Press.

Altug, Sumru, Richard A. Ashley, and Douglas M. Patterson (1999). Are technology shocks nonlinear? *Macroeconomic Dynamics* 3: 506–33.

Andersen, Torben M. (1985a). Price and output responsiveness to nominal changes under differential information. *European Economic Review* 29: 63–87.

Andersen, Torben M. (1985b). Price dynamics under imperfect information. *Journal of Economic Dynamics and Control* 9: 339–61.

Andersen, Torben M. (1986a). Differential information and the role for an active stabilization policy. *Economica* 53: 321–38.

Andersen, Torben M. (1986b). Pre-set prices, differential information and monetary policy. *Oxford Economic Papers* 38: 456–80.

Andersen, Torben M. (1994). *Price Rigidity: Causes and Macroeconomic Implications*. Oxford: Oxford University Press.

Andersen, Torben M. (1998). Persistency in sticky price models. *European Economic Review* 42: 593–603.

Arnsperger, Christian, and David de la Croix (1993). Bargaining and equilibrium unemployment: Narrowing the gap between New Keynesian and "disequilibrium" theories. *European Journal of Political Economy* 9: 163–90.

Arrow, Kenneth J. (1959). Toward a theory of price adjustment. In M. Abramowitz, ed., *The Allocation of Economic Resources*. Stanford: Stanford University Press, pp. 41–51.

Arrow, Kenneth J., and Gérard Debreu (1954). Existence of an equilibrium for a competitive economy. *Econometrica* 22: 265–90.

Arrow, Kenneth J., and Frank H. Hahn (1971). *General Competitive Analysis*. San Francisco: Holden-Day.

Ascari, Guido (2000). Optimising agents, staggered wages and persistence in the real effects of money shocks. *Economic Journal* 110: 664–86.

Balasko, Yves (1979). Budget-constrained Pareto-efficient allocations. *Journal of Economic Theory* 21: 359–79.

Ball, Laurence, and David Romer (1990). Real rigidities and the nonneutrality of money. *Review of Economic Studies* 57: 183–203.

Barro, Robert J. (1972). A theory of monopolistic price adjustment. *Review of Economic Studies* 34: 17–26.

Barro, Robert J., and Herschel I. Grossman (1971). A general disequilibrium model of income and employment. *American Economic Review* 61: 82–93.

Barro, Robert J., and Herschel I. Grossman (1974). Suppressed inflation and the supply multiplier. *Review of Economic Studies* 41: 87–104.

Barro, Robert J., and Herschel I. Grossman (1976). *Money, Employment and Inflation*. Cambridge: Cambridge University Press.

Bean, Charles (1984). Optimal wage bargains. *Economica* 51: 141–49.

Bean, Charles (1989). Capital shortages and persistent unemployment. *Economic Policy* 8: 11–53.

Bellman, Richard (1957). *Dynamic Programming*. Princeton: Princeton University Press.

Bénassy, Jean-Pascal (1973). Disequilibrium theory. Ph.D. dissertation and Working Paper. University of California, Berkeley. Hungarian translation in *Szygma* (1974).

Bénassy, Jean-Pascal (1975a). Neo-Keynesian disequilibrium theory in a monetary economy. *Review of Economic Studies* 42: 503–23.

Bénassy, Jean-Pascal (1975b). Disequilibrium exchange in barter and monetary economies. *Economic Inquiry* 13: 131–56.

Bénassy, Jean-Pascal (1976a). The disequilibrium approach to monopolistic price setting and general monopolistic equilibrium. *Review of Economic Studies* 43: 69–81.

Bénassy, Jean-Pascal (1976b). Théorie néokeynésienne du déséquilibre dans une économie monétaire. *Cahiers du Séminaire d'Econométrie* 17: 81–113.

Bénassy, Jean-Pascal (1976c). Théorie du déséquilibre et fondements microéconomiques de la macroéconomie. *Revue Economique* 27: 755–804.

Bénassy, Jean-Pascal (1977a). A neoKeynesian model of price and quantity determination in disequilibrium. In G. Schwödiauer, ed., *Equilibrium and Disequilibrium in Economic Theory*. Boston: Reidel.

Bénassy, Jean-Pascal (1977b). On quantity signals and the foundations of effective demand theory. *Scandinavian Journal of Economics* 79: 147–68.

Bénassy, Jean-Pascal (1978). Cost and demand inflation revisited: A neo-Keynesian approach. *Economie Appliquée* 31: 113–33.

Bénassy, Jean-Pascal (1982). *The Economics of Market Disequilibrium.* New York: Academic Press.

Bénassy, Jean-Pascal (1984). A non-Walrasian model of the business cycle. *Journal of Economic Behavior and Organisation* 5: 77–89.

Bénassy, Jean-Pascal (1986). *Macroeconomics: An Introduction to the non-Walrasian Approach.* New York: Academic Press.

Bénassy, Jean-Pascal (1987). Imperfect competition, unemployment and policy. *European Economic Review* 31: 417–26.

Bénassy, Jean-Pascal (1988). The objective demand curve in general equilibrium with price makers. *Economic Journal* 98 (suppl.): 37–49.

Bénassy, Jean-Pascal (1989). Market size and substitutability in imperfect competition: A Bertrand-Edgeworth-Chamberlin model. *Review of Economic Studies* 56: 217–34.

Bénassy, Jean-Pascal (1990). Non-Walrasian equilibria, money and macroeconomics. In B. Friedman and F. H. Hahn, eds., *Handbook of Monetary Economics.* Amsterdam: North-Holland, pp.103–69.

Bénassy, Jean-Pascal (1991a). Microeconomic foundations and properties of a macroeconomic model with imperfect competition. In K. J. Arrow, ed., *Issues in Contemporary Economics: Markets and Welfare,* vol. 1. London: Macmillan, pp. 121–38.

Bénassy, Jean-Pascal (1991b). Monopolistic competition. In W. Hildenbrand and H. Sonnenschein, eds., *Handbook of Mathematical Economics,* vol. 4. Amsterdam: North Holland, pp. 1997–2045.

Bénassy, Jean-Pascal (1991c). Optimal government policy in a macroeconomic model with imperfect competition and rational expectations. In W. Barnett, B. Cornet, C. d'Aspremont, J. J. Gabszewicz, and A. Mas-Colell, eds., *Equilibrium Theory and Applications: A Conference in Honor of Jacques Drèze.* Cambridge: Cambridge University Press, pp. 339–52.

Bénassy, Jean-Pascal (1993). Nonclearing markets: Microeconomic concepts and macroeconomic applications. *Journal of Economic Literature* 31: 732–61.

Bénassy, Jean-Pascal (1994). Le rôle de la mobilité du travail dans un modèle macroéconomique de sous-emploi avec concurrence imparfaite, négociations salariales et anticipations rationnelles. *Economie et Prévision* 113–114: 57–66.

Bénassy, Jean-Pascal (1995a). Money and wage contracts in an optimizing model of the business cycle. *Journal of Monetary Economics* 35: 303–15.

Bénassy, Jean-Pascal (1995b). Nominal rigidities in wage-setting by rational trade-unions. *Economic Journal* 105: 635–43.

Bénassy, Jean-Pascal (1995c). Classical and Keynesian features in macroeconomic models with imperfect competition. In H. Dixon and N. Rankin, eds., *The New Macroeconomics: Imperfect Markets and Policy Effectiveness.* Cambridge: Cambridge University Press.

Bénassy, Jean-Pascal (1995d). *Macroeconomics and Imperfect Competition*. Aldershot: Edward Elgar.

Bénassy, Jean-Pascal (1996). Analytical solutions to an RBC model with imperfect competition, increasing returns and underemployment. *Recherches Economiques de Louvain* 62: 287–97.

Bénassy, Jean-Pascal (1997a). Imperfect competition, capital shortages and unemployment persistence. *Scandinavian Journal of Economics* 99: 15–27.

Bénassy, Jean-Pascal (1997b). On the optimality of activist policies with a less informed government. Cepremap, Paris.

Bénassy, Jean-Pascal (1998). Optimal monetary and fiscal policies under wage and price rigidities. Cepremap, Paris, forthcoming, *Macroeconomic Dynamics* (2002).

Bénassy, Jean-Pascal (1999). Monetary policy rules as a second-best exercise. Cepremap, Paris.

Bénassy, Jean-Pascal (2000). Staggered contracts and persistence: Microeconomic foundations and macroeconomic dynamics. Cepremap, Paris.

Bénassy, Jean-Pascal (2001). On the optimality of activist policies with a less informed government. *Journal of Monetary Economics* 47: 45–59.

Binmore, Ken, Ariel Rubinstein, and Asher Wolinsky (1986). The Nash bargaining solution in economic modelling. *Rand Journal of Economics* 17: 176–88.

Blanchard, Olivier, and Kiyotaki Nobuhiro (1987). Monopolistic competition and the effects of aggregate demand. *American Economic Review* 77: 647–66.

Blinder, Alan S. (1982). Inventories and sticky prices: More on the microfoundations of macroeconomics. *American Economic Review* 72: 334–48.

Brock, William A. (1975). A simple perfect foresight monetary model. *Journal of Monetary Economics* 1: 133–50.

Bruno, Michael, and Jeffrey Sachs (1985). *Economics of Worldwide Stagflation*. Cambridge: Harvard University Press.

Bulow, Jeremy, and Heraklis M. Polemarchakis (1983). Retroactive money. *Economica* 50: 301–10.

Bushaw, Donald W., and Clower, Robert W. (1957). *Introduction to Mathematical Economics*. Homewood, IL: Irwin.

Burda, Michael C. (1988). Is there a capital shortage in Europe? *Weltwirtschaftliches Archiv* 124: 38–57.

Cahuc, Pierre, and André Zylberberg (1991). Niveaux de négociations salariales et performances macroéconomiques. *Annales d'Economie et de Statistique* 23: 1–12.

Cahuc, Pierre, and André Zylberberg (1996). *Economie du travail: La Formation des salaires et les déterminants du chômage*. Brussels: De Boeck.

Calmfors, Lars (1982). Employment policies, wage formation and trade union behavior in a small open economy. *Scandinavian Journal of Economics* 84: 345–73.

Calmfors, Lars, and John Driffill (1988). Bargaining structure, corporatism and macroeconomic performance. *Economic Policy* 6: 13–61.

Calvo, Guillermo (1983). Staggered prices in a utility-maximizing framework. *Journal of Monetary Economics* 12: 383–98.

Carlton, Dennis (1986). The rigidity of prices. *American Economic Review* 76: 637–58.

Carlton, Dennis (1989). The theory and facts of how markets clear: Is industrial organization valuable for understanding macroeconomics? In R. Schmalensee and R. Willig, eds., *Handbook of Industrial Organization*, vol. 1. Amsterdam: North Holland, pp. 909–46.

Chamberlin, Edward H. (1933). *The Theory of Monopolistic Competition*, 7th ed., Cambridge: Harvard University Press, 1956.

Chari, V. V., Patrick J. Kehoe, and Ellen R. McGrattan (2000). Sticky price models of the business cycle: Can the contract multiplier solve the persistence problem? *Econometrica* 68: 1151–79.

Cho, Jang-Ok (1993). Money and the business cycle with one-period nominal contracts. *Canadian Journal of Economics* 26: 638–59.

Cho, Jang-Ok, and Thomas F. Cooley (1995). Business cycles with nominal contracts. *Economic Theory* 6: 13–34.

Cho, Jang-Ok, Thomas F. Cooley, and Louis Phaneuf (1997). The welfare cost of nominal wage contracting. *Review of Economic Studies* 64: 465–84.

Christiano, Lawrence J., Martin Eichenbaum, and Charles Evans (1999). Monetary policy shocks: What have we learned and to what end? In J. Taylor and M. Woodford, eds., *Handbook of Macroeconomics*, vol. 1A. Amsterdam: North Holland, pp. 65–148.

Christiano, Lawrence J., Martin Eichenbaum, and Charles Evans (2001). Nominal rigidities and the dynamic effects of a shock to monetary policy. National Bureau of Economic Research, Cambridge, MA.

Clarida, Richard, Jordi Gali, and Mark Gertler (1999). The science of monetary policy: A new Keynesian perspective. *Journal of Economic Literature* 38: 1661–1707.

Clower, Robert W. (1960). Keynes and the classics: A dynamical perspective. *Quarterly Journal of Economics* 74: 318–23.

Clower, Robert W. (1965). The Keynesian counterrevolution: A theoretical appraisal. In F. H. Hahn and F. P. R. Brechling, eds., *The Theory of Interest Rates*. London: Macmillan, pp. 103–25.

Clower, Robert W. (1967). A reconsideration of the microfoundations of monetary theory. *Western Economic Journal* 6: 1–9.

Cogley, Timothy, and James M. Nason (1993). Impulse dynamics and propagation mechanisms in a real business cycle model. *Economics Letters* 43: 77–81.

Cogley, Timothy, and James M. Nason (1995). Output dynamics in real-business-cycle models. *American Economic Review* 85: 492–511.

Cooley, Thomas F., and Gary D. Hansen (1989). The inflation tax in a real business cycle model. *American Economic Review* 79: 733–48.

Cooley, Thomas F., and Lee E. Ohanian (1991). The cyclical behavior of prices. *Journal of Monetary Economics* 28: 25–60.

Cooper, Russell, and Andrew John (1988). Coordinating coordination failures in Keynesian Models. *Quarterly Journal of Economics* 100: 441–63.

Cournot, Augustin (1838). *Recherches sur les principes mathématiques de la théorie des richesses.* Paris: Hachette.

Crettez, Bertrand, Philippe Michel, and Bertrand Wigniolle (1999). Cash-in-advance constraints in the Diamond overlapping generations model: Neutrality and optimality of monetary policies. *Oxford Economic Papers* 51: 431–52.

Cuddington, John T., Per-Olov Johansson, and Karl-Gustav Löfgren (1984). *Disequilibrium Macroeconomics in Open Economies.* Oxford: Blackwell.

Danthine, Jean-Pierre, and John B. Donaldson (1990). Efficiency wages and the business cycle puzzle. *European Economic Review* 34: 1275–1301.

Danthine, Jean-Pierre, and John B. Donaldson (1991). Risk sharing, the minimum wage and the business cycle. In W. Barnett, B. Cornet, C. d'Aspremont, J. J. Gabszewicz, and A. Mas-Colell, eds., *Equilibrium Theory and Applications: A Conference in Honor of Jacques Drèze.* Cambridge, Cambridge University Press, pp. 299–318.

Danthine, Jean-Pierre, and John B. Donaldson (1992). Risk sharing in the business cycle. *European Economic Review* 36: 468–75.

D'Aspremont, Claude, Rodolphe Dos Santos Ferreira, and Louis-André Gérard-Varet (1990). On monopolistic competition and involuntary unemployment. *Quarterly Journal of Economics* 85: 895–919.

D'Autume, Antoine (1985). *Monnaie, croissance et déséquilibre.* Paris: Economica.

Debreu, Gérard (1959). *Theory of Value.* New York: Wiley.

Dehez, Pierre (1985). Monopolistic equilibrium and involuntary unemployment. *Journal of Economic Theory* 36: 160–65.

Devereux, Michael B., Allen C. Head, and Beverly J. Lapham (1993). Monopolistic competition, technology shocks and aggregate fluctuations. *Economic Letters* 41: 57–61.

Dixit, Avinash K. (1978). The balance of trade in a model of temporary equilibrium with rationing. *Review of Economic Studies* 45: 393–404.

Dixit, Avinash K., and Joseph E. Stiglitz (1977). Monopolistic competition and optimum product diversity. *American Economic Review* 67: 297–308.

Dixon, Huw (1987). A simple model of imperfect competition with Walrasian features. *Oxford Economic Papers* 39: 134–60.

Dixon, Huw (1988). Unions, oligopoly and the natural range of unemployment. *Economic Journal* 98: 1127–47.

Dixon, Huw (1990). Imperfect competition, unemployment benefit and the non-neutrality of money: An example. *Oxford Economic Papers* 42: 402–13.

Dixon, Huw (1991). Macroeconomic policy in a large unionized economy. *European Economic Review* 35: 1427–48.

Dixon, Huw, and Phillip Lawler (1996). Imperfect competition and the fiscal multiplier. *Scandinavian Journal of Economics* 98: 219–31.

Dixon, Huw, and Neil Rankin (1994). Imperfect competition and macroeconomics: A survey. *Oxford Economic Papers* 46: 171–99.

Dixon, Huw, and Neil Rankin (1995). *The New Macroeconomics: Imperfect Markets and Policy Effectiveness.* Cambridge: Cambridge University Press.

Dornbusch, Rudiger, and Jacob A. Frenkel (1973). Inflation and Growth: Alternative Approaches. *Journal of Money, Credit and Banking* 5: 141–56.

Drèze, Jacques H. (1975). Existence of an exchange equilibrium under price rigidities. *International Economic Review* 16: 301–20.

Drèze, Jacques H. (1979). Demand estimation, risk aversion and sticky prices. *Economics Letters* 4: 1–6.

Drèze, Jacques H. (1991). *Underemployment Equilibria.* Cambridge: Cambridge University Press.

Drèze, Jacques H., and Charles R. Bean, eds. (1990). *Europe's Unemployment Problem.* Cambridge: MIT Press.

Drèze, Jacques H., and Christian Gollier (1993). Risk sharing on the labour market and second-best wage rigidities. *European Economic Review* 37: 1457–82.

Drèze, Jacques H., and Heinz Müller (1980). Optimality properties of rationing schemes. *Journal of Economic Theory* 23: 131–49.

Erceg, Christopher J., Dale W. Henderson, and Andrew T. Levin (2000). Optimal monetary policy with staggered wage and price contracts. *Journal of Monetary Economics* 46: 281–313.

Fischer, Stanley (1977). Long-term contracts, rational expectations, and the optimal money supply rule. *Journal of Political Economy* 85: 191–205.

Friedman, Milton (1969). The optimum quantity of money. In M. Friedman, ed., *The Optimum Quantity of Money and Other Essays.* London: Macmillan.

Gabszewicz, Jean Jaskold, and Jean-Philippe Vial (1972). Oligopoly "à la Cournot" in a general equilibrium analysis. *Journal of Economic Theory* 42: 381–400.

Gary-Bobo, Robert (1987). Locally consistent oligopolistic equilibria are Cournot-Walras equilibria. *Economic Letters* 23: 217–21.

Glustoff, Errol (1968). On the existence of a Keynesian equilibrium. *Review of Economic Studies* 35: 327–34.

Gottfries, Nils, and Henrik Horn (1987). Wage formation and the persistence of unemployment. *Economic Journal* 97: 877–84.

Grandmont, Jean-Michel, and Guy Laroque (1976). On Keynesian temporary equilibria. *Review of Economic Studies* 43: 53–67.

Grandmont, Jean-Michel, and Yves Younès (1973). On the efficiency of a monetary equilibrium. *Review of Economic Studies* 40: 149–65.

Gray, Jo-Anna (1976). Wage indexation: A macroeconomic approach. *Journal of Monetary Economics* 2: 221–35.

Greenberg, J., and H. Muller (1979). Equilibria under price rigidities and externalities. In O. Moeschlin and D. Pallaschke, eds., *Game Theory and Related Topics.* Amsterdam: North Holland.

Grossman, Gene M., and Elhanan Helpman (1991). *Innovation and Growth in the Global Economy.* Cambridge: MIT Press.

Grossman, Herschel I. (1971). Money, interest and prices in market disequilibrium. *Journal of Political Economy* 79: 943–61.

Hahn, Frank H. (1978). On non-Walrasian equilibria. *Review of Economic Studies* 45: 1–17.

Hahn, Frank H., and Takashi Negishi (1962). A theorem on non tatonnement stability. *Econometrica* 30: 463–69.

Hairault, Jean-Olivier, and Franck Portier (1993). Money, new-Keynesian macroeconomics and the business cycle. *European Economic Review* 37: 1533–68.

Hansen, Bent (1951). *A Study in the Theory of Inflation*. London: Allen and Unwin.

Hart, Oliver D. (1982). A model of imperfect competition with Keynesian features. *Quarterly Journal of Economics* 97: 109–38.

Hénin, Pierre-Yves, and Philippe Michel, eds. (1982). *Croissance et accumulation en déséquilibre*. Paris: Economica.

Hénin, Pierre-Yves, and Thomas Jobert (1993). Profits, investissement et chomage. In P.-Y. Hénin, ed., *La Persistance du chômage*. Paris: Economica.

Hercowitz, Zvi, and Michael Sampson (1991). Output, growth, the real wage, and employment fluctuations. *American Economic Review* 81: 1215–37.

Hicks, John R. (1937). Mr. Keynes and the "classics": A suggested interpretation. *Econometrica* 5: 147–59.

Hildenbrand, Werner, and Kurt Hildenbrand (1978). On Keynesian equilibria with unemployment and quantity rationing. *Journal of Economic Theory* 18: 255–77.

Honkapohja, Seppo (1979). On dynamics of disequilibria in a macro model with flexible wages and prices. In M. Aoki and A. Marzollo, eds., *New Trends in Dynamic System Theory and Economics*. New York: Academic Press, pp. 303–36.

Hornstein, Andreas (1993). Monopolistic competition, increasing returns to scale and the importance of productivity shocks. *Journal of Monetary Economics* 31: 299–316.

Howitt, Peter W. (1974). Stability and the quantity theory. *Journal of Political Economy* 82: 133–51.

Huffman, Gregory W. (1993). An alternative neo-classical growth model with closed-form decisions rules. *Economics Letters* 42: 59–63.

Ireland, Peter N. (1996). The role of countercyclical monetary policy. *Journal of Political Economy* 104: 704–23.

Ito Takatoshi (1980). Disequilibrium growth theory. *Journal of Economic Theory* 23: 380–409.

Iwai, Katsuhito (1974). The firm in uncertain markets and its price, wage and employment adjustments. *Review of Economic Studies* 41: 257–76.

Jacobsen, Hans-Jörgen, and Christian Schultz (1990). A general equilibrium macro model with wage bargaining. *Scandinavian Journal of Economics* 92: 379–98.

Jacobsen, Hans-Jörgen, and Christian Schultz (1994). On the effectiveness of economic policy when competition is imperfect and expectations rational. *European Economic Review* 38: 305–27.

Keynes, John Maynard (1936). *The General Theory of Employment, Interest and Money.* New York: Harcourt Brace.

King, Robert G. (1982). Monetary policy and the information content of prices. *Journal of Political Economy* 90: 247–79.

King, Robert G. (1983). Interest rates, aggregate information, and monetary policy. *Journal of Monetary Economics* 12: 199–234.

King, Robert G., and Charles I. Plosser (1984). Money, credit and prices in a real business cycle. *American Economic Review* 74: 363–80.

Koop, Gary, and Simon M. Potter (1999). Dynamic asymmetries in U.S. unemployment. *Journal of Business and Economic Statistics* 17: 298–312.

Kydland, Finn E., and Edward Prescott (1982). Time to build and aggregate fluctuations. *Econometrica* 50: 1345–70.

Laroque, Guy (1981). On the local uniqueness of the fixed price equilibria. *Review of Economic Studies* 48: 113–29.

Layard, Richard, Stephen Nickell, and Richard Jackman (1991). *Unemployment: Macroeconomic Performance and the Labour Market.* Oxford: Oxford University Press.

Leijonhufvud, Axel (1968). *On Keynesian Economics and the Economics of Keynes.* Oxford: Oxford University Press.

Licandro, Omar (1995). A non-Walrasian general equilibrium model with monopolistic competition and wage bargaining. *Annales d'Economie et de Statistique* 37–38: 237–53.

Lindbeck, Assar, and Dennis Snower (1988). *The Insider–Outsider Theory of Employment and Unemployment.* Cambridge: MIT Press.

Long, John B., and Charles I. Plosser (1983). Real business cycles. *Journal of Political Economy* 91: 39–69.

Lucas, Robert E. Jr (1972). Expectations and the neutrality of money. *Journal of Economic Theory* 4: 103–24.

McCallum, Bennett T. (1989). Real business cycle models. In R. J. Barro, ed., *Modern Business Cycle Theory.* Cambridge: Harvard University Press.

McCallum, Bennett T. (1999). Issues in the design of monetary policy rules. In J. B. Taylor and M. Woodford, eds., *Handbook of Macroeconomics.* Amsterdam: North Holland.

Malinvaud, Edmond (1977). *The Theory of Unemployment Reconsidered.* Oxford: Blackwell.

Mankiw, N. Gregory (1988). Imperfect competition and the Keynesian cross. *Economics Letters* 26: 7–14.

Marschak, Thomas, and Reinhard Selten (1974). *General Equilibrium with Price-Making Firms.* Berlin: Springer.

Mills, Edwin S. (1962). *Price, Output and Inventory Policy.* New York: Wiley.

Molana, Hassan, and Thomas Moutos (1992). A note on taxation, imperfect competition and the balanced budget multiplier. *Oxford Economic Papers* 44: 68–74.

Muellbauer, John, and Richard Portes (1978). Macroeconomic models with quantity rationing. *Economic Journal* 88: 788–821.

Muth, John F. (1961). Rational expectations and the theory of price movements. *Econometrica* 29: 315–35.

Neary, Peter J. (1980). Nontraded goods and the balance of trade in a neo-Keynesian temporary equilibrium. *Quarterly Journal of Economics* 95: 403–30.

Neary, Peter J., and Joseph E. Stiglitz (1983). Towards a reconstruction of Keynesian economics: Expectations and constrained equilibria. *Quarterly Journal of Economics* 98 (suppl.): 196–201.

Neftci, Salih (1984). Are economic time series asymmetric over the business cycle? *Journal of Political Economy* 92: 307–28.

Negishi, Takashi (1961). Monopolistic competition and general equilibrium. *Review of Economic Studies* 28: 199–228.

Negishi, Takashi (1972). *General Equilibrium Theory and International Trade.* Amsterdam: North Holland.

Negishi, Takashi (1977). Existence of an under-employment equilibrium. In G. Schwödiauer, ed., *Equilibrium and Disequilibrium in Economic Theory.* Boston: Reidel, pp. 497–510.

Negishi, Takashi (1979). *Microeconomic Foundations of Keynesian Macroeconomics.* Amsterdam: North Holland.

Nickell, Stephen J., and Martyn J. Andrews (1983). Unions, real wages and employment in Britain 1951–79. *Oxford Economic Papers* 35: 507–30.

Nikaido, Hukukane (1975). *Monopolistic Competition and Effective Demand.* Princeton: Princeton University Press.

Nishimura, Kiyohiko G. (1986). Rational expectations and price rigidity in a monopolistically competitive market. *Review of Economic Studies* 53: 283–92.

Nishimura, Kiyohiko G. (1989). Indexation and monopolistic competition in labor markets. *European Economic Review* 33: 1605–23.

Nishimura, Kiyohiko G. (1991). Differential information, monopolistic competition and investment. *International Economic Review* 32: 809–21.

Nishimura, Kiyohiko G. (1992). *Imperfect Competition, Differential Information and Microfoundations of Macroeconomics.* Oxford: Oxford University Press.

Oswald, Andrew J. (1979). Wage determination in an economy with many trade unions. *Oxford Economic Papers* 31: 369–85.

Oswald, Andrew J. (1982). The microeconomic theory of the trade-union. *Economic Journal* 92: 576–95.

Patinkin, Don (1956). *Money, Interest and Prices.* New York: Harper and Row.

Persson, Torsten, and Lars E. O. Svensson (1983). Is optimism good in a Keynesian economy? *Economica* 50: 291–300.

Picard, Pierre (1983). Inflation and growth in a disequilibrium macroeconomic model. *Journal of Economic Theory* 30: 266–95.

Portes, Richard (1981). Macroeconomic equilibrium and disequilibrium in centrally planned economies. *Economic Inquiry* 19: 559–78.

Portier, Franck, and Luis Puch (2000). The welfare cost of fluctuations in representative agents economies. Gremaq, Toulouse.

Quandt, Richard E. (1982). Econometric disequilibrium models. *Econometric Review* 1: 1–63.

Quandt, Richard E. (1988). *The Econometrics of Disequilibrium.* Oxford: Blackwell.

Rankin, Neil (1998a). Nominal rigidity and monetary uncertainty. *European Economic Review* 42: 185–99.

Rankin, Neil (1998b). Nominal rigidity and monetary uncertainty in a small open economy. *Journal of Economic Dynamics and Control* 22: 679–702.

Robinson, Joan (1933). *The Economics of Imperfect Competition.* London: Macmillan.

Romer, Paul M. (1990). Endogenous technical change. *Journal of Political Economy* 98 (suppl.): 71–102.

Rotemberg, Julio J. (1982). Sticky prices in the United States. *Journal of Political Economy* 90: 1187–1211.

Rotemberg, Julio J. (1983). Aggregate consequences of fixed costs of price adjustments. *American Economic Review* 73: 433–36.

Rotemberg, Julio J., and Michael Woodford (1992). Oligopolistic pricing and the effects of aggregate demand on economic activity. *Journal of Political Economy* 100: 1153–1207.

Rotemberg, Julio J., and Michael Woodford (1995). Dynamic general equilibrium models with imperfectly competitive product markets. In T. F. Cooley, ed., *Frontiers of Business Cycle Research.* Princeton: Princeton University Press, pp. 243–93.

Rothman, Philip (1991). Further evidence on the asymmetric behavior of unemployment rates over the business cycle. *Journal of Macroeconomics* 13: 291–98.

Samuelson, Paul A. (1958). An exact consumption-loan model of interest with or without the social contrivance of money. *Journal of Political Economy* 66: 467–82.

Samuelson, Paul A. (1967). A turnpike refutation of the golden rule in a welfare-maximizing many-year plan. In K. Shell, ed., *Essays on the Theory of Optimal Economic Growth.* Cambridge: MIT Press.

Samuelson, Paul A. (1968). The two-part golden rule deduced as the asymptotic turnpike of catenary motions. *Western Economic Journal* 6: 85–89.

Sargent, Thomas J., and Neil Wallace (1975). Rational expectations, the optimal monetaryiInstrument and the optimal money supply rule. *Journal of Political Economy* 83: 241–54.

Sargent, Thomas J., and Neil Wallace (1976). Rational expectations and the theory of monetary policy. *Journal of Monetary Economics* 2: 169–83.

Schulz, Norbert (1983). On the global uniqueness of fixprice equilibria. *Econometrica* 51: 47–68.

Silvestre, Joaquim (1977). A model of general equilibrium with monopolistic behavior. *Journal of Economic Theory* 16: 425–42.

Silvestre, Joaquim (1982). Fixprice analysis in exchange economies. *Journal of Economic Theory* 26: 28–58.

Silvestre, Joaquim (1983). Fixprice analysis in productive economies. *Journal of Economic Theory* 30: 401–409.

Silvestre, Joaquim (1985). Voluntary and efficient allocations are Walrasian. *Econometrica* 53: 807–16.

Silvestre, Joaquim (1988). Undominated prices in the three good model. *European Economic Review* 32: 161–78.

Silvestre, Joaquim (1989). Who benefits from unemployment? In G. Feiwel, ed., *The Economics of Imperfect Competition: Joan Robinson and Beyond.* London: Macmillan, pp. 462–81.

Silvestre, Joaquim (1993). The market-power foundations of macroeconomic policy. *Journal of Economic Literature* 31: 105–41.

Silvestre, Joaquim (1995). Market power in macroeconomic models: new developments. *Annales d'Economie et de Statistique* 37–38: 319–56.

Smith, R. Todd (1992). The cyclical behavior of prices. *Journal of Money, Credit and Banking* 24: 413–30.

Sneessens, Henri R. (1981). *Theory and Estimation of Macroeconomic Rationing Models.* New York: Springer.

Sneessens, Henri R. (1987). Investment and the inflation-unemployment tradeoff in a macroeconomic rationing model with monopolistic competition. *European Economic Review* 31: 781–808.

Sneessens, Henri R., and Jacques H. Drèze (1986). A discussion of Belgian unemployment combining traditional concepts and disequilibrium econometrics. *Economica* 53 (suppl.): 89–119.

Snower, Dennis (1983). Imperfect competition, unemployment and crowding out. *Oxford Economic Papers* 35: 569–84.

Solow, Robert M., and Joseph Stiglitz (1968). Output, employment and wages in the short run. *Quarterly Journal of Economics* 82: 537–60.

Svensson, Lars E. O. (1986). Sticky goods prices, flexible asset prices, monopolistic competition and monetary policy. *Review of Economic Studies* 53: 385–405.

Taylor, John B. (1979). Staggered wage setting in a macro model. *American Economic Review* 69: 108–13.

Taylor, John B. (1980). Aggregate dynamics and staggered contracts. *Journal of Political Economy* 88: 1–23.

Taylor, John B. (1993). Discretion versus policy rules in practice. *Carnegie-Rochester Series on Public Policy* 39: 195–214.

Taylor, John B. (1999a). The robustness and efficiency of monetary policy rules as guidelines for interest rate setting by the European central bank. *Journal of Monetary Economics* 43: 655–79.

Taylor, John B., ed. (1999b). *Monetary Policy Rules.* Chicago: University of Chicago Press.

Triffin, Robert (1940). *Monopolistic Competition and General Equilibrium Theory.* Cambridge: Harvard University Press.

Turnovsky, Stephen J. (1980). The choice of monetary instrument under alternative forms of price expectations. *Manchester School* 48: 39–62.

Uzawa, Hirofumi (1962). On the stability of Edgeworth's barter process. *International Economic Review* 3: 218–32.

Van de Klundert, Theo, and Anton Von Schaik (1990). Unemployment persistence and loss of productive capacity: A Keynesian approach. *Journal of Macroeconomics* 12: 363–80.

Walras, Léon (1874). *Eléments d'économie politique pure.* Lausanne: Corbaz. Definitive edition trans. by William Jaffe as *Elements of Pure Economics* (1954). London: Allen and Unwin.

Weiss, Laurence (1980). The role for active monetary policy in a rational expectations model. *Journal of Political Economy* 88: 221–33.

Weitzman, Martin L. (1982). Increasing returns and the foundations of unemployment theory. *Economic Journal* 92: 787–804.

Weitzman, Martin L. (1985). The simple macroeconomics of profit sharing. *American Economic Review* 75: 937–52.

Younès, Yves (1975). On the role of money in the process of exchange and the existence of a non-Walrasian equilibrium. *Review of Economic Studies* 42: 489–501.

Young, Alwyn (1998). Growth without scale effects. *Journal of Political Economy* 106: 41–63.

Zabel, Edward (1972). Multiperiod monopoly under uncertainty. *Journal of Economic Theory* 5: 524–36.

Index